EDWARD T. HALL

An Anthropology of Everyday Life

AN AUTOBIOGRAPHY

ANCHOR BOOKS
DOUBLEDAY
NEW YORK LONDON TORONTO SYDNEY AUCKLAND

AN ANCHOR BOOK
PUBLISHED BY DOUBLEDAY
a division of Bantam Doubleday Dell Publishing Group, Inc.
666 Fifth Avenue, New York, New York 10103

ANCHOR BOOKS, DOUBLEDAY, and the portrayal of an anchor are trademarks of Doubleday, a division of Bantam Doubleday Dell Publishing Group, Inc.

An Anthropology of Everyday Life was originally published in hardcover by Doubleday in 1992. The Anchor Books edition is published by arrangement with Doubleday.

Library of Congress Cataloging-in-Publication Data

Hall, Edward Twitchell, 1914–
An anthropology of everyday life: an autobiography
Edward T. Hall.—1st Anchor Books ed.
p. cm.
Originally published: New York: Doubleday, 1992.
Includes bibliographical references and index.
1. Hall, Edward Twitchell, 1914– . 2. Ethnologists—United States—Biography. 3. Intercultural communication. 4. Personality and culture. 5. Ethnopsychology. I. Title.
[GN21.H24A3 1993]
301′.092—dc20
[B] 92-39059
CIP

ISBN 0-385-23743-x

Printed in the United States of America
First Anchor Books Edition: March 1993

1 3 5 7 9 10 8 6 4 2

This book is dedicated to the people I have known and worked with from all parts of the world, who took me in, who were kind enough to share their life experiences with me, and from whom I learned all I know about what is important in life.

ACKNOWLEDGMENTS

HOW DOES ONE acknowledge the contributions that others have made to the corpus of one's lifetime? This entire book, in a sense, is an acknowledgment of what others have contributed to my life and work. However, the creation of a book itself is a task involving the active participation of many people, without which it is doubtful that this or many other books would see the light of day.

My first acknowledgment is to my long-time editor at Doubleday, Sally Arteseros. Jana Oyler worked for me as an assistant and associate, critic and coach, and provided editorial assistance of an unusual, creative, and insightful type. Kimberly Sheasby is my assistant and has also provided the sort of dedication and skills that are rare to find. Rosemary Lincoln edited parts of the manuscript in its early stages. My friend Gerri Reid Skjervold, a talented artist and a former assistant, helped me choose the right course for this book in its early stages. I owe her a deep debt of gratitude. When I write, I quite frequently have Gerri in mind because I know that if I am addressing her, what I say will be true. I also wish to acknowledge the cheerful and gifted support of Martha Levin, publisher of Anchor Books.

The last acknowledgment and the most important of all is to Mildred Reed Hall, my lifelong partner, whose contributions are so varied and important as to make them impossible to list.

CONTENTS

INTRODUCTION

THIS BOOK is a record of one of the several stories of my life. There are other stories and I hope that someday they will be written also. I wanted to be sure this one got told because at age seventy-six I find that my life goes faster with every year and I know that one of these days I will reach a velocity sufficient to overcome the pull of the earth and fly off into the unknown.

In the perspective of the years I can see that mine has been an unusual life—in fact, a remarkable one, endowed with a luminosity. Not that I had all that much to do with its overall design. There were events that were served up to me: years on the Navajo and Hopi reservations in Arizona in my youth, the Depression, World War II where I did service in a black regiment, my training for and working as an applied anthropologist, working for the State Department during the McCarthy years in Washington, and my psychoanalysis. But it was from my association with different ethnic and professional groups that I have learned the most. For me, life has been an ever-changing environment made up of people who came across as searing hot deserts, fertile plains, alpine meadows, mountains, impenetrable jungles—each person imposing his or her own laws and rules of survival, so that while I have not always done as well as I would have liked, I have learned, and because I learned, I survived. But I have only recently reached a point where I can understand how atypical my life has been—atypical and productive enough to warrant telling.

This has been the most difficult of all my books for me to write. Ordering my thoughts and writing about ideas has never been easy. But describing the evolution of my own deep true self as reflected in the mirror of everyday life has been even more difficult. It is a task much like excavating a prehistoric Anasazi kiva: you must work with agonizing care because not only do you not know what you will find buried in all that debris but you must be mindful not to damage anything in the process of discovery, and, even more important, you must have the proper respect and reverence for what you are uncovering—a sacred record of the past.

Some remarks concerning where I stand philosophically are necessary for those of my readers educated only in the legacy of Western thought. My approach to life and to the study of culture is metaphilosophical, alien to philosophies growing out of the analytic, word-based tradition of Aristotle, Plato, and Socrates. When it comes to philosophy, all of us inhabit at least two worlds: the world of explicit statements—an outgrowth of scholasticism, learned in schools, which makes up the corpus of what is thought to be our "cultural heritage"—and the ever evolving unconscious world of everyday behavior which guides all informal activities of daily life. The latter is so much a part of us that, like culture, it is not thought of as anything special, but simply the way we are.

My study (and hence my philosophy) has been rooted in this overlooked, often disdained, uncultivated soil. Because this soil has rested undisturbed over the centuries, built up by successive generations of living, it has proved to be phenomenally rich. Working in these pastures requires special techniques and skills. Instead of controlled experiments to test a hypothesis, it is more important to guard against projecting one's own habits and worldview onto others, and to pay less attention to what people tell you and more attention to what they do. The architect Mies van der Rohe was fond of saying "God is in the details," and it is my emphasis on the details of everyday life over theory, or even policy, that distinguishes my work from that of most anthropologists of my generation. It is the details of the rules underlying common behavior that govern the world.

Therefore, my philosophy, if it can be dignified by such a term, is that of the vernacular, rooted in the unstated rules of everyday life. It is the infinitely varied philosophy of the grass roots—reminiscent of the "dust of history" school of the French—in which there is no judgmental statement of what should and should not be, only an observation of what is. Paralleling my work are the pioneering studies of J. B. Jackson on vernacular landscape, which he contrasts with the crafted landscape of the establishment. Jackson and I agree that the products of everyday life have been neglected in favor of the more prestigious, traditional, ordered, and controlled world of the manifest culture of institutions. But to discover the order (and there is order) in the vernacular is the wave of the future.

As I said before, this is only one of my stories. It is the nucleus of what was going on in my life from childhood until early middle life—the soil out of which my ideas grew. It is also the story of the men and women who encouraged me to see beyond or behind the mask of explicit, learned culture into that much more vast, less artificial world acquired in the deeply personal process of life as it is lived by human beings as they interact naturally with each other with neither thought nor artifice. It is a story of my gradually increasing awareness of the richness of the grammar and vocabulary of everyday culture, the unwritten rules that provide what order there is to daily life.

It is my hope that my story will reveal to others something of the vast world of unconscious culture in its relation to the unconscious self. In the process, perhaps some of my readers can not only begin their escape from the oppressive walls of culture, but can also see through the manipulations and violations of culture's tacit rules when they are used against us by others. As they inevitably will be!

Part I

Early Days
1914–1931

ONE

Growing Up in the Twenties

MY BEGINNINGS were hardly auspicious. The first of four children, born at the beginning of World War I, I had survived diphtheria and then Spanish influenza by the time I was three. The combined effect left me with asthma and made me prey to bullies and, like the runt of the litter, a target for schoolmates' aggression.

Four memories mark my early years. First, there was the German nurse who took care of us during the World War I flu epidemic, the only nurse my mother could find in that time of universal sickness. She had a stern authoritarian voice and was fond of saying, "I am telling you! You vill *DIE* if you don't take your medicine!" Dying never seemed so real and terrifying as it did then. Then there were the nightmares, which are still puzzling: I would wake up in the middle of the night in my crib in a panic because the sheets were wrinkled, rough, and disordered—a perverse version of the tale of the princess and the pea. The third memory was of repeatedly falling down the narrow back stairs to the kitchen when I was groping my way down the hall to the bathroom. My mother was annoyed at being awakened, but nobody did anything to correct matters, like putting in a night light or a small gate at the head of the stairs.

Then there was the dog that came as close to killing me as I hope anything ever gets. It was early summer after dinner, at dusk, when it was beginning to cool off a little. Mother and Dad wanted to retrieve a bridle they had loaned to a man who ran a stable down by the railroad tracks and had taken me along. It was only a short distance to the stable, where we were met by a man I had never seen before, who immediately opened the stable door, letting out his police dog. The dog, of course, was overjoyed; frisking about, barking and wagging his tail, he greeted everyone and was petted by everyone, including me—he was just like our "lobo," a German shepherd. All four of us entered the stable as the man explained that he should feed his dog. The next scene is all in slow motion. The man is bent over, head down, rooting around in the straw in a manger looking for the bridle. Between him and me are my parents standing together forming the base of a triangle. At the apex of the triangle, a good seventeen feet away, is the dog, eating. Like all children I know, I am watching the dog eat. The next thing I know I am on my back looking up into those horrible flashing teeth and jaws. The dog had grabbed me by the waist, thrown me down on my back, and was astride my body making the most horrible frightening noises. Looking for my parents to save me, I saw them standing there immobilized, unable to do anything. I could see that they were not going to do anything, which made my situation even more desperate. Just when I had about given up hope, the man raised his head out of the trough of the manger, bridle in hand, and whistled. The dog withdrew.

From this I learned three things, only one of which was explained to me. Mother told me that I should not look at strange dogs when they are eating because they might think I was going to take their food. This was my first experience with eye behavior; I have been an observer of it ever since. The other thing I learned was that when the chips were down (still hard to realize), my parents would not risk themselves in any important way to save me. And if they wouldn't, who would? Third, if that dog hadn't been well trained and if his owner who knew the proper commands had been absent, I wouldn't be here. You must know the proper language in order to survive. I also wondered why my parents would lend anything, to say nothing of an expensive bridle, to a man who would toss it into a manger where the horses ate their hay and slobbered on it.

The doctor who dressed my wounds had practiced medicine in Africa and told my parents that they were worse than many of the wild animal wounds he had seen inflicted on humans when he was there. Despite this early traumatic experience—and despite a short period when I was afraid of dogs—I still relate to them on a fundamental level. I love dogs—in fact, I love most animals, even wild ones. You just have to know their language, what to do and what not to do. (The two exceptions, in the wilds of North America, are badgers and bears.)

In my earliest years we lived on Gore Avenue, in Webster Groves, Missouri, a suburb of St. Louis. Our Victorian house was clapboard with generous proportions and large verandas. It sat at the top of a slope, back from the street behind an expansive lawn enhanced by giant oak and chestnut trees inhabited by bushy-tailed gray squirrels that spent their time gathering acorns, which they tucked away in their cheeks on the way to some secret hiding place in our attic. Behind the house was a barn with a stable, a place for the carriage and stalls for the horses, and a manger for the cow. Beside the barn was a chicken house with attached yard. The cow produced milk, the chickens eggs and pullets to eat. The horses were for my mother and father to ride. I don't think we had a carriage—the MOPAC (Missouri Pacific Railroad) commuter trains were ten minutes' walk away and there was also a streetcar that ran from Kirkwood to midtown St. Louis. One evening we heard a horrendous noise in the driveway beside the house. We all rushed out to see what had happened. Dad had brought home a 1917 Model-T Ford four-door sedan which looked like a glass showcase. Model-T Fords were never well known for the quietness of their motors—this one sounded more like a cement mixer than an automobile. And it had a horn that went *ooga* as it rasped out warnings to pedestrians.

Our nearest neighbor was a Civil War veteran who hallucinated battles from his front porch. Depending on his mood, my sister Delight and I used to play or fight with him, throwing curses (which we learned from him) and horse chestnuts as ammunition. The boundary between our two houses was no-man's-land. Occasionally, by working together, attacking from two sides at once, D and I could invade his territory, but not often. When we succeeded, his daughter would intervene, calling him into the house. Otherwise, we would withdraw when we were tired to the safety of our own lines.

At other times my sister and I would bake potatoes in a small pit by coating them with mud and building a fire on top. The best potatoes I ever ate!

Of my two parents Dad was the easier to understand. Of medium height, with blue eyes and thinning sandy hair, poorly proportioned (narrow shoulders, broad hips, large hands and feet), he was energetic, imaginative, and curious. Reared by New England women in near poverty, ambitious, inherently shy and unsure of himself, lacking in social skills, his spirit was a battleground of two sets of opposing forces. Driven by grandiosity, he did everything he could to wrap himself in the trappings of the big shot—the spiffiest Packard roadster, the most expensive suits, the most stiffly waxed mustache. Then one morning he would wake up, shave off the mustache, put on his old clothes (the older, more dowdy and threadbare the better), pick out an old tie, come down to breakfast, look at us all to be sure we had noticed him, and say, "I'm nothing but a simple New England boy!" This phase would last a short time until ambition and grandiosity would take over again.

Dad's parents were New Englanders dating back to the *Mayflower.* Since they were poor, their ancestry was a point the family made much of. Grandmother Hall was a Twichell[1] before she married my grandfather, a Congregational minister who was also one of New England's early photographers. When he died he left a widow, two daughters, a maiden aunt, and his twelve-year-old son, my father. Born in Meriden, Connecticut, in 1884, reared in a strict Puritan atmosphere on the edge of poverty, my father was ambitious, energetic and resourceful, and eventually worked his way through Amherst. He grew up never having enough of anything—warmth and affection, good wholesome food, material goods, sweets, fireworks, strawberries, status. As a defense he built an impenetrable mask. In Jungian terms he would have been classed as a thinking and sensing type. (Mother, however, would have been feeling and intuition—not the best combination in the world. Not only were there these differences in temperament but my parents were far apart in culture and class as well.) Energetic and resourceful, Dad could do anything with his hands. He was impressed from the start with big business, because it provided an outlet for his energy and offered him security, money and prestige, but he managed to succeed and then fail in a pattern which dogged him to the end of his days. His grandiosity inevitably tripped him up.

Dad must have been extremely shy. He was somewhat gauche and ill prepared to deal with people like Mother, who turned her nose up at much of what he represented as well as what he did. My mother's disapproval included his family and particularly my Aunt Delight, a spinster who was one of the best-hearted souls I have ever known. She was as typical an example of the poor New England gentry as one could find. Because she was good to the core, kind but unsophisticated and awkward, Aunt D pushed all the wrong buttons in Mother.

The daughter of a Philadelphia banker, Mother had a will of her own. Grandfather John Jay Gilroy, of Scottish ancestry, had been a lieutenant in the U.S. Navy and was one of the founders of the Philadelphia Zoo and a thirty-third-degree Mason. He lost everything when, succumbing to gold fever in the 1880s, he invested his bank's assets in Colorado mines. As an upright and respected citizen, Grandfather Gilroy took his obligation to his depositors seriously and promptly set to work repaying the bank's debts which, in his view, outweighed his obligations to his family. Mother never forgave him for losing the family fortune.

Mother and Dad met while they were both working at the Curtis Publishing Company in Philadelphia. He was thirty-one, she twenty-nine—old not to be married in pre–World War I days. Curtis was a publisher of popular magazines such as the *Saturday Evening Post* and the *Ladies' Home Journal*. Dad was in advertising. Mother signed her columns J.A., which in those days was how a man would have done it. When I questioned Mother and Dad about their courtship, the information vein, sandwiched between two granitic layers of reticence, proved to be thin indeed. Though they didn't say so, all I could elicit was that they both seemed to like canoeing—she being on the water where it was quiet while he liked being in the stern where he was in control.

St. Louis beckoned when Dad was offered a job working for Donald Danforth, a partner of the Mr. Ralston who invented the breakfast food that still bears his name. Danforth was president of the Ralston Purina Company. From that time on Mother never worked again professionally. They had one male child who died; my own birth followed in 1914 and three more children followed.

Like most children I wanted to know as much as possible about my parents and their life before I was born. It was hard going. Dad had earned his athletic letter at Amherst by managing one of the track teams. At the top of her class, Mother was admitted to Bryn Mawr on scholarship. Like many Easterners in those days, particularly Philadelphians, she looked down on St. Louis and all it stood for. Her mother, whose name had been Williams, was from Pittsburgh and felt the same way about Philadelphia.

Normally the status of eldest child in the family carries with it a certain amount of authority over younger siblings. This was not the case in our family. Nervous and self-absorbed, Mother depended on me to keep my younger brother and sisters tranquil. I had to be particularly careful not to disturb or upset them or stand in the way of their childish tyrannies. Crying brought instant retribution—on *ME.* She did nothing to them, and they got what they wanted, at my expense. If I had something and hesitated to give it to them, they would cry, at which point there would be a shriek, Mother would arrive like a cyclone, and I would get beaten with whatever happened to be handy. One time it was a braided leather leash. That particular time her fury was so intense I could see she had lost all control over herself and in that state she could kill. I considered running away but didn't know where to go, so I hid under the floor of the barn and watched through a crack in the wall as, having calmed down a bit, she started looking for me. There were other similar episodes, all of which impressed on me the depth of what I later learned to call her narcissism and the shortness of the fuse that, once lit, would cause her to explode in a fit of fury. These episodes were always preceded by a shriek of rage as, like a caged lioness, she would prowl for the target of her anger, which inevitably seemed to be me.

From my father I inherited energy, curiosity, mechanical skills, and a penchant for trying to figure things out and make them work. Mother developed my aesthetic sense, an appreciation for literature, and a capacity to read between the lines and be sensitive to mood. It's no accident that in my professional life I pioneered the field of nonverbal communication. Neither parent was what one would call conventional, which in American culture can be a mixed blessing. Both parents were stingy, so much so that when, in "Hansel and Gretel," the children are led out into the forest and left to starve, it sounded more like real life to me than a fairy tale.

Both my brother Dick and my sister Delight were victims of my parents' divorce, which happened when I was eleven. This was a shattering event which had a devastating effect on our lives. There were qualities in both of them which I came to value and admire. Dick was four years younger than I. Cute as a child and slightly built, dark and handsome as a man, he never quite found himself. He had difficulty learning to read, probably because of dyslexia—unknown when he was going to school. By the time he was twelve or thirteen some of his innate talent was beginning to become apparent. A particular kind of mechanical genius, he could look at the outside of a machine and see how it worked inside. Dependent and with a craving for love, he attracted first girls and later women as honey attracts flies. He later became an inventor and like most inventors had a rough time of it financially, moving from one exploiter to the next. Innocence as to the true nature and workings of organizations was his greatest liability.

Temperamentally, intellectually, physiologically, spiritually, my one-year-younger sister Delight and I were as different as it is possible to be. Delight took after my father's side of the family, which prejudiced her mother against her.[2] As a compensation for what she was not getting from Mother, as a child she became envy-ridden, straining our relationship. As an adult she was tall, striking-looking, athletic with reddish hair and a fey, even bizarre, sense of humor, enabling her to conjure up original and offbeat ways of getting other people in trouble.

She had as powerful an eidetic memory as anyone I have known, so she did well in school. She could project texts (from books and notes) on a screen in her mind's eye and read them off as though they were in front of her.

Seven years separated Priscilla, my youngest sister, and me. Temperamentally cheerful, cuddly, cute, and beautiful as an adult with a delightful disposition, she was the type that people fall in love with. It was interesting and I suppose not too unusual that Delight and Dick would take after my father's side and Priscilla and I after my mother's. There was a natural affinity between us that has lasted a lifetime. As a woman her beauty blossomed, as did her mind—a fact she kept under wraps because of the times, which have fortunately changed.

Although I didn't realize it until well into adulthood, Mother didn't really like children. They weren't interesting—they neither engaged her mind nor served her vanity—and, I believe, they reminded her of the child within with whom she never came to terms. To a small child she seemed unloving. It wasn't until I was able to talk coherently that her interest in me picked up. Then she began treating me more like an adult. In that sense I had only a part of childhood. What eventually bonded us to each other was our involvement in myths and fairy tales of all kinds: Japanese, Norse, Anglo-Saxon, American Indian, Eskimo, black American, Middle Eastern, German, French, and American. It was a rich and varied diet of which I never tired, and it imbued me with a fascination for the incredible diversity of humankind. There was an extraordinary cast of characters in the stories she read me, each of whom was motivated differently, in keeping with his or her own culture. From Japan, there was "The Tongue-Cut Sparrow" and "The War Between the Crabs and the Monkeys"; from the Greeks, all of Homer's characters: Zeus, Aphrodite, Athena, Theseus and the Minotaur, Hercules and his twelve labors, Hermes, the messenger of the gods, Pan and the centaurs, and crafty Odysseus. From Germany and North Europe, there were Odin (Wotan) and Fria (Freyja); Loki, the clever prankster; Thor with his hammer, who despite his strength and temper beat strands of gold so fine they replicated Fria's hair. Then there were the giants and mythical creatures against whom the gods fought. There were also Little Red Riding Hood, Hansel and Gretel, Cinderella, Snow White, King Arthur and his Knights, Merlin the Magician, Spider Woman, Coyote, and a host of others representing Anglo-American mythology.

The pull of these stories was so powerful that once, when we were on a boat crossing a stormy English Channel and I was turning green, Mother read me the tale of Momotaro the Japanese Peach Boy. The strategy worked. It staved off an attack of mal de mer. I never thought of any of these stories or the characters in them as strange or even exotic, only interesting and different in their own right. But their differences caught my attention.

Even in the European tradition, where there were local versions of the same tale, observable differences characterized each culture. The French stories were so logical and every detail was important: in the French version of "The Sleeping Beauty," when the stepmother decides to eat Beauty's two children for dinner, the clever overseer hides the children and serves up a pair of tender kid goats in their place. But when the wicked stepmother asks to have Beauty served for dinner, he must search and search until he finds a goat old enough and tough enough to fool the stepmother. After all, Beauty had been asleep for a hundred years and she had to be plenty tough. Nor did the French spare children the grisly details of life. Pictures from French versions of Chinese tales showing gory executions with fountains of blood gushing forth were of a sort that I never saw in books of American fairy tales. Later, when I could understand the symbolism, I realized that if you dug deep enough all fairy tales could be gruesome. It was just that the French feeling for detail made a powerful impression on me at the age of seven.

When World War I ended, Mother packed up my sister Delight, my infant brother Dick, and me (I was four) one night and we found ourselves crawling into heavily curtained berths on the Sunshine Special, headed for a place I had never heard of: El Paso. My asthma being unabated, Mother used my poor health as an excuse for leaving my father and St. Louis, which she hated because the climate was terrible, the humidity enervating, and the people "bourgeois." She took us south to Texas, for the warmer, drier climate on the U.S.–Mexican border. How she happened to pick El Paso was never clear. In 1918 El Paso was provincial, dusty, windy, and dreary. The town had an emotional gray overtone that pervaded the atmosphere even when the sun shone. Even the sky, when I could see it through the dust, was not blue but gray.

It was in El Paso that we collected the rest of our menage: Maria, who came to work for us, and her two daughters, Tia, a stringy eleven-year-old, and Juanita, a fat, lethargic teenager. Maria was plump, good-natured, and a devout Catholic. Every day she took the streetcar from Juarez to our bungalow on the northernmost outskirts of town, opposite Fort Bliss, an army cavalry post. Nothing was ever said about Maria's husband. The family must have been dreadfully poor. My mother later learned that they lived for the first week we knew them on the fifty cents Mother had advanced for carfare, which left them about twenty-five cents for food.

Apart from having my tonsils out, watching the army engineers at Fort Bliss blow bridges into kindling wood and rebuild them from the scraps at lightning speed, engaging in a pissing contest against the back fence with two other boys, and visiting a sheep ranch where I fed orphaned lambs from a bottle, not much happened to me in El Paso. There was one small bit of excitement, however. Pancho Villa was roaring around Chihuahua at the time, and Mother was sure he had attacked us one night when she heard bullets whistling by, men shouting, and horses galloping outside our bungalow. She learned the next day it was the guards trying to catch some prisoners who had escaped from the stockade at Fort Bliss.

In the spring we moved to Santa Fe, New Mexico, taking the train with a night stopover at Lamy (eighteen miles south of Santa Fe). In those days there was a wonderful little Harvey House hotel on the railroad platform at Lamy—a hacienda with rooms around a court and a well in the middle with a small lunchroom off the lobby.

My first unforgettable impression of New Mexico was out the window of my room in Lamy the next morning. Seventy years later I can still see that luminous hill of sparkling fragments of red granite. Chamisa, tufts of grama grass, a piñon tree here and there—all bathed in fresh early morning light. What gave it life and meaning was the miraculous quality of that light. I had never dreamed there could be such light. It wasn't just the altitude and the clean air (St. Louis was even then smothered in a continuous blanket of smog) but some other ineffable components which I have yet to identify. The difference between that light and what I had known before was like the difference between the muddy Mississippi at flood stage and the crystal clear waters of the Caribbean. A bright, intense, blue cloudless sky was supported by red granite terrain which glittered unobscured by smog, moisture, or haze in unfiltered sunlight. For the first time in my life I experienced air that was pure, clean, fresh, and invigorating. Later, when I went outside, the sky opened up, the world expanded and went on forever.

Here before me was a country that spoke to me. What it said was Here I am and here you are. You are home now where you belong. It was a miracle telling me that there could be happiness in the world.

About ten o'clock that morning, we boarded another train which took us the remaining eighteen miles to Santa Fe. We unloaded at the Santa Fe railroad depot and were taken by horse-drawn coach to an old Victorian hotel surrounded by an immense veranda, on the corner of Marcy Street and Lincoln Avenue.

Santa Fe in 1919 was little more than a large village. Most of the town's businesses were on the plaza. Cowboys still rode into town on horseback and watered their horses at the trough at the corner of Lincoln and Palace avenues. There were no paved streets, no grass except behind a low wall around the federal building between Washington and Lincoln, few trees and little shrubbery. Two weeks after our arrival we moved up the street to 213 Marcy to a bungalow sandwiched between a poor Hispanic family on one side and the wealthy Oteros on the other. Across from us was a large meadow with a stream running through it; watercress grew along the banks. We had white rabbits in hutches in the back, and Mother made dandelion wine. Maria, Tia, and Juanita lived with us, as did my mother's sister, Aunt Blanche, an emaciated little woman who, like my mother, was inclined to be hysterical.

I went to kindergarten in the basement of a brick school two blocks down the street where Mother left me after bemoaning my "high squeaky voice." Particularly irksome was when she overheard me telling the kindergarten classmates that she was making dandelion wine and inviting them to see our rabbits.

For transportation mother rented a spavined gray mare that was harnessed periodically to a buckboard carriage. Once we were settled in our house Mother bought me a pair of featherweight beaded Indian moccasins which I wore constantly. Most of the time I was not content to ride in the carriage and would jump out and run behind. It was no time at all before I became addicted to the pleasures of running in the dusty road behind that buggy. For the first time in my life, I was healthy and happy.

There were different kinds of interesting people in New Mexico, not only the *ricos* Oteros next door and their two little girls but also Juan Pino and his wife, Laurencita, from Tesuque Pueblo whom I met, I suspect, when Mother saw some fine little line drawings of the pueblo which Juan was trying to sell on the plaza. They were quiet, mild people. When you were around them they didn't talk much and when they did their voices were soft and their rhythm was much smoother than ours, which was jerky and irregular.

On one of those bright sunny early summer days so typical of Santa Fe, I had climbed the back steps of our house and pushed my way into the kitchen where Maria stood by the sink, cleaning a chicken. I already knew all about the innards of chickens because I liked to hang around the kitchen watching the cook prepare meals and had made a nuisance of myself questioning the cook as to the anatomy of chickens' internal organs. I could identify the heart, the liver, lungs, gizzard, intestines, and stomach, and marveled at the chain of eggs like a string of graded pearls, moving down nature's assembly line as they approached the stage at which they were complete and ready to be laid. There lying on the counter this morning were two bright yellow chicken legs with feet waiting to be discarded. When I asked Maria if I could have them, she replied, "*¿Cómo no?*" (Why not?). In typical Spanish manner she didn't interfere by asking what I was going to do with the legs. Perhaps she should have, because a plan had begun to take shape in my head.

The plan included eleven-year-old Tia. I had long known that Tia and I were very different. It wasn't just that her mother worked for us but that somehow the two of us came from and were still living in very different worlds. When I saw those two chicken legs divorced forever from the chicken that had walked on them, I was overcome by an urge to test one of those differences between Tia and me.

I thought I could scare Tia. Chicken legs in hand, I started by raking together some loose soil at the base of a tree where I made a conical mound about two feet in diameter and a foot high. Inserting black pebbles for eyes, nose, and mouth and sticking the chicken feet as arms midway between the face and the base of the mound in an "I'm going to get you" arrangement, I stood back to survey my creation. It was pretty spooky and still looks devilish in my mind's eye. Admiring my handiwork, the next step was to see if it would do what it was designed to do and the only way to find out was to find Tia. She was in the kitchen, leaning against the sink idly watching her mother, standing with one leg curled around the other.

Taking her hand in mine and not wanting to give her a chance to spoil things by seeing my spook at a distance, I said, "*Tía, ven aca.*" I led her out the back door, down the steps around toward the street, and right up to the tree, where I pointed to my creation and said, "*¡Tía, mira!*"

"AIEEEEEE*eeeeee*," she screamed and jumped. Turning in midair, Tia hit the ground running back to the kitchen. Her reaction sobered me. I hadn't realized it was possible to produce such an effect with so little effort. Mulling this over, I somehow understood that this kind of experiment was risky at best and probably wrong. I hadn't counted on really scaring her. Slowly and carefully I dismantled my little shrine to the devil, put the chicken legs in the garbage where they belonged, and as a finishing touch, flattened my cone of earth. I had already known instinctively that Tia and I differed in fundamental ways and now I knew that, of the two of us, she was the more vulnerable.

TWO

The Mueller and Los Alamos Schools

FOLLOWING our spring and summer in Santa Fe, Mother brought us back to my father and our house on Gore Avenue in Webster Groves. By then I was five and old enough to go to school. At some point I had learned to read, although I don't remember when or how, but it was in school that I really learned what it means to be small and weak and picked on by those who are more robust. Children from the age of five on can be pretty terrible to each other.

First there were the bullies. Bullies seemed to have a sixth sense which told them they could pick on me without getting in trouble themselves. Some kids would scream and yell and make such a fuss that it attracted attention. What a bully wants is a polite well-disciplined little kid who simply stands there and takes it: a punching bag for displaced aggression. Apparently I was an easy mark. Schools then as now did little to discourage bullying. Yet I noticed that there were other little kids who did not attract the bullies' attacks the way I did. I had to ask myself what I was doing that caused these oversized hulks to rough me up for the pure pleasure of it. Often they acted as though there was something sinful about me, that I had done something wrong and that they were punishing me for it. I knew this wasn't the case and that if someone had challenged them they would be unable to justify their position. But I did feel there was something different about me and that, because I couldn't defend myself, I was being beaten up.

It was when I was in the third or fourth grade at a private school in St. Louis run by two German women that the bullying came to a crisis. It started with Fritz. Fritz was the son of Germans who had immigrated to St. Louis and become successful. He was oversize for his age, or perhaps he had been held back in school and was just bigger because he was older. Red-faced and fat, he had a clumsy, awkward, aggressive way about him. I don't remember his playing with anyone, but whenever he found me alone Fritz would grab me and start pummeling. Our school playground was too small for baseball so we played soccer instead. For some reason best known to Fritz, he never played. But when there was no game in progress he would make a beeline for wherever I happened to be, and the beating and harassment would begin. In desperation I screwed up my courage and went to complain to Miss Mueller, the headmistress. I didn't know it but I was about to learn a practical lesson in the unstated rules of culture. Looking for support from above, I got a disdainful reproach: "Handle it yourself. You must have done something to cause the fight." I later learned that when dealing with Germans you really are expected to handle things yourself on your own level, and if you can't, too bad!

I don't know how long I would have stayed locked in a hopeless losing struggle with my nemesis Fritz if my mother, who must have guessed that things weren't going well, hadn't for once in her life taken action. She announced that my friends and I were going to take boxing lessons. Recoiling at the thought, I wondered where in the world she had gotten such an idea. I wasn't a boxer! I didn't even like to fight (which may have been part of the problem). Anyway, half a dozen of us fellows found ourselves lined up on the grass facing our boxing instructor, outside the south wing of our house. By then we had moved from our comfortable Gore Avenue house into a fancy new one which my father had built on Berry Road across from the Algonquin Country Club. The house was of stone, a replica of a Normandy chateau with seven acres of lawn, shrubs, porte cochere, and studio for my mother as well as about fifteen acres of woods, orchard, and vegetable garden.

Mac, our instructor, was a genuine pug, like the kindhearted, gentle Joe Palooka who appeared in the 1930s funny papers. Like Palooka, Mac even said "youse guys." There was only one of our group who was able to really hit. If you can't hit, and most people can't, you'd better stay away from boxing. After working with us awhile, I think Mac realized the problem. Mac had already told us how he grew up in a tough East St. Louis neighborhood where he had to be able to defend himself. Mac said, "Now listen, youse guys." We were standing in a row in our shorts, all spindly arms and legs, facing him. "When I was a kid there was always bullies. Big stiffs who was beating up on anyone who'd let 'em. Now what youse guys gotta know about a bully is, he's like a bull. He'll charge you, sometimes it's like he has his eyes closed. You don't gotta be able to box or even to t'row a hard left. All you gotta do is t'straight-arm 'im, to stick out your fist and let him run into it. Dere ain't nothin' to it. Dat's all you gotta know. When he runs inta da fist, he won't bodder you no more. He'll go find somone else t'pick on who don' know about bullies."

The next time I looked up and saw Fritz coming at me, it was just the way Mac said. Fritz's arms were flailing about like a windmill. Terrified, I backed away until I could go no farther. With my back to the wall, elbows locked, I stuck out both arms, aiming at Fritz's nose. Then I waited and watched through squinted eyes while Fritz's nose connected with my two clenched fists. Fritz stopped, rubbed his nose with a kind of surprised expression, turned around without saying a word, and walked away.

Mac wasn't an anthropologist, but he was one hell of a good observer. He knew his bullies and he gave me as clear-cut and accurate an example of patterned behavior as I have ever had.

It wasn't only Fritz, however, that I had to contend with at Miss Mueller's school. A much more formidable foe was Mueller herself. She was always down on me. No matter how hard I tried nothing ever seemed to suit her. It might have had something to do with my refusal to blindly accept what the teachers said; I had instead an irrepressible need to find the sense in what they were telling me. When things didn't make sense—which was often—I started asking questions, a trait I still possess. To some people it makes little difference how things work or why things are the way they are. To me it has always mattered, which has been one of the drives behind my constant need to understand the patterns in other cultures.

A major source of my trouble with Mueller was the fact that I couldn't spell. My difficulties in spelling were traceable to the inconsistencies between English orthography and the way words are pronounced, and were further complicated by dyslexia. In most European languages there is a reasonable equivalence between the way words are said and how they are spelled, but anyone who is looking for sense or reason in English is bound to be mystified. I desperately looked for rules governing spelling, but I found none. My difficulty with spelling was seen as a refusal on my part to learn to spell. My poor performance was taken as outright rebelliousness against the core values of the school, which of course were sacred. Subversions of this sort must be dealt with severely. I never thought of myself as subversive, but that was the way I was being treated.

Later, much later, I learned that to the Germans, the written word is sacred. One learns the rules and obeys them. One does not complain, and it annoys them if you are weak. I was simply being subjected to a classic example of the more rigid variety of North German behavior. Unfortunately there was no one to interpret Mueller for me. And she would have been the last person in the world to recognize that, in spite of all her efforts to be a "good American," she was still acting like a German and treating students the way she had been treated in Germany when she was young. In her defense I should say she was just trying to run a school as best she could and to see to it that all of her charges could perform. So here I was, dyslexic before we knew about learning disorders, confronted with an impossible system, yet my failure to come up to snuff was seen as my being a subversive bent on undermining the authority of the headmistress—a woman who was not a receiver but a sender, who would brook no interference in her image of how the world was supposed to be. Unlike any other student in the school, I was required to spend hours in her office, cowed, squirming, and sometimes silently weeping under her stern and watchful eye. She probably really did care, otherwise I wouldn't have been there in her office. The trouble was that neither of us knew how to reach the other. So we remained forever alienated like two dogs in adjacent kennels restrained by culture's chains.

Christmas season was an occasion I looked forward to—a time of relief from the agonizing quotidian routine of class. I still like the sound of Christmas carols because they remind me of the short periods when we would take a break from class and practice singing them in preparation for the school's Christmas program for parents. That little thirty minutes or so was the only relief from the inescapable and constant torture occasioned by class routines and the uneasiness of being called on. There was no doubt about it that school and I were on a collision course and neither was going to give up. If I had known how to do what was wanted, I would have. But something in the situation left me with the feeling that I was utterly and congenitally incapable of performing in a manner acceptable to that German headmistress.

Then, in 1927, my world fell apart. I was eleven, almost twelve. One Saturday in February, I was in my father's study reading because it was raw and cold outside. I looked up and saw Mother standing in the doorway. She told me she wanted me to go for a ride in her car. She backed her blue Hupmobile out of the garage, hooking back to the right in order to reverse direction. She then swung left through the porte cochere and followed the driveway around the north end of the living room and east between all the shrubs my father had planted on the left and the duck pond on the right, down to the gate on Berry Road. I was glad to be alone with her for a change, free of the continuous bickering of my brother and sisters, which always made her nervous. Her Hupmobile was expensive and solid, well finished on the inside, with a smooth powerful motor. Sitting there beside her on the front seat, I was daydreaming about the time two years before when I was ten and had taught myself to drive our Dodge touring car in Santa Fe where we had spent the summer. (Santa Fe traffic in those days was virtually nonexistent. No driver's license was required. It was not unusual to see two apparently driverless automobiles approach each other. Looking closely, one could then see two little boys—one in each car—arms and necks stretched to bridge the gap between the seat and the steering wheel, avoiding burros, pedestrians, and an occasional car.)

I was thinking about how it would be to drive that big Hup 8. We had hardly gotten past the gate when I realized Mother was saying something. I heard her say that she would be leaving me, that she and Dad were getting a divorce. I heard the words and I knew what they meant but I could not take them in. She said that she would be taking my little sister Priscilla (who was too young to leave behind) and that she and Heinz—a German sculptor who had been around a lot for the past couple of years—would be getting married. This seemed unreal too. Why would she want to marry someone else? She was already married to my father. I could feel my stomach turning first to jelly and then to lead. I didn't make a scene—I was too well behaved—I only sank deeper into my seat trying to take it all in, to fathom what it meant. While I sat there in her blue car, my future simply vanished. The world closed in. I couldn't visualize my life without Mother.

There would be other times when it seemed as though my world would fall apart, but this was and will always be the worst. It took thirty-one years and endless analysis before the grief which had been so much a part of me that I didn't even know it existed finally broke through to the surface.

Ignorant of the ways of the world and still in a state of shock, Dad shipped me off to Los Alamos Ranch School where I had camped the summer before. Dad used to expound on how much he admired Teddy Roosevelt. Roosevelt was robust and "gung ho." He had mastered his asthma. He walked softly and carried a big stick, he had the iron hand in the velvet glove, and so on. It was part of the times. Fathers felt it their duty to inspire their sons to be something they were not. The sons were seldom fooled. To please Dad I should be like President Roosevelt. Riding alone on the Santa Fe Railroad's Grand Canyon Limited to Lamy, New Mexico (where I had spent my first night in New Mexico seven years before), I felt anything but robust or gung ho.

Standing next to my luggage on the blue brick platform at Lamy, I was met by a well-turned-out man in an immaculate Studebaker Phaeton. After stowing my gear the two of us drove through Santa Fe and crossed the Rio Grande over a narrow rickety suspension bridge at Otowi. In the course of our trip we climbed almost a thousand feet to Santa Fe, then descended from seven thousand feet to a little over five thousand at the Rio Grande, and then began an eighteen-hundred-foot climb. From the bridge crossing the Rio Grande, the road narrowed to two ruts in a tufa base.

Flanked by basalt-capped mesas, the road threaded between piñons and ponderosa pines, finally switching back and forth up the face of a steep mesa, until it topped out at seven thousand feet, a few miles east of the school. Rustic log buildings were situated in a clearing at the edge of a western yellow pine forest overlooking the Rio Grande Valley. It was a magnificent view. But so remote, and so very far from St. Louis.

Familiarity with the ambience as well as with the masters and staff was reassuring. I knew where I was. Apart from some new boys, there were familiar faces. Best of all there was Bensis, a Hispanic from Española, who clerked in the store in winter and was our camp cook when we were on the trail in summer. Bensis's face, like many New Mexicans' then, was pockmarked. He made the best sopaipillas any of us had ever eaten (or were to eat) and had the disposition of an angel. He was always smiling (though I know his life was not easy), always glad to see me, always cheerful and willing. Because of his status, I don't think many people there recognized what an important person Bensis was. But I did.

At Los Alamos I was simply one of a number of other boys whose parents had shipped them off to boarding school. There were twenty-four of us and approximately an equal number of staff and support personnel. Each boy had his own horse and tack for which he was responsible. Every other week saddles were cleaned and oiled as were bridles and any other gear, such as leather chaps and rifle holsters.

The school (later displaced by the Los Alamos atomic laboratory) had been founded by Ashley Pond, a Santa Fe idealist, who hired A. J. Connell, a temperamental, red-faced, obsessively neat

Irishman, to run it. A tough taskmaster, Connell demanded strict obedience. If you didn't get out of line everything went well.

The mountains were friendly and enveloping, the boys typically upper middle class, transplanted away from their protected, suburban homes. Classes were small—usually four or five boys to one master—and traditional in subject matter as well as treatment. The school was not very engaging, but was good enough to get you into any college or university in the country. What I enjoyed most was riding in the virgin pine forest behind the school, visiting the nearby ruins, fishing for trout in Ashley Pond (there were ten-to-twelve-inch steelhead trout in that pond that could bend your rod double), and the pack trips in the mountains. My father had given me money for a .22 rifle, which Mr. Curtis, one of the masters, selected for me and taught me to shoot; he also taught me the whole corpus of skills, rules, and cautions about guns, as well as a great deal about how guns are designed and made, such as the relationship between the ammunition and the way the bore is grooved. Many of the boys had rifles, including my friend William Burroughs, whom we called Bugs because of his interest in biology. Our uniform was simple: khaki shorts, shirt, bandanna, brown leather ankle-height shoes, Stetson hat, chaps, spurs that jingled, and a yellow slicker when on horseback.

When that school year ended I stayed on for the summer camp. Three pack trips were scheduled so that altogether we spent between six and seven weeks traveling and camping all over the Jemez Mountains. We visited or camped in or at the Valle Grande (the largest caldera in the world), the hot springs above Jemez Springs, Los Posos, Redondo Peak, Cebolla, Rio las Vacas, Vallecitos de los Indios, San Pedro Parks east of Cuba where the best trout fishing in the state was to be found, and Chicoma Peak, which is a sacred place to some of the Rio Grande Pueblos, who had left prayer plumes at the shrine on the mountaintop. On the pack trips we did everything including pack the mules, using a diamond hitch to tie our gear together securely.

My first year at camp I had ridden somewhere in the middle of our seventy-five-animal pack train. This summer it was assumed that I now knew all the trails we would be following, so Connell put me at the head of the pack train "to keep me away from the dust" and to clear the trail when necessary. The miracle was that I could remember all those trails covering over two thousand square miles after going over them only once from the middle of a mile-long train of animals. When confronted with the reality of being out in front and having to choose which fork to take, I really did choose faultlessly. But how did Connell, who had chosen me as leader, know I could do it?

I liked being in front for several reasons, one of them being that when we were crossing open country as in the Valle Grande I could ride and talk with Ted Mather, a short, swarthy wrangler who was half Indian and half English. Instead of carrying his .45 Frontier Colt in a holster, he had a special holster built into his chaps. I queried him on that one, of course. "Well, you see, if you have your gun on a cartridge belt you are likely to hang it on your saddle because it's heavy. But you don't ever take your chaps off until you're through work. Well, one time I had roped a horse out on the range and my leg got caught in rope. There I was being dragged by that horse goin' as fast as he could go. If I hadn't had that gun there in my chaps I wouldn'ta been able to shoot that horse." I didn't ask how Ted managed to draw a bead on the horse while being tossed, turned, and bounced along that uneven ground cover. Just a dead shot and a cool customer to boot, I imagine.

The first year I had had my own horse, a mare named Frisk. I had left her at Los Alamos with their herd during the winter. She was with foal when they transferred the horses to the summer pasture in the mountains and didn't survive a late spring snowstorm. The snow was so deep that they had to dig the horses out. The telegram reached me just before my parents split up. She wasn't a great horse but she was all mine, and I had ridden her bareback all the first summer in Santa Fe so that some bad saddle sores could heal. She would do anything I asked her to do and she had taken me all over both the Sangre de Cristo range east of Santa Fe and the Jemez mountains.

To replace Frisk they had given me a young gelding—a strawberry roan that was "not quite broke yet" as the cowboys used to say. That meant that he wouldn't buck when you got on him but that was about all. There were a lot of things that horse didn't know and others that he was not used to. I was able in my own quiet way to teach him how to behave and not to spook when you threw a saddle on his back. After a while I was able to walk all around him and under his belly if I wanted and he would take the bridle without throwing his head up. In fact, he had become a well-mannered horse, except for one thing: when riding along the trail the slightest movement on either side, like a gum wrapper or even a leaf blown by the wind, would release the most incredible shy in that horse. One minute we would be going straight ahead; the next minute he had moved sideways a good four to six feet. Ted used to watch that performance and laugh. And then he would say, "That horse is going to unseat you yet. You'll be riding along thinking about something, and a squirrel will jump up and run up a tree and before you know it you're sitting on the ground brushing the dirt off. Happened to me once. Never could break that horse of shying." Well, neither did I but I did find out, years later when working on *The Hidden Dimension*, why some horses couldn't be broken of shying. It's a matter of the circuitry in the peripheral part of the retina which actually amplifies motion in the peripheral field, releasing an immediate "hard-wired" response called shying. Without this built-in device the ancestors of my horse would have been much more vulnerable to predators on the African plains. He was treating a moving piece of paper as though it were a lion hiding in the grass. This experience with that horse made the whole matter of the sensitivity of the peripheral field (even in humans) so much more real to me than it might have otherwise been.

That second summer in the mountains meant as much to me—even more in fact—as the first one. There is something about living outdoors in the forest for weeks on end that is unlike anything else I know. Everything is so real! Much of what you do is in your hands and not the hands of others. No one could have told me how to stick on that horse; I had to build in reflexes to meet the horse's reflexes on my own. I did, however, learn to spot potential sources of movement that might spook him so that I would be prepared when he jumped sideways. But then some things are not in your own hands and can't be controlled.

That fall before school started again, Connell took me out for a ride by myself in his car and told me that my father had written that he couldn't afford the tuition at Los Alamos, so I was to be sent to another school in the Sangre de Cristo Mountains on the east side of the Rio Grande. This was a shock. I was just beginning to get settled and to feel at home in Los Alamos. But shock could not take away what I had learned in Los Alamos: a lifelong obsession with doing things right, with the maintenance of all equipment, and with the importance of quality. These ideals were shared by most of my classmates when I met them later in life.

THREE

The Aspen Ranch School

WHEN I ARRIVED at a house on Hillside Avenue in Santa Fe a large, rough-hewn man about fifty-five years old welcomed me and introduced himself. Robert C. Ten-Eyck, while large-framed and rugged, was not completely the outdoor lumberjack type. He had an air of competence and self-assurance that told me he not only was comfortable around men but was used to managing them. Ten-Eyck had owned one of the hundreds of small railroads crisscrossing the country in the early part of this century. His two trains linked Santa Fe to the Estancia Valley to the south, but had been replaced by roads and the new trucks which were rapidly taking the place of wagons and horses.

I later got to know Mr. Ten-Eyck while guiding him around the mountains during deer season. My initial impression of him was correct. Like many self-assured, competent people he could recognize and accept the expertise of another human being without injecting himself into the equation. Not once, after having climbed up and down over a couple of dozen ridges and valleys for an entire day, did he ever question his young guide as to whether we were on the right trail or not. It has been my experience that the less secure and less familiar people are with a subject the more likely they are to interfere with ongoing processes. This is particularly true of getting around in strange territory. People often become instant experts and will challenge anyone. But Ten-Eyck and I had no trouble communicating and hence no trouble relating to each other.

At our first meeting, Ten-Eyck explained that Larry, one of the cowboys, would be by in a little while to take me to the ranch, after he had picked up groceries and other supplies for the school. Ten-Eyck's daughter Carolyn had married Norman Appleton, a young man who wanted to start a school in the mountains. Ten-Eyck had put up the money.

Sitting there next to the living room window, I heard a truck drive up at the same time that Ten-Eyck pushed himself up out of his chair. Larry was driving a Dodge Power Wagon outfitted as a greengrocer's delivery truck. There was quite a contrast between that truck with its wire sides and back and the Los Alamos School's immaculate Studebaker Phaetons. The truck was only the first of the differences between the two schools.

Larry tossed my gear into the back of the truck next to the groceries and some sacks of grain, slammed the rear gate, and pushed aside the clutter on the front seat to make room for me. That done, he climbed in, settled his tall, thin frame behind the wheel, and sat there, looking straight ahead, saying nothing. Then, glancing at me sideways, he breathed a sigh and said with sadness in his voice: "Well, I guess we might as well get going. It sure was good to be in town."

Driving north on the road to Taos, we passed through Tesuque and turned right on the road to Rio en Medio and Aspen Ranch, about three miles north of Tesuque. The road as it headed for the mountains dwindled to nothing but two wagon tracks through the foothills. It climbed up one hill and down another through the parched, chamisa-covered open range[1] until we reached the top of a ridge overlooking the Tesuque drainage on one side and the Rio en Medio on the other. Dropping down into the Rio en Medio drainage, we soon entered a dark, granite-walled, spruce-filled canyon. Nosing down into the stream at the bottom of the canyon and then scrambling over boulders, we swayed, rocked, and bumped in low gear as we clawed our way up the opposite bank. After about a dozen of these crossings, the driver announced with pride that "there are twenty-one stream crossings in a mile!" Later I learned that the crossings were duck soup compared to working our way through that narrow gorge in the winter when the truck was replaced with a wagon pulled by two magnificent Percherons called Bill and Dandy. Not only were the ups and downs still there, now covered with snow, but there were hundreds of feet of glare ice where the stream had overflowed, which had to be chopped with an ax to keep the horses from falling, and all this at ten to twenty degrees below zero.

The canyon seemed endless. I thought we would never leave that dismal, dank, closed-in space. The forest of fir trees was old, and having never been cut, was choked with a nearly impenetrable mass of underbrush and fallen timber. Eventually a bit of sunlight appeared on the red granite walls above the treetops, and it looked as though we might break out of the gloom. Sure enough, cresting the last rise in the canyon floor, we were suddenly at the edge of a mountain meadow surrounded by aspens. The wagon trail then turned north up the side of the slope, ending at a crest covered first with scrub oak and then with a wonderfully open stand of mature western yellow pine *(Pinus ponderosa)*. My spirits began to rise; the sun was warm and I could see again.

As we climbed along the crest of that ridge, I could tell we were gaining altitude (Larry said ten thousand feet, but it was closer to nine). I was beginning to wonder where the ranch could possibly be. Some of those meadows that we passed looked like good locations. Why wasn't it in one of them? The truck ground along in low gear, bouncing off rocks, climbing out of ruts, but always climbing. Then without warning the truck's hood, which had been pointed upward, dropped away as we plunged down the side of a steep ravine. There we were back again among the spruce trees and all the tangled undergrowth surrounding their thick black trunks. Bouncing and skidding, the truck worked its way around a steep sharp turn to the right, down a straightaway, taking another turn this time to the left, then approaching yet another stream crossing on the edge of a meadow. Breaking out of the forest at the meadow's edge I could see two log buildings on the side of a hill facing south. The ranch was in the bottom of a canyon. No forty- to fifty-mile view this time; one-fourth of a mile would be more like it. The last quarter mile from the stream to the larger of the two houses was a steep climb in and out of ruts in black loamy soil.

We were met by a tall, thin man dressed in fancy cowboy garb (Pendleton shirt and pants, red cowboy boots with four rows of stitching, neck scarf and white Stetson hat) who greeted us with a smile, introducing himself as Norman Appleton.

A biologist who had been to Bucknell during World War I, Appleton later told me, with some pride, how he had managed to escape the draft by enrolling in the divinity school (ministers were exempted from the draft). Since there was no popular antiwar movement at the time, why he would boast about it was not clear. Avoiding the draft in those days was not something a man would vaunt in front of others, especially in the West. Yet in these off-hand remarks about his past, there lay a strong clue as to how the man's psyche was organized and how it worked against him much of the time. Figuring him out took a while. But even the first time we met, I sensed there was something bizarre about Appleton. The first incongruities I noticed were in the clothes he was wearing. They were all of good quality, but of the kind men only wore when they dressed up. His saddle, which he showed me almost immediately, was of stamped and hand-carved leather. Both the cantle and swell were trimmed with silver. Those who knew the difference would note that Appleton had chosen a three-quarter rig for his saddle when a double rig would have been more suitable in our mountains. Appleton's choice of clothes and equipment screamed that he had had no real cowboy experience other than that of a dude. For the most part Appleton's persona was made up of a kind of foolish bravado to hide a man who had never been able to understand what the world was all about nor where he fit into it. There were times when Appleton's bumbling attempts to act the cowboy were lethal. And it soon was apparent to me that if anything was done right on the "ranch" it wasn't because of Appleton.

. . . .

The Aspen Ranch School consisted of two buildings. The first was a log cabin built on the slope of a steep hill with a wide porch in the front. To enter the building one had to climb at least nine feet up a broad series of steps. It was almost like going from the main deck to the poop deck on a square-rigger, and anyone standing on the porch commanded that small domain. Inside were the captain's quarters: a large living-dining area with a huge stone fireplace opposite the door. To the left were two rooms, one in the front of the house where Appleton and his wife slept, and the other which was occupied by various people, including the cook. To the right of the door was the dining area, adjacent to the kitchen. There was also an attic, which was reached by climbing a ladder on the outside. The second building was an L-shaped bunkhouse with separate rooms in a row like an old-style tourist court. This was where we boys slept. Each pair of boys occupied a room opening directly onto a porch where the boys and one master slept outdoors with temperatures in the winter dropping to thirty or more degrees below zero. The cowboys bunked in the attic of the main building.

The contrast with Los Alamos was beyond belief. The first clue was in the equipment and how it was maintained, such as that old beat-up Dodge delivery truck with wire mesh around the back. Then there was the physical plant, which could only be described as minimal. The corral for the horses and the attached barn were a good half mile from the main lodge. The corral, because it was substantial with a full-size snubbing post in the middle, was at least up to standard. Each boy had a horse assigned and the tack was adequate—not fancy, hand-carved stuff with tapaderos almost to the ground such as Appleton sported, but solid, well made, of good leather and reasonably new.[2]

The Sangre de Cristo Mountains were much more rugged and tougher to get around in than the Jemez had been. Nor were the Sangres as open as the Jemez. We did ride in the mountains—north to Rancho Viejo and along the Windsor Trail toward Cowles on the other side of the mountains—but nothing like the extended rides we used to take at Los Alamos.

One day, Appleton, one of the cowboys, and I rode through the aspen grove next to the ranch, following a steep climbing trail which broke out into a beautiful alpine meadow nestling in a bowl some two thousand feet below Lake Peak.[3] From there we picked our way up a two-thousand-foot climb to the top of the mountain. The horses had to get over an interlocked mass of tree trunks felled during a massive forest fire fifty years before. From Santa Fe the fallen trees looked like matchsticks strewn over the side of the mountain. Today, another sixty years later, most of the trunks have rotted and returned to the soil.

Reaching the crest at twelve thousand feet we worked our way down a narrow rocky path so steep and rough that it was necessary to dismount and lead the horses as they picked their way foot by foot. Below us was a beautiful little blue-green lake.

Santa Fe Lake is at the headwaters of the Santa Fe River and the head of Santa Fe Canyon. Standing there in the clear mountain air, listening to the breeze as it whistled through the branches of the spruce trees, I watched Appleton as he bent down and carefully filled a mason jar with water from the lake. Naturally curious, I asked him what he was going to do with that water, to which he replied, "Wait and see. You'll be surprised."

A week later Appleton opened the jar and, using a medicine dropper, put a single drop of the water on a glass microscope slide over which he then placed a thin covering glass. Seating himself at a workbench next to a window he carefully slid the slide onto the stage of a microscope. He adjusted the mirror and then the lens, then examined the droplet from the jar with intense concentration. After what seemed like an interminable period he looked up and beckoned me to come over and sit down. After explaining how to use the mirror to get light on the slide from below and to focus the microscope without breaking the cover glass, he invited me to take a look.

There before my eyes I saw, for the first time, an active world of small creatures scurrying in all directions. I had never seen anything like it, anything that active and alive before. They were amoebas that put out pseudopodia into which they then flowed as a way of getting about. Anything edible and small enough was ingested as an amoeba flowed around it, incorporating that morsel into its protoplasm. There was no mouth, no head or tail, only protoplasm edging its way around in the tiny world under the lens of my microscope. Paramecia with thousands of hairlike cilia that could move the organism in any direction had a form like a bedroom slipper with an oval slit in the side for ingesting food. *Euglena viridis* (on the border between plant and animal) was a flower-shaped cup attached to a whiplike flagellum which worked like a strung-out propeller. There were cilia around the rim of the cup which swept smaller organisms down into the mouthlike area of the cup. I was so fascinated that terms like "mitosis" (cell division) and "conjugation" (an early form of sex in which paramecia revitalize themselves after numerous cell divisions) soon became part of my everyday vocabulary.

Appleton got me some prepared slides of different stages of the entire process. Looking at the prepared slides was not the same as watching the process unfold before my eyes. It was possible to see, even at that early stage, that the information in the chromosomes was what made it possible for the organism to grow and develop in an orderly manner. In mitosis it was also evident that, as the chromosomes split down the middle, the information was being divided equally so that each daughter cell would have what it needed to grow, to live, and to reproduce. For me to learn how the information was coded would of course have to wait until much later. While there was no way I could have known it at the time, the mystery of the information coded in those chromosomes would set me on a course which I was to follow for the rest of my life.

Appleton liked to do drawings of human anatomy, but he was also very good at drawing protozoa. He taught me how to make stippled ink drawings of the details as well as the gross anatomy of these tiny creatures, drawings which identified the microanatomical structures controlling the metabolism of these microscopic beings, how they ingested their food and eventually evacuated the waste products. Once I was started he would leave me alone to draw and to learn. If I had a question I would wait until he arrived and ask it. Learning and school for the first time in my life were combined with those magic ingredients: complete absorption, concentration, and fun. Now there was something in school that was alive, which really interested me, in which I could be totally lost to the outside world. As I peered through that microscope, there was even a hint that some of what was going on might make a little bit of sense.

The rest of the curriculum was standard for prep schools of the time: history, mathematics, Spanish, English grammar and composition, all taught by either Appleton, his wife, or Captain Terry, who had come to us from a military school. Terry had a drinking problem which was probably why he had left the previous school. Actually he was not a bad guy and apart from Appleton's biology was the better teacher. Carolyn Appleton wasn't the worst teacher I have known but certainly couldn't be ranked with the good ones either.

Even though Appleton opened my eyes to the magic of biology, I never really warmed to either the Appletons' school or to them as a couple. Mrs. Appleton was tickle-brained and neither of them knew anything about running either a ranch or a school. As a less mature human being than I am now I was inclined to categorize Appleton according to the stamp which our culture placed on him —he was inept, and like many others had little feeling for congruence and for the deeper levels of human ties to their culture. Many Americans are brought up in a white hat/black hat tradition in which people are seen as either all good or all bad—for us or against us. Yet life is not that way—so many talented people are misunderstood because of traits and mannerisms which if viewed on a larger screen become relatively unimportant compared to what they are really doing. Picasso was one of those. His life was less than perfect. But he changed the way we look at the world.

While Appleton was no Picasso and will remain relatively unknown he did make a contribution; the other side of Appleton's nature, which I am sure he did not fully appreciate in himself—and in this I can sympathize—was that he had a sense of what the geneticist Barbara McClintock called "a feeling for the organism." In this context both McClintock and Appleton were decades ahead of their times. Appleton did the right things without knowing why he did them. He understood biological systems *as systems* and by so doing transcended the compartmentalizing tendency of most of our science. His fragile ties to the culture, in this instance, worked to the advantage of the human species in the circumstance I am about to describe. In the thirties and early forties the Rocky Mountains of the southwestern part of the United States were suffering a horrendous infestation of "tent caterpillars," which were wiping out the aspen trees that spring up following forest fires. The aspens' function is to protect the seedling conifers as they grow up to replace those trees destroyed in the fire. So far nothing had worked on the tent caterpillars. Appleton took an approach which became known years later. By studying sick caterpillars, he managed to identify and isolate the organism which was killing the caterpillars. By making a culture of these natural enemies he demonstrated that this organic treatment, specific to the infestation, really worked. Unfortunately DDT, which was so popular after the war because it killed practically anything, became the insecticide of choice.

All of this was, of course, years after Appleton was a part of my life. But it was this very quality in Appleton that made it possible for me to learn from him and which gave biology the comprehensiveness so characteristic of living systems and so *uncharacteristic* of the way it was taught in most schools. Another point which I keep finding examples of in the course of my life is that there are many people like Appleton in this world and it is about time we stopped throwing them away because of what are relatively minor character flaws. Sure, many of them appear to be losers, and they are frequently difficult to love or to like, mostly because of their goofy behavior, their bull-in-the-china-shop attitude, and the fact that they don't fit easily into our white hat/black hat categories.

Viewed in this larger context, I am much more at ease with the memory of Appleton than I would have otherwise been. Also, I learned a good deal about what to avoid from him. He was a wonderful model of what not to be when it came to just plain getting ahead in this world.

There were real cowboys at Aspen Ranch. They related to me quite differently and did their best to toughen me up as I spurted into and through puberty. My transition from boy to young man was fast. It was over almost before I knew what had happened, and it left me with new problems. Most of the cowboys had lived lives which were about as unpredictable as my own had been, so there was a sort of kinship there, plus the dubious advantage of well-defined sex roles, which ensured, for example, that the female cook would never go out into the wood yard and gather wood for the stove. We would saw logs on a massive circular saw run by a Cushman Cub gasoline engine that went "whump whump whump wuf wuf wuf wuf whump whump." The saw screamed a high-pitched note as it chewed its way through a twelve-inch pitch-pine log. The note was lower for aspen, which was softer. At some point one of us would look up and see the cook standing in the open kitchen door with her hands on her hips. This was the sign for one of us to run over to see what kind of wood she wanted, return, pick up the wood, carry it in, and stack it in the wood box next to the stove.

Apart from Appleton, the ranch was run by the cowboys and there was a reason for doing everything in a particular prescribed way. These ways were built on a solid foundation of experience—years and years of trial and error, accidents and deaths that had happened when things were not done as they should be, mistakes to be avoided in the future. None of these rules were ever explained, but were implicit in the way in which procedures were demonstrated and the way they were followed by a little story illustrating what had happened to "poor old Mike" when he was snaking a pitch-pine log down off the ridge with a team of horses. "The team got spooked by a bear and he got caught in the middle." The cowboys and their rules were a refreshing relief from Appleton's mistakes and the confusion of life in the cities and towns.

The only people I didn't seem to have problems with in those days were the cowboys at the Los Alamos and Aspen ranch schools. I understood them and they understood me. The fact that I really knew how to ride and handle horses, even those that were still in the bronco stage of their training, helped, of course. In addition I looked up to these grown men and was always eager to learn. Many of them shared with me difficulties in dealing with Easterners who looked down on us at the same time that we were forced to put up with their incompetence on the trail.

It was pretty obvious to me that the ranch school could not operate forever. There was discontent among the boys Connell had sent to Aspen Ranch from Los Alamos. The food was poor and disorganization was endemic—accidents were always waiting to happen and did happen.

Dad visited me only once in the twelve months I was there and I didn't get the impression that he paid much attention to what was actually going on around me—he was too tied up in his own problems, which were mostly concerned with why Mother had left him. For reasons having nothing to do with the school or Appleton's incompetence as a manager, Dad took me out in the fall and moved me into Santa Fe to live with a couple he knew, Theresa Dorman and Josef Bakos.

I didn't really want to stay at the ranch much longer. Yet there were important ties: the biology and the fact that I had suddenly metamorphosed from a slight kid into what would soon be a reasonably solid grown-up man.

I moved into Santa Fe with Bert, one of the cowboys, taking my saddle, chaps, guns, and a Stetson hat which I still have. It was fiesta time and no one was at home to receive me, so Bert and I spent the first night sleeping with our heads on our saddles under the portal of Joe Bakos's house on the Camino del Monte Sol.

FOUR

Living with the Artists

THERESA DORMAN, her nineteen-year-old son John Dorman, and Josef Bakos lived together in Joe's house, home of the Cinco Pintores (the Five Painters) and center of the original Santa Fe art colony made up of painters, sculptors, writers, and poets.[1] They were the community in which I lived and to which I related and kept returning from 1928 until 1942 when I joined the army.

Bakos painted in the style of the Impressionists and made furniture. Theresa drank and schemed. A voluptuous dark-haired woman of Italian descent, Theresa told everyone she was an Italian countess and had been cheated out of her inheritance by her husband. While considered a corker by some men, Theresa had a hungry, dissipated look. Too much food and an excess of alcohol had taken their toll. But Theresa was a skilled practitioner in the art of wheedling and conniving and she could still make a sucker out of a certain type of gullible male. Unfortunately, my father was such a man.

At one time Theresa had been a friend of Mother's, but having discovered that my father had a little money, she directed her charms toward him instead. She had known Dad for about five years when I was sent to Aspen Ranch. I became an unwitting player in a new scheme. Hearing about my schooling so nearby in the mountains, she said to Dad, "Why not have Ned move to Santa Fe and stay with us? Then he would be with a family. Why spend all that money on tuition and board? If you just gave us what you are spending on Ned's education, he could go to public school in Santa Fe for nothing, and we could hire a maid to cook and clean up. It would be much better all around. That way you would know what was going on and wouldn't have to worry, knowing that he is in responsible hands." Dad bought it.

Joe Bakos, a second-generation Pole, was a square-shouldered, rough-cut man with a false joviality which served him well with those who did not really know him. He had grown up on the streets of Buffalo, New York, fighting with the Germans, which I think was the high point in his life because he talked about it all the time. Actually he was damn good in a gang fight (I saw him in action once during a brawl between two softball teams) and he could make furniture and build adobe houses. As a painter he was mediocre. As a human being I would rank him about two cuts below Appleton, although Bakos was more successful at hiding what he was really like.

The Dorman/Bakos house was of adobe, on a slope on the west side of the Camino. Joe had built the house and furnished it with his own Taos-type furniture. A high adobe wall protected the house from the street. Joe and Theresa had a bedroom and bathroom and there was another room for Theresa's son. On the south side of the kitchen, adjacent to the neighbors' property, was a large, dark, nondescript room used for storage. I was given that room. It was evident that any accommodation to my presence on Theresa's part was purely symbolic. In the two years I lived there, I never did have a place, to say nothing of a room, I could call my own.

I slept in this large dark room surrounded by junk for perhaps two months. Then Bakos built a lean-to against the adobe wall dividing his property from that of Will Shuster, who made etchings. A lean-to is open to the outdoors on one side. In this case the open side was to the north. I spent the rest of my two years there sleeping in the lean-to. I was told I would be healthier sleeping outside, but in reality the presence of a strange teenager in the house was cramping Joe and Theresa's style. Both of them liked to drink, which was especially apparent when they were visited by Duff Twysden (this was the woman on whom Brett Ashley in Hemingway's novel *The Sun Also Rises* was based). Duff was a real drinker. People swore it took at least a quart of gin to get her drunk, but by then she would be off and running. Why Theresa thought that by moving me outdoors I wouldn't hear what was going on in the patio was puzzling. One message did come through loud and clear: my status had been reduced to that of the stepchildren and orphans in the fairy tales my mother used to read to me.

By the time I had arrived on the scene Theresa had deteriorated from the svelte, curvaceous brunette she had been when she married Dorman. The two had teamed up to work a gullible public for whatever they could get. She attracted the men and when sufficiently softened, turned them over to Dorman. He and his get-rich-quick schemes did the rest. He was the brains and she was the bait. Piecing together fragments dropped by Theresa and later by Dad, I reconstructed a partial picture of what was going on. After working with Dorman for several years, Theresa had chosen, for whatever reason, to remain in Santa Fe and move in with Bakos. But whenever a live sucker appeared, Theresa would contact her husband (a shadowy figure who waited in the wings to appear in whatever guise might be appropriate to the situation). Dad told me that Dorman had visited him in his office in St. Louis and had managed to get him to invest in what later turned out to be a scam. While it was not at first clear what was going on, the pattern did unfold, mostly I suppose because Theresa and Joe thought I was just a dumb kid. I used to sit and watch while they maneuvered and schemed, setting a series of traps which Dad always seemed to miraculously avoid (usually through comical misunderstandings, such as the time he was supposed to meet them in San Diego and turned up in Santa Barbara).

Theresa, Bakos, and Dorman would hold conferences and get-togethers, some of them in California, some in El Paso and Juarez, but always near the border between Mexico and the United States. One scheme, involving a whole cast of characters, was to buy an entire deserted, remote border town reputedly owned by a single man. The town was half in Mexico and half in the United States. Dad really liked this idea because it gave his imagination free play and fed his grandiosity. He would sit at the kitchen table in Bakos's house and talk about how he would bedazzle the town's owner by presenting him with a suitcase full of bills (just like in the movies). Dad had visions of casinos and drinking—it was Prohibition time in the United States—and, while he never said so, I was sure he was thinking of bordellos. All this on the Mexican side, and a fancy "exclusive" resort on the American side, and Dad would own it all. Imagine owning a whole town! Well, the scheme almost made it that time. I assume their plan was to have someone in their group play the owner of the town. Others would be bogus recorders of deeds, attorneys, a couple of ranchers, Mexican bartenders. The real owner, if there was one, would have been paid to stay out of town for a short period while the scam was run. Possibly because they were too greedy, impatient, or fought among themselves, they tipped their hand.

Shortly after my arrival at the Bakos ménage I was sent to the public high school on Marcy between Grant and Lincoln streets. There I was directed to the office of Raymond Patrick Sweeney, the principal. A short, intense, dark-haired man with a casual air, he still had the look of the coach he had once been. Reviewing my records as I sat opposite him he said, "I guess you'll be a junior. You'll be taking Latin from me, history from Miss McKenna, physics from Greiner, English from Miss Dring, and algebra from Mr. Roberts." No biology and no Spanish.[2] I could hardly believe my ears: a junior, no less. Because I could go at my own pace at Aspen Ranch, I had actually managed to cover three years in one. I was overjoyed. For once I had done well in school.

I was eager to report the good news when I got home. But instead of congratulating me, Theresa acted as though I had done something wrong, which was puzzling. I had not yet considered the effect of my good fortune viewed from Theresa's perspective: by advancing two years more than expected, I had just cut two years off her sinecure. She had been counting on milking my father for at least four years, and now it would be only two!

What I liked best about Santa Fe High was the size of the school (there were about twenty-five in my class) and the ethnic mix of the student body—about half Hispanic and half Anglo with a couple of blacks. The curriculum was not particularly challenging. The teachers, as in most schools, were fair to average with a couple of real teachers thrown in. Nevertheless the total mix was good enough for those who got A's and B's to get into good colleges. I made friends instantly, which was wonderful and could be explained in part by western openness and the fact that the students were basically friendly and accepting. Unlike the other small towns I had known, Santa Fe kids had become used to the fact that the world was made up of all sorts of people with different kinds of knowledge. Danny Shuster, for example, could name all the bones of the body by the time he was six. When it came time for everyone to tell what his father did, Danny said his father, of Zozobra (Old Man Gloom) fame, made *etchings*, which he sold for cents apiece! Danny had to explain to the teacher what an etching was, so the whole class knew too.

So that her son John, a six-foot-four beanpole of a youth, would have a car to ride to school in, Theresa prevailed on my father to buy me a Model-T Ford coupe. I was only thirteen, but I had been driving since I was ten. Having a car of my own opened up an entirely new and pleasurable chapter in my life. I could now drive wherever I wished, limited only by my ability to buy gasoline. I was free to explore the country I loved and I used to drive members of my school athletic teams to meets in different parts of the state. But beyond the freedom, the car also brought me a new way of thinking about machines.

Model-T Fords were unusually simple—in fact, quite elegant—in design, but you had to know how to keep them running. There was, for instance, a carburetor adjustment on the dash. People were always twisting it to see what would happen, which either made the gasoline mixture so rich the car would stall or so lean that it would cough, spit, and then stall. Either way the car wouldn't run unless the carburetor was adjusted properly. The points needed adjusting, as did the spark plugs and the timing. It was inevitable that my car would have to be taken to Walter Miller, the mechanic who checked it over for my father before he bought it.

Walter was no ordinary mechanic. At his shop on East de Vargas Street (where a community theater is now located), there was a ten-foot wooden gate that hid a bare yard, a windmill, some old cars in an open shed, and a tall nondescript adobe structure with a peaked tin roof and dirty industrial-type steel windows. When I drove up in my Model T everyone within a mile knew I was there. By the time I had shut the motor off and opened the door, Walter had emerged from his lair to identify the source of the racket. A stocky Germanic-looking man wearing steel-rimmed glasses, Walter had an unassuming but thoughtful way about him. Dressed in a mechanic's typical striped overalls and duckbill cap, he acknowledged my greeting. Our first real conversation went as follows:

Walter: "What seems to be the matter?"

Me: "I don't know, Walter, she's just not running right. I thought maybe you could fix it."

Walter: "Why don't you fix it?"

Me: "Walter, I don't know how. Besides I don't have any tools."

Walter: "I'll *show* you how. You can use my tools. Can you get her home all right?"

Me: "I think so."

Walter: "I see you tomorrow then."

Walter then turned on his heel and reentered the shop. I still have some of the tools I bought working on automobiles under Walter's educated watchful eye over sixty years ago.

Walter's garage was more like an immense old barn than a garage and I really grew to love that place. At times I would go down there just to hang out. Inside the garage was a treasure trove of old automobiles, including some late-nineteenth-century "horseless carriages": a classic Apperson Jackrabbit roadster, one of the first Studebakers, a number of predecessors of the Model-T Ford, and an old Stanley Steamer (the first in the state—you had to be a licensed steam engineer to drive it, which Walter was, of course). There were a couple of old motorcycles and dusty motors of every vintage—nothing was ever thrown out. I eventually learned that all the men worth knowing in town ended up at Walter's because there wasn't anything Walter couldn't make or fix. A silent misogynist, he was polite and respectful whenever a woman appeared. But in general women stayed away from Walter's garage—I imagine it was the dirt and disorder and the general matrix in which Walter was set. The total effect of Walter's place was that of a jewel fashioned in one of Max Ernst's dreams: a happening, but still a work of art impossible to duplicate.

I used to love being there because of all the things different people would bring in to have fixed; the scene changed weekly and was an accurate index of what was breaking down in the community. "I see you got one of those new power lawn mowers in here again, Walter." "Yup, not too well made. People don't seem to be able to keep 'em running. You got to be careful of rocks when you're using them things. Hard to get the blades off, too."

Walter was not one to show emotion, but I soon learned to read him more reliably than many more demonstrative people I knew. We grew to be friends in the old-fashioned sense and, whenever I had been away, the first person I would go see on my return would be Walter. There he would be, standing at his workbench in front of that dirty window just as he had been when I left. I would close the sliding door to keep the warm air in if it was winter or the hot air out if it was summer, pick my way through the most recent collection of contraptions that needed Walter's particular magic, walk over to where he was standing, and wait. When he had finished what he was doing or came to a stopping place he would look up, and it was possible to detect the shadow of a fleeting smile on his lips, and then it would be as though no time at all had passed since our last visit. Around Walter I was able to learn how to relate properly to machines and to learn the principles on which they operated.

Walter never set out to teach me anything in the traditional sense. He just shared his knowledge and insights as well as his mental processes on the way to a solution. Just sitting there in that dusty mess of mechanical leftovers, I learned about a wide range of subjects. Who would believe in 1928 that cultural differences would crop up in an old garage where nothing ever got thrown out? But when Ted Asplund (the son of a neighbor on Marcy

Street dating back to our 1918 stay) was getting his start as a mechanic he worked under Walter's watchful eye and picked up, along the way, the key to working on foreign cars. Someone would bring in a 1925 or 1926 Fiat that was overheating. No one between Mexico City and Santa Fe had been able to fix it. They had tried everything—radiator, water pump, ignition timing (they overheat when retarded too far), the works. Yet nothing made a difference.

Walter would say, "Ted, you better check out that muffler. You know, over there, they make the inlet pipes on the muffler the same size as the outlet pipes and it's just possible that someone got the muffler on backwards when it was replaced in Mexico."

It would be the muffler, all right! But only Walter could see what was most important, that not only did Mexicans or other people "not do things over there the way we do" but what it was about the *way* they might be doing them differently that could cause a problem.

Another time Ted was rebuilding a motor on a Renault, vintage 1920–25. He had sent away for new oversize pistons and was boring out the engine block to accommodate the new larger pistons.

Walter said, "Ted, did you mike those pistons you got in for that Renault? You know we make our pistons all the same size so that when you order five thousandths oversize, that's what you get, but you can't always depend upon it in France and Italy." Sure enough, all the pistons were different sizes. Each cylinder had to be bored to fit a particular piston. The people whose car was being overhauled had no idea how lucky they were. The car ran like a sewing machine when it left the shop. If it had been in the average shop it would have left with a rebuilt motor but sounding like a cement mixer. How and where Walter picked up his knowledge of European culture is anybody's guess.

Years later, Peach Mayer, who had been one of my few good high school teachers and who lived in a wonderful Spanish colonial compound adjacent to Walter's garage, told me the following story. When her son Jimmy (now a well-known Santa Fe physician) was a boy, he used to visit with Walter and his pals. The old men and the little boy would hang out in Walter's little box of an office built up against the wall of the garage, drinking coffee and chocolate. It was typical of Walter that the same status would be accorded the child as the men. Though no one ever said so, the office was the sanctum sanctorum and was reserved for the sacred serious moments of sharing and feeling each other's presence. To be in that office signified membership in a select company.

One day following World War II, Jimmy, just home from school, had scooted over for his regular visit to Walter's place. Peach noted that coming home early, he hadn't stayed as long as usual. At first he said nothing to his mother but she knew something was wrong. Finally, unable to contain himself any longer, Jimmy, tears in his eyes, blurted out, "Walter's *dead!*"

Walter had had a heart attack driving to work in his specially built car, a Rube Goldberg assemblage of parts of other automobiles. Peach told me that the people who ran the *New Mexican*, the town newspaper, didn't know who Walter was, even though he was the state's first mechanic, the owner of the second automobile and the first motorcycle and the first Stanley Steamer in the state, the designer and builder of Dr. Aling's centrifuge for separating the components of blood, and goodness knows how many other specially built and designed pieces of research equipment. And, of course, he was one of the few people in the state who could really think and, in his own unassuming way, could guide others to do likewise. But none of this appeared in his obituary—who would imagine citing such talent in an obituary of a common garage mechanic?

I keep remembering things that I first learned from Walter. Both of us found human beings difficult to understand. He was born in another era and his skills and talents gave him pleasure. He knew who he was. He knew what he could do and he knew what he liked to do. He was one of the most effective teachers I have ever known. I still remember almost everything I learned from him. Walter was a bit out of place even then, in the late 1920s, but there was still a niche which he could and did fill. I am not certain whether that niche still exists, but I know the world could use more Walters.

. . . .

In the early years of the twentieth century there used to be a cartoon strip called "The Toonerville Trolley." One of the characters was a woman of tremendous girth (as wide as she was tall) named Aunt Eppy Hog. My neighbor Mrs. Jensen was as close as one could get in real life to the cartoon character. Her husband, Nels Knutsen Jensen, was six foot four and taught manual training at the high school. Their son Carl, a six-five young blond called "Swede" (they were Danish, so naturally he was called Swede), and I were schoolmates. He was one of the nicest, most easygoing fellows in the entire school. His right trapezius had been torn during birth, and his shoulder sagged to such an extent that his right arm was immobilized. Sports were all that really counted at Santa Fe High, yet Swede and his gentle laugh were always welcome despite the fact that he couldn't participate in sports.

Mrs. Jensen was famous for two things: her Danish coffee cake and the table at her boarding house. And therein lies a story. As soon as Theresa Dorman was sure that the checks for my maintenance were still coming in regularly, and since John was away at school at Pomona College, she and Joe took off for California, leaving me in the house with strict instructions not to let anyone in or to have any parties. I was told I could get my meals at Mrs. Jensen's. Although common in rural America, boarding houses were new to me. Reluctant at first, I soon learned that there was much to be said for Mrs. Jensen's fare over that provided by Theresa. Not only was the food good, but the company was an extraordinary mélange of character and talent. There we were, squeezed in like sardines with all that incredible food. There was a weird assortment of Santa Fe's gentry, including the pianist at La Fonda Hotel, who was so thin he couldn't sit on anything without a cushion. There were three of the teachers from my school (one beautiful and very smart, one handsome and nice, and one from New England with her tweeds and ground gripper shoes who was intelligent, strict, demanding, well educated, and one of the finest teachers I have known). Then there was Al Dasburg (son of the artist Andrew Dasburg), who was my friend and schoolmate. Al, like me, was a functional orphan—neither of us had parents with whom we lived. Al lived in a tent behind the boarding house.

Mr. Jensen, who was really an ornithologist, was also a rich source of information about the Indian school where he used to teach, telling how two little Indian boys once sneaked up on a bobcat sleeping under a bush and killed it with a stick! Tom Dodge, a full-blooded Navajo, often joined the table. Tom was the son of Chee Dodge, chief of all the Navajos in those days. Tom was a quiet type who wore tweeds and plus fours, practiced law and played golf. He had been to Oxford and was probably the only Oxford graduate in Santa Fe at that time. Tom's fiancée was a redheaded, attractive, diffident, well-brought-up young Englishwoman. Then there was a mousy accountant who could always be counted on to present the commonsense straight side of any issue. The meals were just plain fun: a combination of good food, good company, and good repartee.

The most important thing I gleaned from Mrs. Jensen was another of those difficult to learn and still more difficult to accept facts concerning the communicative aspects of culture. Like many North European women she was curt and abrupt in her speech. To our rather casual relaxed western ears she could sound gruff, as though she were trying to distance herself. There was none of the feminine softness in her speech that American women generally had when addressing people they liked or who weren't doing anything wrong. At first it was difficult to keep from being put off by the way she spoke to me; having been brought up to be polite and attentive I had become accustomed to women addressing me in a more "friendly" manner. It wasn't long, though, before it hit me. Mrs. J wheezed up to my place with a serving dish full of food and passed it to me in her usual gruff manner. Right then I knew (in the gnostic sense) that behind that gruff facade was a heart of gold and a depth of warmth. All I needed to do was to translate from the Danish style of presentation to middle-class western American. This is not an easy lesson to learn. I have had to remind myself again and again that the way a person speaks to you does not always reflect, in your terms, how he or she is feeling toward you.

Mrs. Jensen's boarding house proved not only to be interesting, diverting, and educational, but friendly as well as supportive. In some respects, the only other place where I encountered so much diversity was years later in the army. Of course, I began to realize I was better off when the Bakoses were out of town. Naturally Theresa didn't want Dad to know that they were not fulfilling their part of the bargain and were leaving me pretty much to my own devices. Worse, they weren't even providing a warm house for me to stay in. To keep me from saying anything, not even breathing a word, she let me know that I could count on retribution if my father found out that they were in California or even Ojo Caliente for weeks at a time and not in Santa Fe.

FIVE

Impressionism in New Mexico

TOWARD THE END of my junior year the boys in high school were all talking about getting summer jobs with the Highway Department. The idea of earning my own money was appealing. Whenever I had tried to make money before Dad had managed to obstruct my efforts because of his unconscious need to keep me dependent and also to demonstrate how soft I had it (compared to him). Now he wasn't around to intervene (or so I thought as I pushed ahead with my plans). The most common summer job as well as the easiest to get, because no experience was required, was that of rodman on a survey crew. Rodmen are the ones you see along the sides of highways holding a long narrow rod. If you look closely you can see numbers on the rod. The job involves little more than scrambling around over a variety of terrain, grasping the stadia rod in one hand and any convenient shrub, bush, or rock in the other to maintain your balance. Once you have gotten into approximate position, the engineer, looking through his transit, signals you just where he wants you to be. Then you must hold the rod very still so that the surveyor can read the distance from the numbers on the rod.

Since little skill was needed to qualify as a rodman, what were the requirements? You shouldn't go to sleep on the job, you must be able to move with some alacrity when necessary, you must not get too bored standing around in the hot sun and, most important, though no one said anything about it, you must be able to get along with the other members of the survey crew.

At the Highway Department just off Don Gaspar Street in the state capitol building, I started by asking questions about where to go to apply for a job. After the usual false leads, I was directed to the appropriate desk. An Anglo male in a white shirt recorded my name, address, age, education, and answers to questions concerning my experience and why I wanted a job with the Highway Department. Then he looked up at me, bobbed his head, and said, "That will be all. Check back with us when school is out and we will see what we can do." I thanked him and said goodbye. I was now a certified job applicant with the New Mexico State Highway Department. The pay was ample and you were paid for your own keep. The workweek was five days with the weekend off but you might be almost anywhere in the state, up to two hundred miles from Santa Fe. It sounded fine to me. Not too stimulating, but then given my age and experience, what did I expect? The main thing was the job—a real job and real pay. Driving home to tell the Bakoses I mentally reviewed what I would say to Dad and how glad I was to be able to relieve him of the load of my upkeep, even if it was for only three months.

In person and by pen (people weren't used to telephoning long distance then, except in emergencies, and even then they were more apt to send telegrams) Dad had showered me with laments of poverty and how pressed he was with having to support us children and what a difference it would make if he didn't have the expense of our upkeep.

By then I had begun to realize that my father was inconsistent in his drives and motivations and was pulled in at least two opposite directions. I had to take into account his own need to control and to keep me dependent, counterbalanced by his deep-seated penuriousness which took the form of a fantasy in which he was rid of all responsibilities, especially those inescapable ones associated with raising a family. I think there were times when he simply felt sorry for himself because Mother had left him. The result, regardless of motives (conscious or unconscious), was to emphasize that I was a burden. Proving that I could work and be on my own for a while was therefore important to me.

There was also the question of how to deal with Theresa. My strategy, developed from past experiences, was to shut myself off and to involve her in my life only when absolutely necessary. This was one of those times, since I had to tell her about the job. As I entered the house, she came out of the kitchen and placed herself in the doorway between the kitchen and living room with her hand on the frame, effectively barring the entrance to the kitchen and the room where I kept my things. I had wanted a little more time but since she wanted to know where I had been, I had to tell her. As my story unfolded she expressed more and more dissatisfaction. But why? Wasn't she delighted that I had taken the initiative and applied for a summer job? Apparently not. I couldn't remember Theresa ever complimenting me on anything so there was no way of judging where I stood with her at any given moment.

In the two years I spent with the Bakoses I was unable to detect, at any time, even a modicum of enthusiasm from Theresa about me. So I was not surprised when her reaction to the news of my summer job plans was far less than enthusiastic. Her negative response didn't bother me too much, as there had been little tendency on her part to interfere in the past. Nevertheless, the unexpected chill in the air and a hint of distress at the thought that I might actually get the job should have told me something.

Sure enough, the next week I received a letter from Dad saying that he didn't approve of what I was doing, adding in very uncharacteristic terms that I would be associating with rough construction types and that after all I was young and didn't know the score and could be led astray by associating with unsavory characters. Just how this was to be accomplished was not specified. I realized I had never heard Dad, under any circumstances, use arguments of that type before. His letter sounded more like something originating from an overly protective woman than a man. At that time, I had neither the insight nor the inclination to devote time to psyching out my parents (it would have been a full-time job), so I said nothing. I did not reply to his letter. From past experience I knew it would be useless to try.

I don't remember whether the news came from Dad or Theresa, but I was told I had been enrolled in Cyril Kay Scott's art class. I didn't know Cyril personally but I knew that he was part of the Santa Fe scene. I had seen clutches of art students with their easels —they all seemed to be women—wearing cotton dresses and straw sun hats, hunched over, dabbing paint from a watercolor box, painfully constructing washed-out versions of adobe houses with hollyhocks along sun-drenched walls. And there I was, freshly imprinted with a cowboy's image of what a man should be. A superabundance of energy and restlessness made me unsuited to sitting around on a canvas stool all day surrounded by middle-class women. I was dismayed, but then I hadn't been consulted and, never having been able to resort to the open rebellion of some of my more normal peers, it never crossed my mind that there were other options.

So how did I end up in Cyril's class instead of working as a rodman? It seemed that Theresa had done some quick calculating and had seen that she stood to lose the money my father was giving her for board and room (and a maid who seldom appeared). She had to have some way of keeping me at home and not in the field where I would be paid a per diem. She wrote—or possibly even telegraphed—my father, giving reasons why he should squelch my plans to work and at the same time suggesting the great advantages of having me enrolled in Cyril's class. I am not certain of the details but there were enough of her tracks and they were easy to follow. It was one of the many times in my life when things worked out for the better, but for the wrong reasons.

Cyril Kay Scott was a smallish, energetic man with graying sparse hair, a goatee, and small potbelly. If he had been an authoritarian, take-charge type he would have placed himself differently in the studio than he did. A take-charge type sets up rows of chairs and then puts himself at the head of the class facing the students. Instead, Cyril placed himself in the northeast corner of the room so he could refer to his notes and keep an eye on things. The rest of us scattered ourselves and our easels in a double semicircle catty-corner to the main axis of the room. As a silent tribute to the master, I don't think that there was anyone closer to him than twelve feet. Cyril's voice was clear and relaxed and carried with it the right amount of reassuring authority, the kind that knows but doesn't have to tell you so.

Since his son Creighton (Jig) and I were the same age, we grew to be good friends over the years. As a result I learned a good deal more about Cyril than I might otherwise have known. An Englishman, he did not speak with the upper-class public-school accent which was so characteristic of the other Englishmen I had known, nor do I remember his having any noticeable class or ethnic dialect. He had started professional life as an engineer and later switched to medicine. Clearly as a young man he had been searching for something, because he gave up medicine and received training as a psychoanalyst (it was rumored that he had been analyzed by Freud), which, in the 1920s, was an unusual thing to do.

The analysis, I assume, and a restless spirit deflected his interests from medicine to art. Paris at the beginning of the century was roiling with change and Cyril was the type who would have been in the middle of it. He told us he had studied with one or two of the better-known Impressionists, and since the names didn't mean much to me then I didn't pay much attention to which ones. From his art it would have been impossible to tell, because his painting was unlike that of any Impressionist I can think of. At the time of our art class Cyril had just moved to Santa Fe, bringing his two wives with him, one of whom was Jig's mother. This ménage à trois occupied an old adobe house on upper Canyon Road just below the reservoir.

My mother had always painted, as had her sister Blanche (a nervous wisp of a woman married to a sculptor). Heinz Warneke, my stepfather, was a sculptor of some note. Josef Bakos painted, as did everyone else on the Camino del Monte Sol: Will Shuster, Willard Nash, William P. Henderson, Andrew Dasburg, Fremont Ellis, Datus Meyers, and others, so that the activity of painting was not new to me. Even the paint-covered studio floors were a part of the familiar scene. It had just never entered my head that *I* might be doing it. I already knew I had no talent and couldn't draw, though I could make the very fine-grained stippled renderings of bones and protozoa like those in biology textbooks.

Our class was held in an ideal studio, an unused chapel on lower San Francisco Street. The only adaptation in the shift from chapel to studio was to replace the north wall with a large, clear glass window so there was plenty of light. The chapel was suffused with an aura of the particular comfort associated with pleasant, totally absorbing work. Years later I was to work there for Martha Field, Catherine Gay, and Ann Webster, who were sculpting and needed someone who could do their casting for them and pose for figure studies from time to time. Prior to Cyril's time, my mother had taken classes in that same chapel from B. J. O. Nordfeldt, a Norwegian painter who had studied with and was deeply influenced by Cézanne. It seemed that everyone who had anything to do with the art scene in Santa Fe had held classes or studied or worked in that studio. I don't know exactly when the chapel was demolished, but when I tried to find it in the 1950s it was gone, replaced by a cheap imitation adobe structure, and with it a very real part of Santa Fe's past had vanished. It was far from a public landmark, but there are places that don't need public recognition because their memorial is in the hearts of people.

With a minimum of fuss Cyril taught us the vocabulary and the grammar on which the Impressionists' system of painting was based: the isolates, sets, and patterns, an analytic method and classification system that I was to explain thirty years later in my first book, *The Silent Language.*

Cyril's method was to lecture from a voluminous set of notes in the morning and to allow the afternoon for painting. He explained that the Impressionists were inspired by the remarkable strides being made in late-nineteenth-century science (mostly physics). Using science as a model they analyzed what was happening when they looked at the world around them and experimented with how to express what they saw.

One of their preoccupations was with light—the quality of light; in New Mexico, this was something with which I could identify. They started with the assumption that if one concentrated on the quality of light and analyzed it carefully enough and didn't just look at things in a stereotyped way but really tried to see the relationship between the light, the surface of the object, and the image perceived by the eye, then something new would happen. They were right. They even studied sunlight as it was broken down into its components by prisms, discovering three things: that natural light, as in sunlight, is not the same as a pigment; that there is a carryover in such matters as primary and complementary colors; and that somehow they had to bridge the gap between the way in which natural light behaves and is perceived and how to treat it on a flat surface with pigments that don't act the same as natural light but would give the "impression" of a natural scene screened through different conditions of light. The famous paintings by Monet of the cathedral at Rouen at different times of day is a classic example of their discoveries. One might say that the Impressionists' gift to the Western world was that they taught us to look at that world in a more intelligent and perceptive way. No longer could visual perception be taken for granted.

The Impressionists' observations told them that colors could be arranged on a scale from warm to cool, which was the way we students would lay out our palettes. It was essential to know which colors gave the best impression of distance—which colors to use in the background, which in the middle distance and in the foreground. Right at the start each of us was forced to make a choice between warm and cool as to where our emphasis would be. I favored the close warm range (even though I dearly loved to be able to see a hundred miles from the top of any New Mexico mountain).

We were also told that by using the Impressionists' procedures, it was possible for a novice painter to produce a painting that "worked" the first time. It was stressed that we wouldn't produce a masterpiece but a painting in which the eye was led around the painting naturally by the composition, and in which the colors balanced and didn't clash, but stayed where they should be, not jumping off the surface of the canvas.

While lecturing, Cyril would make references to the work of different artists: Cassatt, Rouault, Seurat, Renoir, Gauguin, Matisse, Cézanne, van Gogh, Dufy, Vlaminck. We were never shown any pictures. He had his reasons—nothing could take the place of the original. And he didn't want us using reproductions of other artists' work as models. The extreme diversity of styles among the Impressionists is explained by the way they attacked their problem, and it is also evident that each of them got caught up in a different aspect of the subject. Matisse was a student of edges (lines); Seurat liked to work with the relationship of small bits of color as they built up an impression of light, Monet with the total effect of different lights on the same subject.

Expecting that our first paintings would all be quite similar, I was unprepared for the results. Difficult as it might seem, I didn't want to be influenced. I had deliberately avoided studying what was on the other easels in the room. But when the time came, the differences were so pronounced that it was hard to believe the paintings had all been done of the same subject in the same time and place. In Impressionist land it was mandatory to be oneself.

We did a number of additional paintings that summer, each one better than its predecessor. Each of mine represented a new challenge and revealed new sides of myself, though I didn't realize that until later. In many ways our small group was one of the most congenial (and the most diverse in composition) that I have ever worked with. There was a quiet, healthy, relaxed rhythm to our outings (after the first still lifes we spent most of the summer outdoors). Also, we were treated as professionals, expected to perform like professionals. I began to feel comfortable in this setting. It had certain things in common with the Los Alamos School, and, most surprising, was also reminiscent of working on a ranch. Cyril believed there was a reason for everything and he spent little time on philosophizing—fantasy and philosophizing were left up to the individual and were private matters. What went on in the studio had a no-nonsense air, a far cry from what I had feared from my observations of summer art classes for amateurs.

It was also interesting to note that while Cyril was unusually effective as a teacher, like many art teachers he was not a first-rate painter. His works were drab and colorless with little form or character. Nevertheless, he was later appointed dean of the University of Denver and director of the Denver Art Museum. The debt that I owe to him is incalculable. That man really knew what Impressionism was all about. Ever since then, art has run like a golden thread throughout the fabric of my life.

In retrospect, I find that the foundations of patterns important in my later life were laid down during that summer's work with Cyril. A great strength of the Impressionists was that there was *no* dogma attached to the movement as I learned it from Cyril. From that summer on, whenever I sketched with other artists they inevitably tried to get me to do it *their* way, whether or not I liked it or it fit. Later on I couldn't help noticing that this is also the hidden trap in the academic world. It is so ubiquitous that it is taken for granted that this is what professors are supposed to do. If professors could ever give up trying to produce clones of themselves and go deeper into their fields—explore how things are really put together, what really makes them work, and how different impressions are created—the implications for the academic world would be mind-boggling. First, of course, it would be necessary to subject most of the fields now taught to a rigorous reexamination, the same kind of rigorous analysis the Impressionists went through when they set out to discover what painting was all about.

Then there was the process itself. Not only were we taught that everything was interconnected but our experience with painting substantiated that premise. Paintings had to "work right"—the colors and the composition had to be congruent. A change in one color altered the perception of the color next to it. This may not sound like much but in a culture where everything is compartmentalized and linear and where people have trouble making connections there is a great need for what Buckminster Fuller used to call "comprehensive thinking." If there was ever a time when I was taught to think comprehensively it was in Cyril's class, where it was implicit that every part of a painting affects every other part. As Faber Baren, the colorist, demonstrated later, there is no such thing as a constant color, because the color changes depending on the context in which it occurs.

Another important lesson gleaned from the summer's work was "If you can live without doing it, accept that fact and do something else." This rule is not restricted to art but applies to practically any profession I can think of. I learned it first from the artists; I lived with and around artists most of my early life (I later married one[1]). There is something about their work that makes it possible to draw conclusions that might not be obvious in other fields. For one thing you can *see* the work. It is there before your eyes. I am not talking about taste in art styles, for most artists, if they are worth their salt and are not being vicious or vindictive, know the difference between those who can paint and those who can't, regardless of style. They have little difficulty distinguishing a serious painter from a potboiler. Artists—whom Plato would have excluded from his republic—are as deeply involved with the meaning of truth as he was. Being a virtuoso with words, Plato apparently had little appreciation for the visual sense. Many people are like that. This should not be held against them, but they should be reminded that no one has a right to put down the talent of another and that what truth there is in the world is expressed in many ways.

A spinoff from my long and deep association with artists is that whenever I come up against a tough, virtually insoluble problem in my own work and am really stymied, I turn to the artists. There isn't much they haven't thought about or tried to do, few problems they haven't tried to solve or shed some light on.

In the 1960s I was struggling with the idea of boundaries in connection with my work on proxemics (the study of distances between humans) and I needed something against which to check my own observations. I knew that there must be more than simply the distances as we see them in street scenes and other scenes of people interacting with each other. Consulting a linguist friend who was well read in art and art theory, I was referred to Maurice Grosser, author of *The Painter's Eye.* Grosser had made a detailed study of how artists in the past had depicted personal distance, which was precisely what I was researching in everyday situations. Here was an artist whose insights provided the kind of detailed descriptions I was looking for.

The artists also have provided me with data on how people were seeing and thinking at any time in history. The fact that the Impressionists were so deeply influenced by the nineteenth-century advances in physics is a metacommunication (a communication about a communication) concerning the deep importance of these changes in our view of the physical world. Physics then was at the cutting edge of knowledge. The artists, by their very nature, knew in their bones that the physicists had something to say to them. Today artists are looking at a different set of problems, such as how to go about translating important *concepts* and even numbers into a language that can be understood by everybody.

Watching artists struggle for a toehold in society and still not make it economically, and having experienced the difficulty of their task, knowing that talent and the ability to perform were not enough to assure success, I then realized that I now had two fields I could eliminate as possible careers, both of which had been an intimate part of my growing up. I could see I would be neither a businessman nor an artist. Nevertheless, despite my misgivings about a career in art, art has always been an important part of my life and I have never been able to live without it. My second wife and partner, Mildred Reed Hall, and I bought our first painting (a magnificent Nordfeldt) when I was teaching at Bennington. We paid one-third of a year's salary for it. Since I didn't have the ready money, Georgette Passedoit, owner of the Fifty-seventh Street gallery in New York City where we bought it, agreed to take what I could give her from the proceeds of my lectures and articles. We have never looked upon art as an investment but simply as an extraordinarily good statement to have around, rather like so many silent but very communicative friends, constant reminders of the variety and strength of the human spirit.

SIX

Something Alive

AFTER GRADUATING from high school I was faced with the decision of where to go to college. No one—not my parents, not Joe or Theresa or any of my teachers—had said a word to me about college. Wanting to break out of the New England tradition I felt had been stultifying to my father's life, I preferred to go to a small college of good standing as far from New England as possible. I chose Pomona, in southern California. I had friends who would be there, including Al Dasburg—the two of us had pretty much raised each other during our last days in high school. When I applied for admission I found that the registrar had gone to Amherst and was really ambivalent as to whether to admit me or send me to his (and my father's) alma mater. But I was admitted. In the fall, when I registered, I found that my adviser had been my uncle's roommate at Amherst. I had an aunt on the faculty at Pomona and two cousins in the student body as well as more relatives in Pasadena. Apparently in my attempt to distance myself from New England stuffiness I was living out a pattern shared by other family members.

Then there was the other matter—facing Dad with the reality of paying for college. As I remember, the tuition at Pomona was around four hundred dollars a year plus a modest fee for room and board. When I broached the subject, I was as usual faced with that familiar mask my father defended himself with, which I was always trying to penetrate—not for manipulative reasons but because I needed to feel that I was in conctact with a living flesh-and-blood human being and because I loved him and identified with him and his troubles. I wished that I wasn't such a burden but since I had no profession at sixteen there didn't seem to be anything else to do but to continue my education. As was frequently the case, after a struggle I managed to help him defeat his chintzy side so that altruism and parental responsibility could have more leeway in this matter of my education. Of course, I wasn't aware of all this at the time it was going on, so it seemed more like a battle of wills, with me feeling guilty for making demands on him.

Pomona had a good academic rating, but my year as a very young freshman left me with a feeling of emptiness. Something was missing. I had expected great things of college, but this seemed to be just more of what I had done in high school, in larger doses.

Like most young people before they have had to make their way in the world, I had no idea of how naïve, inexperienced, and impressionable I was at sixteen. This naïveté was particularly glaring when it came to politics and the affairs of the world. There was one professor, for example, whom we used to call "High Water" because his narrow cuffed pants stopped slightly below midcalf. He had strong feelings about the oppressed, and having experienced oppression from parents and their surrogates, I swallowed his line. But political philosophy didn't really grab me; it was too abstract—too much in the head—and it didn't have enough to do with situations I could actually see and feel. Even with my genuine identification with the downtrodden, a career in modern history was not for me. Geology was interesting and I was good at knowing what was under the ground by looking at the surface outcroppings. Though I had never excelled in languages, I took it for granted that one learned languages (I had studied French, Latin, and Spanish and would later take Anglo-Saxon), so I chose German. I couldn't have made a bigger mistake. All we did was to memorize grammar without any reference to how it was really used. Since my memory for abstractions was below average I didn't do well. My German professor was a little man with a mean expression. During class he would sit hunched over his books with little concern for the class of approximately forty-five students. Even though I sat in the back of the room near the door, which was as far as I could get from him, there was something about me that simply pushed all the wrong buttons in that man. It was clear from the start that he had no patience for those who couldn't handle language as it was taught in those days. You learned the parts of speech and then were supposed to put the parts together to form something you hoped would turn out to be a sentence. Later I learned why I had reacted so strongly to the unnaturalness of the method. The human brain works better when it can deal with gestalts than when it has to constantly juggle single parts which must be assembled rapidly into different configurations.

I had looked forward to biology, which was all right in the classroom, but my first laboratory session was a disaster. It was taught by graduate assistants who were not too sure of themselves and were therefore very authoritarian. All my previous skills went for naught. Rejecting my stippled renderings, they wanted me to draw everything exactly the way they did, with little lines for shading. The dead frogs and cats reeking with formaldehyde were nauseating. Those dead animals, which had once been so full of life, came to symbolize for me the entire educational process and much of my life as well. There was little that was alive in any of my college courses. Education for me sank back into its old familiar, leaden, mind-numbing, senseless routine.

For this reason I was pleased when a letter from Mother arrived in the spring of 1931 asking me to join her and Heinz, her husband, in Europe for the summer as well as the next academic year, which she said I would spend at the Sorbonne. Priscilla had gone to stay with my father, who had kept Dick and Delight with him.

I had liked Paris the two times we had been there on our way to and from Grenoble, where Mother took us when I was eight, so I looked forward to living there. Also, it would be my first visit with my mother in over four years. While we had corresponded, letters didn't take the place of her physical presence. I had missed her and was really looking forward to being with her again.

In those days if you wanted to go to Europe you went by boat, and I liked boats. To me they always seemed alive. I got myself to New York by train, and I set out for France on the *Rotterdam.* I felt comfortable and at ease as soon as I stepped aboard, as though I were returning home from a long absence. In fact I have had an attraction for almost any way of getting from one part of the planet to another, including walking and horseback. Being on a boat was involving; there was complexity, yet a coherent system into which an incredible amount of diversity had been crammed, all of which must work as a unit. The food was good. The sea was alive and smelled fresh and was never the same. I didn't even mind the sea sickness when the sea was exceptionally rough. No two boats were ever the same. Even sister ships like the *Volendam* of the Holland-American Line had small but noticeable differences in how they were outfitted. Also, on a boat, things had to work and had to be done right and there was a lot to learn. There were storms, and days when it was nice, and there was no doubt that you were out in the weather and at the mercy of the raw forces of nature, as well as dependent on the skill of the captain and his crew. There were passengers to make friends with, people from different parts of the world, as well as people of different classes and educational and occupational backgrounds. (It has been my experience that among the many travelers I have known the proportion of interesting ones far exceeds the norm for nontraveling people.) There were some young people aboard this ship, including a couple of bashful, gangling girls. A young Dutchman took me under his wing and I was amazed at his way with women. He was completely at ease with them, conversationally and in every other way. I knew I could never be that self-assured and sophisticated, but I enjoyed my Dutch friend's company and talking to his girlfriends and looking at their legs, which they kept exposing for his benefit.

Mother met the boat at Le Havre. She hadn't changed and seemed very much in charge as she arranged for our transfer to the boat train which we took to Paris. *Everything* was new and different —the light (dark gray), the sounds (the French language, men shouting, taxi horns of the old toot-toot variety, the noises of the automobiles, buses, and the horse carts pulled over cobblestone streets). The sidewalk cafés were islands of light in dark streets.

In Paris we took a cab to Mother's and Heinz's apartment, a studio on the Left Bank near the Lion de Belfor. They lived in a semi-industrial neighborhood not too far from the famous Café du Dôme where all the artists and intellectuals hung out. I ended up spending most of my time at the Dôme. Those were the days when the waiters brought each drink on a saucer with color-coded rims, a different color for each price. At the end of the afternoon or evening, the waiters added up the tab by adding the rims of the stacked saucers. It was summer and the café was literally on the sidewalk. An awning covered a few of the tables, but by and large we sat out in the sun and enjoyed ourselves. I had never suspected that life could be this way. It was better than any school or university. Every day I heard conversations among artists and intellectuals who talked about everything: history, economics, politics, art, sex, food, the country, the political situation in Germany (would Hitler win the election?). The French I had learned as a child when Mother had taken us to Grenoble for the winter was some help except for the fact that the vocabulary was inadequate. People were used to the fact that they were living in a polyglot world, and they were considerate enough so that they noticed if you weren't tracking and would explain what you had missed. As a result, I could understand much of what they were saying. It was nice to be there with all those minds working like clockwork. And so much fun! There was a Hungarian artist who had a Portuguese girlfriend. The two of them had no language in common. Watching them set up a date with gestures was worth the price of admission.

It was from sitting around talking at the Dôme that I learned some of the basics of economics as a real world discipline. This was brought home to me when England went off the gold standard, stranding English citizens on the Continent. It was quite a while before people were able to cross even the small distance of the English Channel. Mystified, I had to know all about it. What had happened? Why had it happened? Wasn't the paper money backed by the gold? Had someone stolen the gold? All of this provided a chance to get expert briefings as to what was really going on and how it had come about. One could learn more about politics and economics in a week at the Dôme in 1931 than at the average university in a year. People were informed about the real life of politics and economics, not just the theories.

Café regulars would sit around visiting, getting acquainted, meeting new residents, greeting old ones who had been away, exercising their minds while lapping up wine, beer, and liqueurs that tasted wonderful, not at all like the rotgut the bootleggers were dispensing at home. In this atmosphere, surrounded by adults, participating in their lives, sharing their times and places, even though I was just seventeen I began to feel like an adult for the first time.

Heinz took pride in beer. At the Dôme he would ask for *München Bier*, which was his favorite. "Just you vait until ve get to Germany. Then ve vill have some real beer!" Heinz was in his own element in Europe; like many Europeans he never quite felt at home in the United States.

I have difficulty describing Heinz Warneke. His work was wonderful and he had a real feeling for animals and when he described a piece of sculpture he made it come even more alive. You felt what he saw and appreciated in an animal when he sculpted it. First he would make lots of sketches in notebooks, sketches that had a life of their own. Then he made plasticine studies in the round by simply pinching them out with his fingers so that the basic form was there. These had a sort of raw unvarnished life to them. What happened next was determined by the material to be used. If the sculpture was to be cast in bronze, he made a full-size model in plasticine. If the piece was marble, he would start chipping and cutting, ending finally when the surface was smoothed and polished. At times an assistant would help by roughing out wood pieces with a chisel. One time, some years later, when a calf was born on the farm that Mother and Heinz bought in East Haddam, Connecticut, Heinz picked up an ax, sharpened it, and used it to carve an entire piece on the spot from the wood of a dead cherry tree. The same subject done in different materials would result in entirely different pieces. Without really knowing that I had done so, I learned enough from Heinz while watching him work to earn my living a couple of summers later, casting for three Santa Fe women in the same studio in which I had studied painting with Cyril.

When I arrived in Paris, I was still feeling the effects of what Dad had communicated about "the man who ran away with my wife." My identification was with my father and, while Heinz had been around a lot before the divorce, it was not the same as when the marriage broke up and with it our family. I was now facing the man who did it. And while I was secretly ecstatic to be with Mother and didn't want to make scenes or to do anything to detract from the excitement and warmth I was experiencing from being with her again, there must have been some leakage of my feelings about Heinz no matter how hard I tried to cover them up. These feelings and Heinz's narcissism put the two of us on a collision course for my mother's affections. As soon became apparent, he was her baby. In fact, Heinz's need for attention was hard on all her children. He had to be number one, *numero uno*, *eichi ban*, *der Erste*. It's the same regardless of language. All of us children felt shunted aside for Heinz, though I think it might have been harder on Dick and Delight than on myself.

I had hardly gotten settled in Paris when I heard Mother and Heinz talking about going to Germany to see Heinz's family. The big question centered on whether Hitler would win in the elections or not. If he did we would stay in Paris. But Hitler did not win in 1931; in fact, it seemed that he was losing some of his backing at the polls, so the three of us took off for Bremen where we visited with Heinz's mother, two brothers, and sister. They lived in a tiny house out in the country south of Bremen in a small village called Bruckhausen Vilsen where Heinz's father had worked for the railroad as a minor official. Listening to Heinz talking to a neighbor over the back fence I discovered, possibly because of the German I studied in school, that I could understand everything they were saying. The language was that close to English even though the accents were different. They were speaking Plattdeutsch—Low German. The relationship between the English and the Germans became a little clearer the next year when I studied *Beowulf*.

Once he was on his own turf, Heinz seemed to become more

like his real self. To me, of course, everything in Germany was different. You saw it, heard it, tasted it, smelled it, and felt it as soon as the border was crossed. At first it was the surface things that were noticeable, the way things were made, the clothes, the Germans' way of greeting one another and speaking. The trains ran on time and pulled in and out of the stations *on the second*. The roadbeds were smooth and straight so the trains didn't rock and shake. The power of the locomotive was palpable. Later on, I realized that the elements of interaction one took for granted at home were also different: the Germans' manners, tone of voice, the way they moved, their tempo and rhythm, the way they related to each other, the way their minds worked. I had no doubt that the French and the Germans were very, very different, a point which I had an opportunity to study in detail fifty years later when writing a series of books on relationships among the Germans, the Americans, the French, and the Japanese. Recalling those early experiences I realized that the differences were unbelievably real to my seventeen-year-old self, even though I didn't then have a frame into which to put them.

On the first day in Germany, scanning the flat country in which Bremen is situated for something—anything—of interest, I couldn't help being puzzled by kilometer after kilometer of empty locomotives lined up in the railroad yards near Heinz's mother's home. They weren't just empty cars, but expensive locomotives turning to rust. No one seemed to know why they were there, why they weren't being used (Germans tend not to question things that are not their business), but I found a man with the answer. It appeared that following World War I, the French had confiscated all the German locomotives as part of the reparations payment. The locomotives, which the Germans replaced with new ones, were well built and powerful. They were also *heavy*—how heavy the French didn't discover until later, when the light French rails were being pounded to pieces. Hence the locomotive glut. The French should have known, of course, and undoubtedly there were those who did know, but they were overruled by the *fonctionnaires*. The Germans would have known beforehand that the locomotives were too heavy and would have avoided that waste. It was just another one of those differences between the French and the Germans that I was beginning to pick up.

Throughout the entire visit to Germany I was repeatedly caught off guard by what my stepfather found funny or amusing. Once while walking along a cobblestone road in the country we passed a small white block marking the tenths of kilometers. This reminded Heinz of a night when he and some of his friends, feeling no pain as they returned from an evening in one of the local *Bierstübes*, had reached a point when they needed to get rid of that beer. Males will find something to piss on, and there was a small *.1 km* marker showing up in the dark alongside the road. Much to their surprise, no sooner had they begun pissing, than the stone got up and moved away. A couple had been making love beside the road and what the boys thought was the marker was a bit of exposed white panty. Heinz obviously thought this was screamingly funny. The country boy still present in my German stepfather was much closer to the soil than my New England businessman father.

A most vivid memory of North German village life centered on the profound effect of the inflation on the people following World War I. The war's end was only a scant twelve years in the past. Today inflation is an integral part of life; everyone experiences it and knows it is something like the smog that we breathe, one of the costs progress exacts from us. But when inflation struck in Germany, currency was something people depended on to remain constant. It was stored labor, quite frequently representing a lifetime of work and saving. The German feelings about money were not too far from their faith in God. Yet reparations payments and other factors which threw the economy out of gear undermined the mark. Money had to be taken to the store in wheelbarrow loads to buy food. The hub around which all else revolved had suddenly gone berserk. Those serious, solid people were being wiped out by forces and circumstances beyond their comprehension. Luther had preached that success was a sign of salvation and suddenly, without warning, those who had invested in a life of hard work and the success and salvation that went with it were transformed from a state of salvation to one of damnation, a situation which Hitler sensed and exploited and which years later Erich Fromm cited in his book *Escape From Freedom* as one of the heartstrings pulled by Hitler as he manipulated the Germans.

OUR VISIT with Heinz's family ended with Oktoberfest and lots of Rhine wine. Heinz's older brother Johann, who had been a sniper in World War I, got me drunk on Liebfraumilch. By the end of the evening (about 2:30 A.M.) we were all on good terms and I was much more fluent in German. Mother was annoyed.

Three days later the three of us were on the train heading for Paris. The trip was the reverse of the first one. We started with smooth rails, with trains pulling in and out of the stations on the second, with the solid serious air of the bureaucrats running things. Yet as soon as the engines were changed and we crossed the border, we had rough swaying tracks, changes in speed, and higher voices. There was a kind of heaviness in the Germans not evident in the French. Things didn't work as well in France and the French could be difficult, especially in those days, but life had more verve and the people weren't so serious. It was clear to me then that the Germans and the French would always have some problems with each other. They did everything so differently. Their approach to life was not the same.

It was now time to think about the Sorbonne. But there was a problem: Mother, never one to get things straight, had not checked the details of admission to the Sorbonne. A year later, I would have been accepted at the Sorbonne, but as it was, not having matriculated at Pomona, there was no way I could have been admitted. (Europeans required two solid years of college in the States as a condition of admission to a university.) Stymied, and since my French was in need of beefing up, I attended the Alliance Française along with some refugee students from Cuba, and spent my time learning French, visiting the Louvre and other sights of Paris, and sitting at the Dôme with friends like Helen and Langdon (Billy) Kihn.

As though the change in my university plans were not enough there was another piece of bad news. My little sister Priscilla was taken ill, and Mother and Heinz returned to the United States to be with her. While there they decided to buy a farm in Connecticut. Paris was a long way from home for me. It was dark and not too cheerful, and winter was coming on. I was dreadfully lonely and felt abandoned again. Mother and Heinz were gone almost two months, leaving me alone in their studio.

LONELINESS, depression, and the most recent desertion triggered the return of the asthma from which I had been free for many years. Fortunately the French were ahead of the United States in the treatment of asthma. I was given adrenaline for the first time in my life and I recovered slowly, but it was a debilitating, shattering setback. In the grip of that disease one is transformed in a matter of minutes from a strong, healthy, vigorous human being into a helpless incapacitated wreck whose entire energy is spent struggling for the next breath.

On top of my illness, Mother had invited a Chinese exchange student in art, Teng Quay, to stay in their studio for a few days while he looked for a place to stay in Paris. There was one thing about both my parents: either one of them could be counted on, one way or another, to serve up, when least expected and frequently when I was most vulnerable, real-life experiences with other human beings who would shake me to the roots of my psyche. Quay turned up on my doorstep and moved in, made himself at home and took over. I can't say that I ever really understood Quay except that his sense of values was completely different from my own. While there might have been some ties to his family there apparently was no sense of obligation to anyone else. The first thing he wanted me to do was to fire Marie Louise—Mother's *bonne à tout faire*—and use the money I was paying her to hire a young girl to service Quay! There were all sorts of other schemes. What interested me most was his lack of commitment to his government, which had paid the expenses for his entire education in art at American universities. He was seriously considering simply staying in Paris and not returning to the position waiting for him at a Chinese university. At seventeen I can't say that I was really up to dealing with Quay. The fact that I was much more afraid of my mother than of Quay stiffened my spine and increased my resourcefulness. So Marie Louise stayed. When I came down with asthma I told Quay he would have to go.

Paris has a way of getting under your skin. I think it is the greatest city in the world and, like all world-class cities, unique. But at the time, with all its advantages and attractions, there was nothing that could make up for the absence of parents, friends, and a program to exercise my mind. When I was strong enough to travel I returned to America and managed to convince Dad that in spite of the fact that he and my brother Dick and sister Delight were all together in Andover, Massachusetts, New England was not the place for me. I couldn't just say that the entire scene was depressing and that all my brother and sister had done in the past had been to get me in trouble, so I made a strong case that I would be better off in the West where the air was clean and pure and the sun was bright, which was essentially the case.

Pomona had not lived up to my expectations. Strictly on a hunch, since there was no one whose judgment I trusted, I decided not to return to Pomona but to try the University of Colorado. Perhaps the mountain states would hold something for me. Whether it was luck or a deep intuition that has proved to be my mainstay throughout my life, I was right, but not for the reasons I had given myself.

On the way to enroll at the University of Colorado in Boulder, I stopped off in Denver to visit Cyril Scott, my art teacher, and his son, Jig. Cyril was then dean of art at the University of Denver as well as director of the Denver Art Museum. They were glad to see me and wanted to know why I had left Pomona, which I did my best to explain. Cyril, getting the point, urged me to visit any class of an anthropology professor named Renaud at the University of Denver whom he thought I might like.

One exposure was all it took. I hadn't even known that anthropology existed and yet here was what I had been looking for *and* had even been studying in my own amateurish way all my life. From then on there was nothing else that could hold me in its grip the way anthropology has.

At last I had found something *alive* to study. As it turned out

Professor Renaud was more of an archaeologist and cultural historian than a cultural anthropologist, but he had that rare quality of being able to make the subject come alive. There was something about the way he connected things rather than compartmentalizing them that appealed to me. In addition I was intrigued to know that human beings could be studied. Studying what people did (not just their ideas) was tangible and real, not like what I had been previously subjected to in my education.

While still in my first year under Renaud doing an independent study of southwestern (Anasazi)[1] indented cooking pottery, I discovered some things that had not been recorded before. No one had studied cooking pots, possibly because they were so plain—not painted and fancy. What caught my eye was the way they were made with very narrow coils, laid on like the coils of a basket except that as the coils were laid down each new coil was pinched to weld it to the coil below at one-centimeter intervals. Knowing very little about pottery and because it was my first study, I simply measured everything, including the angle of the pinch. An analysis of my figures revealed that occasionally there was a pot in which the pinches were at right angles to the pinches in most other pots. There was nothing complex about it—in fact, it was quite obvious once you had thought about it: these were the works of left-handed potters. Later on things got more complex, but an analysis of collections from different archaeological sites revealed some startling differences in the pottery associated with the culture of the potters. My short paper read before the American Association for the Advancement of Science at Las Cruces, New Mexico, was picked up by the press and carried as an item in *Science News Letters* published in Washington, D.C. My paper, with a typically minimalist approach, showed that the women in one area pinched the coils of their pottery differently than did those in another area and that this difference could only be attributed to their culturally embedded pottery-making traditions. I later realized that in the process of my analysis, I had stumbled on "frozen motor habits" and a way of studying them in the rather limited context of pottery making. A similar statement could be made about the differences in the weaving of textiles or any other technology done with the hands. If the motions of the fingers and hands could be reconstructed by studying the objects it would be comparable to the reconstruction of speech through the analysis of ancient recorded texts.

The indented pottery studies adumbrated a pattern present in practically everything I have ever done. It was as though my work had been directed by the dictum laid down by Mies van der Rohe when he said, "God is in the details." I was studying things that most other people didn't notice. Even though other things were happening in my life I never lost interest in that indented pottery and would return to it whenever the opportunity presented itself. By the time I finished my graduate work at Columbia, I was able to reproduce all of the hundred or more variations in pinching styles. In the end I found that there were only eight ways in which one clay coil could be welded to another—eight different sets of motor habits. I was able to do this because I could identify with the women who made the pottery as they worked—I could reproduce the sensations associated with the different technique of pinching one coil to the next. Some of those women pinched precisely, others less so, and I could feel the precision or the lack of it when I examined their pottery.

Behind all this effort lay the idea that motor habits, like those associated with making different sounds with the voice (phonetics), occur largely outside of awareness and could be a reliable guide to cultural affiliation. This meant it might be possible to plot the movement of the Anasazi peoples on maps at different time periods using my frozen-motor-habits techniques. How one reaches such conclusions is somewhat tedious so I will just say that the process is similar to the biblical test of the pronunciation of the word "shibboleth" or the fact that the inability to pronounce the difference between V and W on the part of many Germans, along with other characteristics, identifies these people as German to most native speakers of English.

A characteristic which differentiated Professor Renaud from most other professors was that he was willing to give a student the freedom to work out ideas on his or her own. In this setting I continued to pursue my study of the Anasazi indented ware for eleven years, from 1931 through 1942. In that interval I dropped out of school to take a job with the Indian Service, took an M.A. at the University of Arizona under Professor Emil Haury, and finally a Ph.D. at Columbia University in 1942.

In 1933, toward the end of my second year at Denver with Professor Renaud, Franklin Roosevelt was the new President and things were beginning to change. Excitement was in the air. The President was in charge and doing things. It never occurred to me that I would in any way be connected with these changes. Yet one sunny spring day, a telegram was sent to me from John Collier, commissioner of Indian affairs. Collier asked if I was interested in his new and innovative program of work on Indian reservations.[2] An attorney, he had been pressing for change in the administration of Indian affairs for years. Roosevelt had originally chosen Harold Ickes to be Indian commissioner, but during his interview with FDR, Ickes' power and sincerity so impressed Roosevelt, that, instead of Indian commissioner, he asked him to be secretary of the interior. Ickes accepted and chose Collier as Indian commissioner.

My affirmative reply to Collier was to change my life. Not only would I be catapulted into manhood but I would learn firsthand about the details and complexities of one of the world's most significant problems: intercultural relations. I would also experience the behind-the-scenes, day-to-day politics of government.

In Santa Fe, friends were working as administrators helping to activate Collier's plans. From them I learned that the job offer had been made because of my interest in and knowledge of Pueblo Indians. I never thought there was anything out of the ordinary about my interest. I took it for granted—like breathing or enjoying New Mexico's sunshine and the clear air, on a par with a good meal, or a beautiful view, not intellectual but natural and from the inside. To me people were just plain interesting. I used to be drawn to the Indian dances because of the power and magic which seemed to surround them. We had had Indian friends when I was a child. Apparently, this background put me in the category of those who were sympathetic to the Indian cause.

Waiting around Santa Fe for confirmation of my job, I learned an old lesson: nothing is ever done rapidly in government, where the bureaucrats are in control and one cannot move a finger without their consent. Raising the question as to what the government would think about my age (I was only nineteen) one of Commissioner Collier's assistants replied, "That's okay, just say you are twenty-one. You look like you could be twenty-one."

As circumstances developed, the greater part of my next four years would be spent living and working in every part of the Navajo and Hopi reservations. Although this area is by far one of the most spectacular in the United States, it was at the time the most remote, least known, and least visited. Today, of course, one can hardly pick up a newspaper without reading something about either the Navajo, the Hopi, or Monument Valley—that breathtaking, strikingly beautiful country one sees as a backdrop for movies of the West and ads of all types, particularly those for cigarettes and automobiles. A great deal of its appeal was its isolation. Here was an entire country unblemished by civilization with some places that were virtually inaccessible. I know it is hard for some people to imagine what a blessing it was to be cut off from "civilization." Kayenta, for example, where the famous Wetherills—pioneer explorers—had their trading post, was forty miles south of Monument Valley and a day's drive of 150 miles in dry weather on deeply rutted and frequently impassable dirt roads north of the railroad town of Flagstaff. It was the most remote post office in the United States.

The Navajo reservation then covered 18 million acres, or approximately 45,000 square miles, 250 miles east and west by 180 miles north and south. The New England states of Vermont, New Hampshire, Massachusetts, and Rhode Island would have fit comfortably within its boundaries. As I bumped across the reservation on a wagon trail from Gallup, New Mexico, my predominant impression was that the country was uninhabited. The landscape at first seemed to be devoid of people—there was no evidence of humanity for hours on end. Even where humans did congregate, there were few whites, only Navajos and Hopis.

Thinking back to those years, I realize that what I remember most is the crystal clear, hot, dry air and the vast distances. The country is desolate and massive in scale. An inflated ego could not have tolerated the Navajo reservation in those days. Indeed, there were people who were made acutely uncomfortable by the country. Moving around in that immense landscape was a constant reminder of how small and insignificant I was. I felt as if I were on the ocean. The ocean is endless and any ship in contrast is finite. Not only was that desert scenery on a monumental scale visually but the reality was there to back up these impressions. It was possible to stand on the high mesa on which the Hopi village of Hotevilla stood, look toward the west, and know that the reservation continued for over a hundred miles where its boundary intersected the Grand Canyon (which continued for another three hundred miles). Years later Alan Jay Lerner would write the song "On a Clear Day You Can See Forever." He must have been out there at some time. But despite the feelings of insignificance, I also perceived that there was something deeply reassuring about all that wonderful space, a feeling that can never be recovered. Out there I was in and of nature and no one could get at me.

No less remarkable than the impressive spaces, but slower to make an impact, were the people. Their settlements were embedded in the landscape, like jewels in a giant's shield, and it took a while to find them and still longer to know them. The towns blended into the barren landscape so successfully that the average white man would drive right by with no inkling that on the mesa top were three entire Hopi villages. Occasionally there would be evidence of the presence of humans. Bright green patches of corn in the arroyo beds, standing in stark contrast to the desert gray, were a cry in the wilderness saying "People live here." That bizarre, surreal world was a cross between a dream and a myth come to life.

I somehow sensed that here in this strange land could be found some of the answers to the meaning of my own life. If I could just let those answers come through I could understand them. Would I ever learn to "read" this mysterious land?

Part II

Indian Country in the Thirties 1932–1935

SEVEN

Spider Woman

Spider Woman is a major deity for the Hopi, who refer to Her as Grandmother. From Her, the Hopi got their major skills and identities. In Her, one also finds the origins of witchcraft and death, for She is both the creator and the destroyer, and is therefore both loved and feared.

For the Navajo She is a major deity and can be both friendly and hostile toward earth people.

The white man does not know about Spider Woman and would not acknowledge Her if he did. But She is there whether he knows it or not.

IN JULY 1933, I was told to report to the Indian agency at Keams Canyon, Arizona, approximately one hundred miles northwest of Gallup, New Mexico, and eighty miles north of Holbrook, Arizona. Keams was just as hot, dusty, and forbidding as it had been the year before when I had driven through on my way to Oraibi and the Grand Canyon.

Excited over having my first real job and being completely independent of my father, I wondered what it would be like to work for the government. I was to be camp manager for the new IECW program.[1] What did I need to know and what did it take to succeed? Approaching Keams and looking over the edge of the canyon at the Indian agency below, I saw a loose cluster of buildings among cottonwood trees on the edge of the Keams wash. A short jolt of anxiety seized my heart. What did the people inside those buildings have in store for me? Taking a deep breath, I slipped the car into low gear, as I eased my way down the narrow dirt road that hugged the canyon wall, crossed the bridge over the Keams wash at the bottom of the hill, and turning right, drove along the valley floor to what would be my home for the next two years.

There is always something a bit forbidding and forlorn about old army posts, with their empty and ill-kept grounds. Keams had this same aura about it, for the Indian Service was originally a spinoff from the army, dating back to the times when white soldiers rounded up Indians and put them on "reservations." The military stamp was still evident in the layout and construction of the post.

The Keams agency looked out of place in the harsh desert grandeur. For as part of the message that they are in charge, government bureaucracies, wherever they are found, do their best to look the same. Adaptation to the environment and locale would violate bureaucratic Rule No. 1: Your primary purpose is to maintain your identity and to stay in business regardless of circumstances. The character of government buildings cannot help but influence the mind-set of employees, and Keams was no different from any other bureaucratic institution in this regard.

The physical plant of the agency comprised a dozen buildings constructed of the grayish tan Wingate sandstone cut from the adjacent rock formations and topped by green-tarpaper peaked roofs. There was a headquarters building in the center; a boarding school with classrooms for Indian children; boys' and girls' dormitories and dining halls; a hospital with a staff of three doctors, a dentist, and a half-dozen nurses; a dismal jail with steel door and iron bars at the back of the large mess hall, specially built in the twenties to house "recalcitrant" Indians; employee housing; recreation facilities; and a garage for maintaining government vehicles. On the west side sprawled a second minor complex: the buildings of the Irrigation Service, responsible for drilling wells and developing springs. Farther west and around a bend in the road, hidden from the agency proper, lay Slim Halderman's trading post, first run by Lorenzo Hubbell, Jr., in the 1890s. Lorenzo would play a prominent role in my reservation experience.

Entering the headquarters building I asked a clerk if I could see the superintendent.

"You mean Mr. Miller?"

"I guess so, if that's his name."

"Sit over there on the bench."

An hour later another clerk said, "Go through that door there," pointing to a door on my left. Superintendent Miller was not what I expected. I had visualized a tall, robust, outdoors, take-charge type, but facing me was a small, red-faced man with a nose like W. C. Fields's, ears that stuck out, and patches of gray hair tufting out of a balding scalp. I could see after a very short time that Miller hated the turmoil and fuss he was being subjected to by the "New Deal crew" that had invaded his peaceful domain.

Before the New Deal, there had been a quiet routine in the isolated desert post. It was a big event when one of the top brass from Fort Wingate on his way to Tuba City stopped by to break the trip and to gossip. The pace at Keams was so ambling and slow, even zombielike, that the entire cadre of post personnel seemed to be playing a collective game of charades. The walk and the pace were also an unconscious communication as to the way to do things if you wanted to keep your job.

Even though Miller was personally a quick-moving man, he still seemed to feel that everything should be kept as it was, which was the way it always had been. But the new directives asked that new programs be started as well as a host of administrative and fiscal matters over which Miller had no control. Like the skipper of a small boat in a squall, he felt he had all he could do to keep his ship afloat, and he certainly had little say over which way the winds of Washington were blowing him and his tiny crew. Without his knowing it, what bothered him most was the mixing of rhythms. These New Deal people—which included me—walked around as though they were going someplace and had a job to do. We acted as though the job was important, and we wanted things taken care of right away. It wasn't that there were so many of us, because we hadn't increased the number of employees by more than fifteen or twenty percent. It was just that all of a sudden here was this influx of what were in his mind foreigners. All of this disrupted his routine and whether he willed it or not, things would change: he was used to Indians who would put up with sitting patiently all day long outside his office and, if he did not see them, would return and resume their silent vigil the next day.

The only recourse he had to express his discomfort with his new employees was to be irritable. Sitting across from him on my first visit, I had hoped to impress him with my seriousness and my eagerness to do well. He was my first real boss and I knew that, like a ship's captain, his word was law on that reservation. I told him I was the camp manager for Collier's IECW program. His response was brief and explicit: "You're new here. Stay away from the Indian traders. Report to the ECW people down under the cottonwood trees by the wash." That was all.

I had no idea what he meant by the admonition about the Indian traders, but later on it was because I failed to obey his directive that I saved him from a tragic and disgraceful end to his career.

Leaving his office, I went down to the tents. Because I had been hired as a camp manager, I had assumed that when I arrived there would be a camp ready and waiting for me to manage. But the camps, which had been modeled after the CCC camps for whites, were not readily adaptable either to the Indians or to the type of work we were supposed to be doing. I soon learned that there were no camps and there were no Indians on the payroll; no projects were under way; nothing was happening. Even in my uninformed state I could see that it was just a matter of time before Washington got upset, and wondered when that would be. In the meantime, all the newcomers sat around outside their hot tents and twiddled their thumbs. The wives made ice cream and the men gossiped, exchanged stories about Washington, and wondered why they were there.

A week went by and nothing changed. I made friends as well as I could, but I felt different from the rest of the crew. Everyone else had been laid off from some government job, none of which had anything to do with Indians. I was just a college kid, new to the ways of government work. I was idealistic and I was not only interested in the Indians but I even knew something about them. Admittedly I was a romantic and I must have seemed pretty dumb to this crew who had so recently faced joblessness. Being low man on the totem pole, I was given jobs that no one else wanted. My first job was to be in charge of a Navajo road-building crew. I was to dynamite boulders so that they could be broken down with sledgehammers wielded by Navajos for further reduction by rock-crushers for use on the roads. At that time Indians were legal minors and as such were not allowed to use dynamite. Fortunately I had picked up experience blasting stumps while working for my father on his property in Missouri. I knew what I was doing, but that was purely coincidental.

WORKING THERE in the hot desert sun surrounded by Navajos, I could feel myself becoming imprinted by the country and the people. I can still see clearly before me the reservation's translucent lapis-blue sky, which offered little shielding from the sun's rays. It was almost as though there was no atmosphere at all between us and the bright, white orb in the sky. The dryness was unbelievable. Hygrometers resting at zero simply didn't record moisture. The boulders were as large as houses, and the white clay earth with little vegetation radiated heat from the ground.

Even though my white skin was being baked to a dark brown crisp, I was conscious of how extraordinarily different I looked from the tanned-leather Navajo men I was working with. I even smelled differently, moved differently, talked differently, dressed differently, and thought differently. Seen through my eyes everything about the Navajos shouted, "We are one thing; you are something else."

Fortunately, one of my crew spoke a little English and was able to act as my interpreter, and we began building rapport. Since then I have had this same experience with Navajos repeatedly—distance combined with aloofness and then, without warning, warmth and friendship. They didn't seem to mind me and I learned that to the Navajo (unlike my own people) one of the least relevant facts about a human being is that he or she is different. For the first time since early childhood I knew what it meant to be completely free to be myself, a rare luxury in white society where there is always someone who feels anxious in the unadorned presence of another, so that much of the genuine relief I felt when I was with the Navajos was due to the escape from having to keep constant tabs on how other people were responding to my presence.

My second job was twenty miles west of Keams, in the middle of the Hopi villages which were nestled together on top of three mesas, extending like fingers of a giant hand resting on the desert below. Three villages occupied the top of each mesa, and there were also newer villages at the foot of the mesas which had split off from the ones on top as a result of factional disputes. My assignment was to repair the road to Mishongnovi, a Hopi Second Mesa village. The road could best be described as two ruts worn in irregular sandstone that climbed the mesa at an angle barely negotiable by horse-drawn wagons or a car in first gear. Even so, the greatest problem was not the steepness of the grade, but rather the stone ruts and high centers requiring careful negotiation every inch of the way. Lack of attention to driving would lead to smashed batteries (in those days the batteries were beneath the floorboards of the car), a punctured oil pan or transmission, or a disabled rear end.

Unlike the sheepherding Navajo, my village-dwelling Hopi crew spoke English, and were loquacious and friendly from the start. We got along well together (at least it seemed that way). I did my best to answer their many questions about the new government work. They picked up on each point with an unfamiliar, but welcome, alacrity. (The Pueblo people I had known in New Mexico living along the Rio Grande were reticent and shy and did not talk that much to whites, even to white friends.) When the Hopis heard that the purpose of the IECW program was to improve the country and to pay the Indians to do the work, they were both interested and enthusiastic and eager to know more.

The road work proceeded with few hitches. I had helped the cowboys at Aspen Ranch repair the road following periodic washouts so I knew what to do. All that was required was the ability to visualize wheels moving over the surface and to eliminate anything that would obstruct their progress. I was happy to be out in the country, away from Keams, and earning my keep, not just sitting around waiting for something to do.

Discussion with the Hopis continued. They thought there should be a meeting to talk about the new work program, which seemed reasonable enough to me. A small Hopi delegation asked me to tell Mr. Miller they were having a meeting the next Monday night at Mishongnovi and that they would like him to attend because they wanted to hear what he had to say about the new program as well as to state their own ideas.

As luck would have it Superintendent Miller drove up fifteen minutes later in an old government issue Chevrolet coupe. He stopped, inspected my work, stretched, and yawned. By then our crew had progressed almost to the mesa top, well past the two large Corn Rocks that looked as though they had been transported by some quixotic genie from Stonehenge. Apparently Miller was pleased. He smiled (which was unusual), looked around at the indescribably beautiful view of the Hopi Buttes to the south, and asked me how things were going. I said they seemed to be going okay and that the repair work would soon be finished. And sticking out my chest with pride I told Miller how interested the Hopis were in our new program, and that they were going to have a meeting Monday night to discuss what they wanted, and that they would like Mr. Miller to attend.

Instead of congratulating me, it was as though I had set off a land mine under his feet. Miller's reaction was instantaneous and violent. His face got red, the veins in his neck began to swell, and as soon as he got his breath he blasted me: "Listen, you little son of a bitch, if I hear about you stirring up meetings among the Hopi one more time, I'm going to run you off the reservation! You got that?" Obviously there was something about Hopis and meetings that I didn't know about. Miller got back into his car, revved up his engine, let out the clutch, and burned all of three inches of rubber on the sandstone slab under his wheels as he took off toward the mesa top. I told my crew that Mr. Miller wouldn't be attending their meeting.

From discreet inquiries and from just keeping my ears open I learned that the Hopis were famous for calling meetings at the drop of a hat and demanding that agency personnel attend. Furthermore, many of these meetings were experienced by Keams personnel as not only tedious and lengthy but loaded with acrimony. The government officials at Keams, as Miller's response had indicated, were fed up with meetings. Even the thought of a meeting could raise their blood pressure. Miller's response, while somewhat extreme, was not unusual for a certain type of Indian Service bureaucrat when he is in power in one context and completely powerless in another. I was sympathetic to the Indians' cause, Miller was not. I represented Washington and interference from Washington. Miller was used to running his own show. It took a while before it sank in but I was like a piece of foreign protein (an irritant that must be gotten rid of) injected into the corpus of the Keams agency. On top of that I was obviously inexperienced; everyone else was a seasoned traveler, fully familiar not only with the written rules but, more important, the unwritten ones as well.

Not long after my contretemps with Miller, Jay Nash arrived from Washington. Apart from the little jobs I had been doing, which could be considered as routine maintenance and not worthy of the status of IECW projects, nothing was happening. Jay, a professor at New York University, was one of John Collier's trusted associates who went into the field and reviewed the progress of Collier's programs. A slight man who wore old-style cavalry pants and high English boots, Nash (unlike many who came out from Washington) was intelligent, matter-of-fact, and quick to catch on. He swung a lot of weight. I was surprised and a bit embarrassed when he turned his attention to me and asked if there was someplace where we could talk, that there were some questions he wanted to ask. I took him to a shady spot under the cottonwood trees where he started his interrogation. "Why aren't there any camps?" It was clear that nothing was being done to get the program underway. I explained that there appeared to be an underground resistance on a number of levels to the whole concept of Collier's new program for the Indians. I told him that the agency people said that because they were traditional enemies, the Hopis and the Navajos would kill each other if they were put in camps together. Since I was at the bottom of the bureaucratic heap, so to speak, there was nothing I could do. Jay then said, emphasizing every word, "Listen, John Collier wants camps! He's committed to camps! And he is going to have camps! If you have to carry those tents out on your back and put them up yourself, I want to see a camp out there in a week!" While I didn't buy into the foot dragging and rationalizing that was going on, I still didn't know what lay behind Collier's obsession with camps and I wasn't about to question it. It was enough that his emissary said that he wanted camps. The camp was to provide a base for crews working on a much needed truck trail from the Keams-Oraibi road to Piñon. The year before, Navajos at Piñon had almost starved to death in a blizzard and food had to be carted in by bulldozers because there was no road that could be cleared. Only ruts in the mud left by wagon wheels. Up to this point nothing that I had been told made sense. Nothing added up.

To me Professor Nash was like a breath of fresh air in that stifled, irrational atmosphere—a welcome change. What I did not understand was by what magic I was supposed to stir that moribund mass of bureaucracy above me into action. Nevertheless, here was an order from the top and I couldn't just brush it aside.

Jay Nash returned to Washington, the agency settled back into its usual lethargy, and I wondered how in the hell I was going to solve the problem he had laid at my feet. I didn't have to be psychic to see that whatever I did could only get me in trouble. My unconscious mind finally dredged up the name of a man I could at least talk to, someone who might be able to advise me. Heart in mouth, I gambled. Ignoring Miller's injunction to stay away from Indian traders, I got in my car and made the thirty-two-mile trip to Oraibi, where the Indian trader Lorenzo Hubbell had his post.

THE PREVIOUS YEAR, I had been told, "If you're going to the reservation, be sure to stop by and see Lorenzo Hubbell. Everyone who is interested in the Indians sees him because he knows more than anyone else."

Lorenzo owned and operated a chain of trading stores running from Ganado to Oraibi on an east-west axis, and from Winslow to Black Mountain (northwest of Chinle) on a north-south axis. In time, when we had become friends, I learned that in spite of the primitive, Spartan surroundings he lived in, his net worth ran into millions. He was a formidable force on the reservation—someone to be reckoned with.

The Hubbell trading post at Oraibi sat perched atop a slight rise in an open, barren area. There was a glass jug-type gasoline pump in front of the store and a screened-in porch through which one crossed to get to Hubbell's office. Entering the shade of the office from the blinding sun was like walking into a movie theater. Stumbling around in the dark, I found a seat in a semicircle of chairs arcing around Lorenzo's desk. Most of the chairs were occupied by an odd (but, as I later learned, typical) assortment of people who had business with Mr. Hubbell.

Lorenzo spoke to each in turn and all business was conducted in public, which was my first experience with a polychronic high-information-flow situation.[2] A good hour after I arrived and he had finished with all the others, it was my turn. I didn't mind the wait —in fact, I had welcomed the interlude because it provided an opportunity to pick up tidbits of background information on reservation affairs, information that exceeded the narrow limits of the scuttlebutt to be garnered at Keams and to see how Lorenzo worked. I was beginning to gain a bit of the picture of the daily stream of reservation life.

A second-generation trader, Lorenzo was the son of a famous father, J. L. Hubbell, one of the first traders to the Navajo. Lorenzo had been given the Navajo name of Nakai Tso (the Big Mexican). A snaggle-toothed man of tremendous girth and immediately obvious appeal, Lorenzo chewed tobacco, which he spit into a coffee can on the floor next to his foot whenever he needed to stop and think. Each conversation was punctuated by a *splat* as Nakai Tso, like a practiced bombardier, zeroed in on that can. His skin was mottled from what must have been a liver disorder; he spoke with a gravelly rasp that was more like a thick whisper than an ordinary conversational voice. He was able to communicate expressively with his left eye while speaking out of the right side of his mouth. When he pushed himself out of his chair, the movement transformed what only a moment before had been a mass of flab into a cross between a ballet dancer and a mountain lion—the grace, ease, and speed of his movements were truly extraordinary. Relatively expressionless of face, he nevertheless had a twinkle in the eye that came and went with the tempo of the conversation. To know what was happening in his head, one had to attend the twinkle. When he encountered lies or fraud, the twinkle became a glint. Like most businessmen in the West, Lorenzo wore the pants of a nondescript gray business suit supported by narrow suspenders, a shirt to match, a tie, and a straight-brimmed four-X beaver Stetson hat. I never saw him dressed any other way. In spite of a rather rough exterior which was typical on the reservation in those times, Lorenzo had an air that set him apart. As I had suspected, he was no ordinary man.

The trading store and the attached, far from untidy living quarters—two rooms, a kitchen and a porch—were an extension of Lorenzo's many-sided, at times enigmatic personality. This meager complex could accommodate up to a dozen guests of both sexes—the men sleeping on the porch in quilts that in daytime were rolled up and rested on the top shelves of the store, the women staying in the two inside bedrooms. The key to the privy hung on a nail by the kitchen door. The kitchen barely accommodated a wood-fired range, refrigerator, china cabinet, sink, and a large oval table (reminiscent of Mrs. Jensen's boarding house table). To get from one part of the kitchen to the other or to the door to the adjoining bedroom it was necessary to suck in one's stomach and edge around the table.

When he needed to speak confidentially, Lorenzo would leave the office with his visitor and they would retire to his bedroom. If the conversation was to be more private still, it was held outside the kitchen door on the way to the privy. With typical Spanish formality, Lorenzo always addressed me as "Mr. Hall." Like everyone else I called him Lorenzo.

Sitting there quietly, I wondered how to bring up all that I had to say in front of strangers. Lorenzo saved me from having to blurt out what was on my mind in front of those who might have told Miller I had disobeyed his injunction about Indian traders or that I had gone over his head. Like a talented lawyer leading a witness,

Lorenzo began questioning me. In no time at all we were in his room behind a closed door, then in the kitchen, then outside the kitchen door. We talked about Collier's program and what was happening at Keams. I told him that the agency's excuse for inaction was that the Indians wouldn't go into the camps and that the agency feared deep and serious friction between the Navajos and the Hopis. He laughed at the notion that the two tribes would kill each other.

He queried me at length about what the camps were supposed to do—how many there would be and for how long. I told him, "Collier has his mind set on camps and he is going to have them. On the other hand, consider the realities. A camp makes sense as long as there is a road to be built and we can haul the men to work in trucks. The road is scheduled to take a couple of months at the most, using perhaps fifty men. The rest of the work falls into two categories: first, building dams scattered all over the reservation, manned by crews of ten to twenty men with teams and five to ten single hands; and second, water development, with even smaller crews of five to eight men at most, developing springs. No one in his right mind would consider camps on this reservation for any job but a road because of the logistics."

I knew that while Lorenzo was a personal friend of Collier's as well as of Secretary and Mrs. Ickes', he would not involve either of them in matters of this sort at our level. It also became increasingly apparent from the questions I was being asked that the traders were behind the resistance to the camps. Lorenzo's reply was typical of him, and surprising to me. He simply said, "When you want your Indians, you let me know and tell me how many you want, and I will see that you get them."

The bureaucratic dam broke, releasing a flood of activity. Carpenters appeared at Keams to build the camp, and they went to work. Supplies were moved, bids for food and supplies were let. It was like magic. At the end of a week there was a camp—tents, screened-in mess tent, cook stoves, storage areas, latrines, and even athletic equipment.

The entire IECW program for the reservation had been stalled for months and no one had known what to do about it. By acting as a surrogate messenger from Washington and setting forth the basic facts of the matter, I had provided an out. Lorenzo did the rest.

How did the Indians take to the camps? Like ducks to water. The only sign of competition between the Hopis and the Navajos was in their singing. The Hopis were practicing songs for a Butterfly dance at First Mesa. Their low-toned, constrained music, heard from a distance, sounded like a large hive of swarming bees. Navajo singing couldn't have provided greater contrast. Their high falsetto voices and great shifts from loud to soft and high to low generated so much energy they could literally be heard for miles. When the Navajos sang, everyone listened. They couldn't help it.

Sports, particularly volleyball, were popular, and it was wonderful to see how happy these men could be. Meals were something else again. Watching our crews eat revealed that they must have been half starved. Unlike Shakespeare's Cassius and his "lean and hungry look," thin Navajos were far from mean.

I had been anxious about my ability to manage a camp. In the end, it turned out to be a piece of cake. It was everything I could wish for. MacCurtain, who was next in line to be chief of the Choctaws, my direct superior, was an amiable, good-natured, gregarious type who could never be blamed for anything because he never did anything. Mac moved out to the camp with me, as did Will Halloran, the civil engineer who was to build the road. Halloran always took his wife with him, and we had a small but congenial group. No sooner had we settled in than another camp was scheduled to be built at Piñon, where the truck trail we were making ended. Taking a cook with me, I supervised the construction and began my acquaintance with George Hubbell, Lorenzo's cousin from Albuquerque. George and his wife ran the Piñon trading post.

It was while I was still at Piñon that work on the road was shut down overnight. Why? Because Halloran had made the road eighteen feet wide instead of nine feet which was the technical width for a truck trail. He had done this because, given the fact that our road graders came equipped with eighteen-foot blades, and the minimal skills of our operators, it was simply not feasible to try to cut such a narrow road with those long blades, especially through that rough rocky terrain. But the regulations only authorized us to build truck trails. Anything wider was automatically the responsibility of the Roads Department!

Altogether the camps lasted only three weeks. The bureaucrats had held that ace up their sleeve and only played it after it was clear that we were definitely on the move and were getting places. Of course our big win was in getting anything going at all. I was really sorry to see Halloran leave. He was intelligent, even-tempered, courageous, experienced, and resourceful. Besides, he had a sense of humor.

By reclassifying the road tying Piñon to the main thoroughfare crossing the reservation and transferring construction of the road to another jurisdiction, the bureaucrats invoked a strategy they had held in reserve. They weren't taking any chances even on that small amount of money. Having built the camps and actually having run them, a gesture had been made. The traders were off the hook. And the whole thing could be laid at our doorstep for making the road too wide! Halloran was the only engineer worth hoot that had been around for months. It was also pretty clear that I would soon go the way of the camps.

My experience with Lorenzo had been an eye-opener. First, in spite of my obvious youth and lack of experience, he had really listened to me. Second, his questions were penetrating and to the point. The two of us could relate as equals even though I was bringing him news of Washington's latest position and not just that of the agency. Lacking experience, I had no notion of how atypical and out of line my behavior was. Only a damn fool or someone with overriding connections at the top would have done what I had done—and, in so doing, circumvented the bureaucratic process. But I had to admit it had been dramatic, seeing the camp come into being as a consequence of a single strategic visit to Lorenzo. Naturally I didn't stop seeing him. In fact, I stopped by every time I was anywhere near Oraibi. That first visit, however, marked the beginning for me of a lifelong pattern of pulling people and ideas together, and it never occurred to me that I should have done things differently.

Working with the tiny threads of information I picked up from

Miller, from the attitude of the government employees, and from sitting around Lorenzo Hubbell's, it was possible to discuss the subtle patterns that made up the fabric of the reservation's unstated, hidden policy. Obstacles designed to circumvent Collier's program had been set in motion and had for a while been successful. But who was responsible? Those threads pointed to a cabal composed of the members of groups that believed it was in their best interest to maintain the status quo, who for ideological, political, and economic reasons were willing to go to almost any lengths to keep things as they were. First, there was the massive inertia of the Indian Service bureaucracy, mobilized quite naturally to resist the Roosevelt-Ickes-Collier reforms. Also, insufficient allowance had been made for, or little attention paid to, the antediluvian attitudes toward Indians on the part of most Indian Service employees.

Second, there were the Indian traders, whose stake in the status quo was political as well as economic. Having underwritten the reservation economy for three years of depression, and with the Indians in hock up to their eyeballs to the traders, the traders were desperately in need of cash to repay overdue bank loans and to finance their purchases of lambs and wool from the Indians (who in turn paid off some of this on their debt to the traders). The IECW program represented the first real infusion of money in several years into a virtually bankrupt Depression economy. In the CCC model for camps, however, the money would be funneled through the camps. If camps were established for work crews, the food for camps would not be bought at the trading posts by Indians, but on bid from wholesalers in the railroad towns of Holbrook and Winslow. If this happened, not only would no money be applied to the reduction of the Indian debt to the traders, but there would be an associated reduction in cash flow. Lorenzo, with lines to all parties, could see that Collier, who was a friend and confidant, was committed to camps. And that it was not worth the risk of opposing him on the matter of camps, because my explanations made it clear that given the worst-case scenario, they would last only a month or so. Furthermore, only a small proportion of those Indians employed would even be in a camp. Knowing all this he took the sensible way out by facilitating the camps.

Because poverty was endemic and the total cash that ended up in the hands of the Indians was so meager even in the best of times, we were dealing with a delicately balanced, marginal, fiscal ecology in which by custom Indians were tied to the particular trader who had extended credit throughout the year. The traders had to trust that the Indians each year would bring in the annual crops of lambs and wool, which was applied to last year's debt. The whole arrangement was precarious, and the camp program threatened the basic relationship of the traders to the Indians. Not much money was involved, but enough to make a difference in that marginal situation. While things would change following World War II, the traders were the keystone in the arch of the reservation economy and the only institution that was keeping that microeconomy going.

Underneath all this was a powerful underground network of traders with strong links to top agency personnel. The purpose of this network was to keep the government from putting the traders out of business, which could be done at any time if a strategically placed superintendent got it in for a particular trader. Lorenzo occupied a strategic place in this network. Miller's injunction to stay away from the Indian traders only made sense if one took into account the fact that I was the only employee on the reservation with lines to the commissioner's office. Everyone else could be counted on not to interfere. I was different and someone to be watched.

On the outside there were bankers, cattle brokers, feedlot operators, and wholesalers. And, of course, the Navajos and the Hopis. Little did I know that when I set out to talk to Lorenzo, I was about to learn some of the basics of the structure and principles of resistance to change that would be applicable to technical assistance projects all over the world. In fact, my training on the reservation would later help me in preparing the State Department technicians working on President Truman's Point IV program for economically underdeveloped countries following World War II. When I finally realized how much knowledge is required to get to the bottom of things even in one's own culture, and how rare a commodity this sort of knowledge is, I eventually began to understand why there was so much difficulty in the transfer of American technical knowledge overseas, and why so many U.S. managers succeed only at home, where subordinates have no choice but to obey orders.

When the camps were abolished, there was a ready-made excuse to abolish my job. I expected to be fired at any moment, but nothing happened. Then I was told I would be working out of Oraibi as a construction foreman building dams. Relieved and a bit surprised, I thought it might be that the government was either inefficient or just plain slow. It was Lorenzo's cousin, George Hubbell, the trader at Piñon, who told me what had happened. George was fat and round like Lorenzo but even more so. A short red-faced man who was as Anglo as Lorenzo was Spanish, he took me aside in front of the store where no one could hear us. Lowering his voice in a confidential manner he said, "When that telegram went to Washington saying that since your job had been abolished when the camps were closed, they wanted permission to fire you, you know what happened? Washington wired back 'PERMISSION DENIED, WE NEED MORE LIKE HIM!' " I didn't know where my clout came from in Washington but there was no doubt it was there. George Hubbell's message was a small clue but an important one demonstrating that the traders had a direct line to the agency which the rest of us were not privy to (I didn't even know a telegram had gone to Washington). It was one more piece to the puzzle. The big one of course was the dramatic change following my visit to Lorenzo's store indicating the presence of a powerful network as well as strong links between Lorenzo and Miller. It was this link that Miller was trying to protect when he told me to stay away from the Indian traders. Lorenzo, being more intelligent and more experienced than anyone else on the reservation, saw the light and gave the go-ahead on the camps after I explained, first, that Collier was going to have camps willy-nilly and second, that the camps could not possibly be justified for more than a month or so, and were certainly not worth threatening the whole program for.

. . . .

WITH MY NEW STATUS as a foreman firmly in place I was assigned three jobs building two Navajo dams and one Hopi. The dams were to be built in what the engineers termed drainage areas that would provide enough runoff after a rain to make it worthwhile to create a catchment basin to hold this runoff by building an earth dam in places where the topography warranted. The sites selected for the dams were 60 miles apart, which meant I would have to drive 180 miles over wagon tracks in the back country in order to visit each dam once. The Hopi crew, made up of men from Second Mesa, was different in a number of crucial respects from the Navajo crews. It was on these projects that I really began to learn what the Navajo and Hopi were all about.

EIGHT

The Navajo and the Hopi

TO THE INDIAN SERVICE REGULARS at Keams, my dedication to understanding the culture and psychology of Indians marked me as an alien. They viewed those espousing the rights of Indians as "Indian lovers," a term of derision applying for the most part to those who romanticized Indians but didn't really know them, and who had a habit of "sticking their noses in where they didn't belong." Of the white men I knew on the reservation there were only three—Lorenzo Hubbell, one young man who had grown up on the reservation, and myself—who really understood the need for a comprehension of Indian psychology and culture.

Today it is taken for granted that to work with people, one should know something about them, but in the early thirties the "deficit model" (a version of Social Darwinism) was in vogue. The deficit model holds that minority peoples or those with poorly developed technologies are simply more primitive, less evolved versions of the dominant group and that all that is needed to "bring them into the twentieth century and make them human" is to get them to discard their "primitive" ideas and adopt the trappings of white culture.

Instead of seeing social and cultural evolution as progressing on several different tracks, each with its own destiny, the European view was that there was only one track—that of European industrial culture—and that the rest of the world was simply several stations behind. Hence, assimilation as a policy.

In the thirties only a few years had passed since white soldiers had been fighting Indians who were thought of as "savages." Stereotypes are slow to die, and at Keams there were white employees who were isolated in a small settlement in a strange, arid, somewhat hostile country, among people they didn't understand. These people spoke "outlandish" languages that even the traders had a hard time learning (none ever mastered Hopi); they lived in primitive dwellings that had not changed form in hundreds of years, and they had religions that were as exotic as one could find anywhere in the world (the Indians believed in witches and spells and communed with snakes). Neither the Hopi nor the Navajo lived in little separate houses on two sides of a street all lined up in a row the way we did. These differences simply made some of the white employees angry. For those who were professionals in the Indian Service, Indians were what made their jobs difficult. Their job, as they saw it, was to keep the Indian Service running smoothly and bureaucratically neatly. Indian needs and demands interfered with the proper working of their well-oiled machine, causing it to rock and sway and at times to stall. The United States, although we didn't know it at the time, was on the edge of one age and about to enter another. There was little real understanding of what is known today as *culture*, so that anything more than a superficial interest in the Indian way of thinking was a sure sign that one was either softheaded, romantic, or subversive. I was someone out of the future and the future was going to turn their world upside down.

The fact that Indian mentalities were formed by historical, cultural, and physical environments totally different from those of white Americans was not seen as relevant. The whites simply did not recognize that there might be valid patterns of thinking and being other than their own.

When I checked in for the dam jobs I was met by Parker, a dark-haired, slick Washington bureaucratic type who looked like an actor in a B movie. Parker had been "riffed" (reduced in force—that is, laid off) from his position in the Department of Commerce. Like many ex-Washington employees, he had been given one of the new temporary jobs that had opened up in the Indian Service. He had been assigned to Keams as project director, and he gave me instructions for the job. He said, "You're going to be a group foreman, building earth dams, stationed at Oraibi. You'll be working under Nichols who's in the Irrigation Service. He's been loaned to us for a while." That said, Parker turned on his heels and walked back into his office.

Having never built a dam before, I went looking for the Shockley twins, our engineers who had staked out the dams, to see what they could tell me. One of the Shockleys clued me in: "You make a three-to-one slope on the back face, two-to-one on the front. Ten feet at the crown. Three feet of free board at the spillway. Barpit ten feet from the base of the dam. It's all on the stakes." That was it.

I was given time-books to record the crew's workdays, an olive drab surplus World War I field level, a list of the men who made up the crews, and was told approximately where my jobs were located. A field level is the simplest of all an engineer's instruments. Mine was nothing but an oblong metal box with an eyepiece at one end and a graduated glass with marks on the face at the other. On top there was a spirit level mounted in such a way that you could see the reflection of the bubble when you looked through the eyepiece. Held steady and level, anything seen through the eyepiece was level with your eye. It was thus possible to tell crews where to add dirt and where to cut.

At one of my dam sites, I could see the outline on the ground marked by stakes where the earth fill was supposed to stop. In the center, there was a triple row of stakes telling how many feet of dirt would be needed—how high the dam would be. The whole relationship between the stakes and the finished product was as though an architect's plans for a house had been translated entirely into numbers. I wondered how, for example, the Navajo were supposed to remember, after they had covered up the stakes in the middle, how many more feet they were supposed to go before stopping.

How was I going to translate all of this, particularly since I couldn't spend much time at any given dam?

But when we had really gotten underway, the nuts and bolts of building small earth dams became clear. With earth beginning to pile up in the proper places, I could see what was actually happening. I was helped by the Navajo (who, like the Eskimo, are blessed with an unusually acute capacity for visualizing), who quickly understood what they were to do and, with no fuss or bother, simply went ahead and did it.

There were still questions, however, such as what I was supposed to do if there was a downpour upstream from the dam while it was being built. I felt powerless, and solutions, if there were any, rested in the hands of the Indians.

ANOTHER VISIT to Lorenzo's gave me the opportunity to update him on my activities. He knew, of course, that the road work had been stopped and that the camps had been closed. We retired into the kitchen and sat down for a cup of coffee from the two-gallon pot simmering on the back of the stove.

Lorenzo's system for making coffee certainly wouldn't have passed muster anywhere else. Whenever the coffee got low in the pot, or every morning, whichever occurred first, the pot was filled with water and a fresh cup of ground coffee was added. Nothing was thrown out. When the pot was filled to the top with grounds and could hold no more, it was taken out behind the kitchen and the grounds were unceremoniously dumped on the hard-packed clay underfoot. Between pourings and brewings, the coffee sat ever simmering, a needed and faithful friend.

Coffee was our social drink and served multiple functions on the reservation. Lorenzo's kitchen, with its ever-present coffee pot, became my informal classroom on the unstated dimensions of culture—the culture of everyday life, the culture of real life as distinguished from theory and classroom anthropology. I couldn't have had a better or more adept teacher. It was at our coffee meetings that Lorenzo would brief me on the ins and outs of trading with the Navajo and the Hopi. Lorenzo knew things that others didn't, and he built his relationship with the Navajo on this knowledge.

He knew there are people who think nothing of changing their minds when matters are already settled and set in motion (markets, agreements, and plans) and then there are those who are upset when things change—even small things—and who build their lives on consistency. He explained, for instance, that the Navajo treasure harmony in all things and one of the enemies of harmony in their world was any change in the price charged by the trader for staples or expensive tools and equipment.[1] It was this fact that had caused him some silent agony because he had bought slip scrapers (simple earth-moving equipment) at one price, which he was selling at a modest markup when the manufacturers doubled their prices. Lorenzo was unable to pass the increase on to his customers. They would have become upset and accused him of cheating them. As the demand grew, Lorenzo was taking a loss on every slip scraper sold in his stores. Lorenzo would absorb the cost, making it up some other way, knowing that disturbing a Navajo's peace of mind could ultimately be much more expensive than taking a loss on even substantial items such as slip scrapers.

I kept thinking of how difficult it would be to explain the Navajo view of pricing to the comptroller or chief financial officer of the average American corporation. Yet this is the very type of shift in values that I later learned must be taken into account when negotiating or doing business with foreign governments and enterprises. Mental patterns of this sort are embedded in the structure of the central nervous system, which is why they are almost impossible to explain to people who have not had extensive cross-cultural experience.

I have not yet mentioned the presence of a most presentable, handsome, and congenial young Hopi woman named Elizabeth, who appeared periodically at Lorenzo's place, washed the dishes, made a quick pass with a broom, and kept the wood stove stoked. Other than these simple tasks, Elizabeth had no other discernible duties. I must say that, given her relaxed manner and looks, it did cross my mind that perhaps Elizabeth had a more personal and pleasurable relationship with Lorenzo. But in the entire course of our friendship, apart from a period when he was considering marriage with a woman he had known in Winslow, Lorenzo never spoke about or alluded to his relationship with any woman.

To ease me into my new job as a foreman, while he said nothing to me about it, Lorenzo recognized that there were three sets of skills which I must master: the skills to be a foreman, the rudimentary engineering required to supervise construction of the dams, and the ability to deal effectively with my Indian crews. Of the three the last was the most important and the one in which the average white man was least effective. He knew that an intelligent, perceptive guide was indispensable for my work, so he chose Sam Yazzie, an alert, cheerful, energetic, curious young man who had all the signs of eventually going places in Navajo politics. Lorenzo told me Sam's strengths and what to look for.

Sam turned out to be a pleasure and provided an easy, painless, natural pathway into the basic intricacies of Navajo culture. It didn't take long before we were friends. Bouncing across the country in our truck like occupants of a small boat in a storm, we explored each other's worlds. He was eager to learn as much as he could about the white world. Driving along across the open and sometimes wild country, Sam would volunteer information on Navajo life that I should know about. He would then ask me questions in turn. Each time we approached one of my job sites, a new situation, or a clan chief seeking employment for his people, Sam briefed me on what was expected of me.

Whenever I had important things to say, or when Sam thought I should clarify something to my crews, we would spend whatever time was necessary going over the question to be sure we both understood exactly what we would communicate and how. It was in this way that I began to see the delicate rules for communicating with the Navajo. Part of what I learned concerned transitions—introducing people into a new situation or in changing frames. The Navajo were not amenable to what the movie makers call a "fast cut"—quick or sudden changes. They preferred to slide into new situations easily and softly.

Nowhere was the need for harmony and slow transitions demonstrated more clearly than in how we arrived at a job site. In the white, narcissistic culture, people have a need to attract attention to themselves. They don't do this deliberately; it's just the way we are. There is also a bit of the little boy in many males that is still trying to get away from the parent who kept after him not to slam the door. Out on the reservation, white males could dispense with manners, which was their way of convincing themselves that they were men. They would play out, for the world to see, a small charade which said, "See how busy I am, how important I am." They would drive up to job sites in a whirl of dust, slam on the brakes, and leap out of the truck yelling instructions.

Yet for the Navajo, if one embraced harmony, there was another way of making an entrance. Arrival at a job was the occasion of a little ceremony that had to take place before anything else could happen. This would not be recognized as a ceremony by the average white, but it was akin to what happens in American culture when two important public figures meet for the first time.

Once I had turned off the motor of my pickup, Sam and I would sit motionless in the cab, not saying a word, letting the dust settle and allowing the feel of the place to penetrate the very pores of our skin.

Once the crew, which was already there, had mentally adjusted to the fact that we had arrived, we could then quietly descend from the cab of the pickup as though we were guests. The foreman would approach in his ambling Navajo gait, greeting us with a smile, a "*Yatahei*," and a handshake, all to make us feel welcome in the proper Navajo way (Yatahei is what you say when you meet someone).

The form of the handshake was also important. For white American males the emphasis is on a firm strong handshake with direct and unblinking eye contact. One must demonstrate mutual respect, equality of status (for the moment at least), strength, sincerity, and dependability. With the Navajo the handshake is different. While it is a greeting in the true sense of the word, the emphasis is on proper feelings rather than image. One does *not* look the other in the eye (to do so signals anger or displeasure).[2] All that is necessary is to hold the other human being in one's peripheral visual field while grasping his hand gently, so as not to disturb the natural flow of feeling between his state of being and yours. These handshakes could be protracted because the Navajo, as I have said, like to ease into things and are jarred by abrupt transitions.

Following the greeting, the foreman would lead the way to the dam or a central location at the campsite. By then, all work would have stopped so the men could form a circle.

Once seated, I would fish out "the makings" (tobacco and Wheat Straw paper for cigarettes) and pass them to the Navajo foreman on my right, who would peel off a paper, fold a crease down the middle, and carefully pour a small amount of tobacco in the paper trough. Passing the tin and papers to the man on his right (who would repeat the same ritual), he would spread the tobacco with the fingers of his right hand and, using the thumb and the first two fingers of both hands, would roll the cigarette into a compact, slender cylinder, lick the side of the paper where it overlapped, press it down, and twist one end to a point while squeezing the other together. Carefully placing the narrow, squeezed end between his lips while lighting the twisted end with a kitchen match, he would inhale. An expression of deep satisfaction would spread slowly over his face. It would be his first smoke in up to a week, and the Navajo have an extraordinarily well-developed capacity to experience the satisfaction of a felt need to the full.

Just watching the pleasure of that first smoke was a reward in itself. The Indians tell me that tobacco is a sacred plant for them and, because of that, the tobacco will not harm them. Everybody would make a cigarette, even though some of them would carefully put theirs away in their shirt pockets to be smoked later. Then we would sit around and smoke and look at each other, glad for the rest from work, glad that we were alive and together.

The ceremony over, the foreman, Sam, and I would review the time-book, naming every man in order and asking which days he had worked. I put an X opposite each name for every day on the job. I realized that I had to trust my straw boss foremen. I would ask that each man be pointed out to me as his name was spoken so I could recognize him. The foreman wouldn't point with his finger, which is impolite, but with his lips and chin. This helped me to become a part of the Navajo world and begin to work the Navajos into my own. In the meantime, the construction of dams continued and data on the costs began to accumulate. I was given more dams to supervise and moved around from one part of the reservation to another.

Working with the Navajo required patience and understanding. They are not an easy people to get to know and they couldn't care less about how a white person feels. However, once someone is "in," the atmosphere changes and becomes warmer and more sympathetic. My analysis of the actual amount of dirt moved in a given month revealed that they were taking advantage of the fact that my time on each job was limited. They were not working all the time they were being paid for, nor were the Hopi crews. By then I had twelve crews to supervise. Dams were costing almost six times as much as they should have. Motivating others is not easy, even in one's own culture, and can sometimes backfire. I knew that the Navajo were not lazy; they could not have survived if they had been. Besides, their value system stressed the importance of hard work and doing one's bit, as did the Hopi's.

Though the supervisors at the agency didn't realize it, there was something wrong in the way we had proceeded. There were things our Indian crews didn't understand about the work. I had tried explaining to the Indians the rationale behind the IECW program and had developed some nice, simple, logical, step-by-step talks. But my carefully prepared talks, given with the best of intentions, backfired and only confused matters. Innocent and energetic, I wouldn't give up. I had to find an answer. I needed expert advice.

From Lorenzo, I learned again that Western logic has no place in the Navajo scheme of things. Socrates would have had quite a time convincing them (that is, if they didn't murder him first for confusing their thinking). I had always thought of logic as a given, as axiomatic, and that one could not proceed in the systematic explanation of anything without it. When I consulted Lorenzo, his reply did not include an explanation of any kind of philosophical treatment. He only said quite simply, "The Navajos understand a bargain."

Starting with this little shard of a thought, I finally managed to transform suspicion and conflicting emotions into a useful explanation to the Navajo of what the government's expectations were and the conditions of their employment.

As luck would have it, a crew to which I had been assigned was working near the major artery between Holbrook and Keams. This road was kept graded when weather was dry, unlike the back roads, which were so bad that it was possible to hear a vehicle approaching anywhere from forty-five minutes to three hours before it actually arrived. Using the Holbrook road, I could reach this particular dam with an alert interval of less than five minutes. When I took over the job, the dam was one quarter finished. The first morning I was there at eight A.M., and the crew was still rounding up their horses and mules. There was a great scramble of hobbled mules running like the wind, men shouting, lassos flailing in the air. It was like a morning at a roundup. By nine all the horses and mules had been caught, harnessed, and hitched to the slip scrapers and the crew was going around in a rhythmic circle, picking up dirt from the barpit and dumping it on the dam. Once the rhythm had been established, I asked the foremen to stop the work because I wanted to talk to the men. I then presented a detailed review of points I knew the Navajo valued. One was the advantages of working one's own land, not somewhere along the railroad far away from friends and relatives. No problem here. Everyone agreed in Navajo fashion, "*O'h! O'h!*" (yes, yes) accompanied by nods. "Maybe you have wondered why the government was giving you this work and what you were going to have to give in exchange," I said. A chorus of "*O'hs*"; I had hit a nerve. The Navajo knew that the government would exact a price at some time in the future, but were anxious because no one had yet told them what the price would be. Apologizing in the name of the government for being so slow to explain the work, I said, "You are right to guess that the government wants something in return, though no one told you what. The government actually has a bargain with you. In exchange for the work near your family, where you can improve your range, your part of the bargain is for you to work eight hours every day."

I knew that the fact they weren't working bothered them and that they had been waiting for the other shoe to drop. I also knew that they would stay up most of the night discussing what I had said. The next day by eight A.M. it was evident that the work had been underway for an hour already. The circle of teams was going smoothly. Every member of the crew stopped, shook my hand, and thanked me for "straightening out their thinking." Word must have gotten around, because after I spoke to the crew, work on all the other dams picked up. The results were phenomenal. The Navajo crews never let me down, nor themselves either. If equipment they needed was not forthcoming on schedule, they improvised.

Each dam had its own problems, its own lessons, and its own examples of how effective and resourceful human beings can be if one will only let them. One of my crews was working on a tremendous dam near Keet Seel, way back in the far reaches of Black Mesa. If the weather was dry for a week, I could reach the Keet Seel dam in a day. As the dam neared completion, the specifications called for fencing the entire area, about a mile square, with five strands of barbed wire. For some reason the government didn't have enough wire stretchers, so I had to shuffle wire stretchers around from one job to the next. A wire stretcher is a block and tackle with fittings at each end so that it is possible to pull the wire bowstring tight. A crew that knew how to stretch a wire fence could make it so tight that it would sing like a plucked violin string —nothing could get through one of those fences. The Navajo, knowing that the fences were there to keep the sheep out at times when the Soil Conservation people wanted to protect the range, would joke about how the jackrabbits couldn't get through.

As luck would have it, the Keet Seel dam was ready for fencing at a time when there were no wire stretchers available. By the time I rounded one up, it had rained hard and not only were the arroyos running but I was knee-deep in mud. Sitting in Piñon waiting for the country to dry out a bit, I had visions of my entire Navajo crew sitting around waiting for that wire stretcher, and all that time and money wasted. Finally the sun came out. Two days later it was dry enough for me to take a chance on getting to Keet Seel. Wire stretcher on the floor of the truck cab, I took off.

The dam was situated in a small valley and hidden by a ridge from the southeast. As my small truck wound its way through the piñon trees I kept thinking about all the Navajos sitting around with nothing to do except gamble and tell stories. I knew that motivated whites would have sent someone to get wire stretchers; unmotivated ones would have simply sat there laughing all the while about how they were beating the system. Disaffected Hopis would have blamed their foreman, regardless of the circumstances, and accused him of wasting "their" money.

As my truck inched its way around the last turn in the trail, I thought I could see a fence between the trees. Were my eyes playing tricks? Was my wishing strong enough to put wires where there had been none? Stopping the truck and walking over, I plucked the wire. It was real, and it resonated with a twang that was music to my ears. The crew, almost a half a mile away on the other side of the dam, appeared to be almost finished with the fencing. I couldn't believe it, nor did I see how the Navajo crew had managed to get the wire so tight without a stretcher.

I learned that my crew had improvised a block and tackle using a lariat. They had run the rope around a thick stick with two offset forks on it, making the mechanical advantage of two sets of pulleys. Tying one end of the rope around the pummel of a saddle and putting spurs to the horse, they could tighten the wire just as effectively as with our manufactured devices.

THE HOPI had been through some rough times with whites. No matter how hard I tried, understanding the Hopi was difficult at best. Reasoning and Aristotelian logic didn't work. Their way seemed to have been laced with a dogmatic pragmatism. Here was a people with a past punctuated by droughts and starvation, carrying an incredible burden of psychic conflicts at least in part the result of their environment of scarcity which amplified contentiousness between individuals and special-interest cliques, of which there were a large number.

The Hopi, as we know them today, had a long history in their current location (at least a thousand years), apparently starting with a core of four or five villages established prior to the Spanish conquest in 1540: Awatovi on the east, Walpi on First Mesa, Shongopovi on Second Mesa, and Old Oraibi at the top of Third Mesa.

More than three hundred years after the Spanish conquest in the 1870s, Major J. W. Powell, explorer of the Colorado River, reported that six Hopi villages and one Tewa village (Hano, from the Rio Grande) occupied the tops of the mesas: Old Oraibi, Mishongnovi, Shipaulovi, Shongopovi, Walpi, and Sichimovi. Since then Polacca, Toreva, New Oraibi and Oraibi, Hotevilla, Bacabi, and Moenkopi have split off from these six.

Judging by the potsherds in the trash mound at Old Oraibi, Oraibi had been inhabited continuously for about a thousand years. I used to drive by the old trash mound at the south end of the village and pick up shards. A road had been cut through the mound, exposing the entire stratified sequence. There it all was laid out before my eyes, layer on layer: charcoal ashes, bones, broken bits of pottery—the story of a civilization. The record from the black-on-gray pottery dating from about A.D. 800, to eleventh-century black-on-white, to sixteenth-century polychrome was unbroken. On the bottom was a plain, rough gray Pueblo I, Lino Black-on-gray pottery; at the top was Sikyatki polychrome made in the 1500s at the time of the Spanish conquest.

Awatovi, the large settlement to the south of Jeddito and the site of an early Spanish mission, would have been inhabited almost as long if the Hopis had not banded together and destroyed their neighbors in 1700. This happened because the Awatovi people had permitted the Spanish fathers to resettle in Awatovi on their return to the Southwest in 1692 following the 1680 Pueblo Revolt.

Quite characteristic of the Hopi, it was eight years before the people of Walpi, Oraibi, Mishongnovi, and Shongopovi carried out their plan to destroy Awatovi. The Awatovi chief, Tapalo, had turned against his own people in disgust and helped plan the raid that brought Awatovi to its knees. Awatovi's fate, while drastic, was well within the pattern of Hopi culture. Factional splits and internecine warfare were endemic. Unlike the Navajo individualists, the Hopi did things collectively and by factions. The result was a proliferation of towns, moving first to other mesas and then off the mesa tops to the slopes and valleys below.

As a newcomer, it was inevitable that I would make mistakes in judgment, behavior, and in the way I was responding, but most of all in my perceptions. Unexpected things would happen and I would be caught unaware of what I had done, such as when I tried to reason with the Hopi to explain why they should not malinger on the job and waste their reservation's funds. As was the case with the Navajo my use of logic as a means of persuasion was rejected, except that this time my arguments were interpreted as harassment. After a while I became overwhelmed by a feeling that I had been unceremoniously dumped in the middle of two surreal worlds: one Kafkaesque, the other akin to Alice's Wonderland.

Driving back and forth across the mesas; passing the Second Mesa towns of Shipaulovi and Mishongnovi several times a week; living in houses rented from Hopis in Oraibi and Hotevilla; watching Homer, Lorenzo's cheerful warehouseman, as he helped manage Lorenzo's business; attending most of the Hopi dances; talking and occasionally arguing with the only prosperous Hopi, Byron Adams (who had his mission on the mesa top in Sichimovi); visiting with my foreman, Peter (chief of Shongopovi), and talking to him about a wide range of subjects; visiting with other anthropologists and the more perceptive civil servants—doing all these things, a picture gradually began to form in my mind as to what Hopi life might be about.

Conceptually the Hopi world is concrete. Abstraction makes them anxious; judged by European standards they would make poor philosophers. This helped explain one Hopi's emotional state when he entered Lorenzo Hubbell's Oraibi store early one fall morning in a blind rage. The previous night James T. had had trouble sleeping and, to keep himself occupied, he reviewed the history of his trading transactions with Lorenzo's store. After reviewing eight years, James believed he was short fifty cents. The trader had not paid him for a coyote skin!

Fortunately Lorenzo, when he had opened his first store at Keams Canyon, had evolved an accounting system of his own design that made it possible to reconstruct every Hopi and Navajo transaction as a linear, step-by-step process, beginning with the customer's first dealing with the store. Going back through all those records for James T. took all day—transaction by transaction. Finally they were there. Each trading session at the counter had balanced. There was the coyote skin and there was a fifty-cent credit. James had forgotten; the trader hadn't cheated him after all. But what Lorenzo *had* done was to dissipate the suspicion and anger in that man's heart, anger which could have stayed there festering for the rest of his life. Now he was satisfied. Leaving the warmth of the store, James T. melted into the early winter dusk; it would not have been natural for him to apologize.

Historical factors had also to be taken into account in order to understand any transaction between the representatives of the two cultures. Following the Spanish conquest the Hopi had split into two factions: the "friendlies" and the "hostiles."[3] There are summer and winter ceremonies, with snake dances alternating with antelope dances, and masked and unmasked dances. The kachina cult has two divisions, powamu and kachina. There are two series of kachina dances: those that occur at night in the kivas during January, February, and March, and those that occur during the day in the plaza during April, May, and June. The kachinas too have their dualism. Chief kachina masks are linked to hereditary chieftainships and are kept in the homes of the chiefs. They are never repainted and do not generally appear in the public dance plaza as part of the dance group.

A 1906 split between the friendlies and the hostiles had accelerated a process of disintegration of the Oraibi clans. Given this obvious divisiveness, one looks for its counterpart, the cohesive element in Hopi life, which is found in their religion. Hopi religion *is* their life; without it and the intertwining relationships of clan, kiva, ceremony, and land, there would be nothing—life would be a void without meaning. The Hopi religious world is a whole; it is tangible, manifest, and very real to them. When I was there, its palpable presence covered and enclosed each village like a giant invisible dome. In many ways the Hopi village was like a cathedral —the architecture was invisible, but it was there, and it was sacred.

Europeans express their religion in their specialized sacred structures; the Hopi expressed it in everything they built and did—in their entire lifestyle. As a consequence, evidences of Hopi religion were ubiquitous: little feathers tied in the tails of burros;

prayer sticks (pahos) at wells, springs, fields, and shrines; men praying to the sun in the east in the early morning; the crier chief announcing the end of the day for all to hear; ceremonies, dances, and sacred cornmeal; the sacred kivas in every village with their ladders, immutable and fixed—like the North Star—pointing toward the turquoise sky in the day and penetrating the dark of night.

Much of the active side of the religion is carried out by the clans. Clan strength is determined by the members who can participate in ceremonies, and clan land makes up a tight-knit, three-part package, somewhat like a finely tuned machine. Remove a vital part, however, and the machine ceases to function.

When I was on the reservation, the Hopi machine was breaking down. The people could see it happening and were doing what they could to keep it going by such measures as holding joint clan ceremonies with other villages.

The disintegration process was unfortunately hastened along by John Roberts, principal of the Oraibi day school. At the time that I knew him, he had the mannerisms of a backwoods high school teacher. A genial man without a trace of rancor in him, Roberts had never "gotten it together." It was as though he backed through life not realizing what he was getting into until the inevitable happened, and by then he would be so deeply involved he couldn't extricate himself. When we met, it was Roberts' second term at Oraibi. At the time of his first tenure, the Indian Service was still actively trying to make Hopis into white people. Their instrument was the destruction of as much Hopi culture as possible.

Roberts was an advocate of assimilation policies, but he had no malice. Unlike some of the more notorious superintendents, Roberts was neither a bigot nor a petty tyrant. He was Mr. Average American, and a sincere agent of his own culture with all the goodwill in the world, plus a sense of righteousness. Yet in his capacity as school principal, he managed to do as much damage to Old Oraibi institutions as any of the more infamous reservation superintendents. I can still conjure up in my mind's eye this big, somewhat blustering man recounting with pride how he had urged the men of Oraibi to employ white logic and efficiency instead of their own custom in the use and allocation of agricultural land. Before he was through, not only would Oraibi be in an uproar, but even Washington would be involved.

By dint of interference Roberts managed to accomplish the equivalent of unplugging the life support system of a critically ill patient. Driving back and forth from Winslow, Roberts would pick up Oraibi men walking to and from their fields up to twenty miles to the south. Quite naturally, he asked them why they had to go so far from the village to tend their crops. The answer was simple. They cultivated their fields in clan-owned lands. A typical conversation as Roberts told it went as follows:

ROBERTS: "What about all that land at the foot of the mesas? Nobody seems to be growing anything there."
SYLVESTER: "That's Bear Clan land."
ROBERTS: "Why aren't the Bear Clan people cultivating those fields?"
SYLVESTER: "Most Bear Clan people are dead or gone away."
ROBERTS: "Well, so what? Why can't you cultivate Bear Clan land if nobody is using it?"
SYLVESTER: "I can only plant in my own clan land where I am told."
ROBERTS: "That's crazy. Why should you walk a half a day down and back when there's perfectly good land right by your doorstep?"

Roberts persisted. Calling the men together, he convinced them that clan ownership of land was irrelevant and that since the traditions were no longer serving a useful purpose, they were no longer viable and it was all right to violate them.

What he didn't know was that Bear Clan was the clan of the Oraibi chiefs; the effect of his campaign was to undermine Chief Tewaquaptewa's authority. Because he was village chief, Tewaquaptewa was not only steward of Bear Clan land, but of *all* lands. His primary duty (when he was not concerned with ceremonies) was the settlement of land disputes. He also had the authority to allot individual plots from a triangular-shaped piece of communal land at the foot of the mesa near the Oraibi wash to the "good" citizens. By attacking the structure of clan land ownership, Roberts not only undermined the authority of the village chief, but he usurped the functions of the chief, thereby denying Chief Tewaquaptewa one of his principal instruments of social control. Roberts stepped in where he didn't belong, and rewrote Hopi history.

In Hopi mythology, Macito, the original head of Bear Clan, led the people from the underworld and received the land directly from the deity Masou'u, the powerful Hopi god of death. All land dealings were traced back to this original transaction. Roberts was nullifying Masou'u's gift. As though that were not enough, there were some twists and paradoxes that made Roberts' intervention in Hopi affairs even more painful for the Hopi. Tewaquaptewa, the chief custodian and steward of Bear Clan land, was a "friendly." The "hostiles," who stood for the preservation of Hopi ways, were the ones who stood to gain by following Roberts' advice. But to do so would put them in a double bind. No wonder there was an uproar in Oraibi. There were meetings and talks and more meetings, then shovings and temper tantrums. All the old wounds were reopened, exposed and bleeding again. The fabric of village organization was rent asunder. How much could Oraibi take? It didn't seem to matter whether the white man was a friend or foe. Either way his presence resulted in torment and the destruction of life's sacred institutions. *It was a direct result of what the white man took for granted, the things he believed in deeply, that seemed to do the most damage*, such as the logic of cultivating unused land.

The repercussions of Roberts' meddling were far-reaching and deep. Oraibi's agony was of such proportion that an investigator was sent from Washington to assess the damage. Told to absent himself from the reservation, Roberts went away during the fortnight of the investigation. Reprimanding Roberts later for stirring up the Hopi, the investigator, reflecting white values and showing that he too had learned nothing from his visit, said, "You shouldn't have done that. But, of course, you were right. In the future, I would go slowly before encouraging the Hopi to change their ways."

Roberts never did go very far in the Indian Service school system. Fifteen years later he was still a community school principal who kept to himself. Nor would Old Oraibi ever recover; from that time on, it went downhill into oblivion. By the midthirties, Oraibi, once the largest and proudest of all Hopi towns, was only a shadow of its former self. The last time I visited Hopi land there was a sign beside the road leading to Old Oraibi stating that because they had desecrated the environment and committed innumerable crimes against nature, whites would no longer be permitted to enter the village.

It is not difficult for me to reconstruct how I felt as I sat in Lorenzo's office while Roberts, with pride in his voice, told me that story. I thought, My God, how can we ever work our way out of this sort of thing? Is there no end to it? Certainly there are no heroes and no villains, only misinformed people who with the best intentions in the world are messing up other people's lives.

THERE ARE MANY LESSONS to draw from this story. One of them is that it can be dangerous as well as sinful to interfere in the lives of others. If we were God, this might be all right. But since none of us is, and since we know so little about ourselves, to say nothing of others, it is more prudent to adopt a nonjudgmental attitude and, even though we may be sorely tempted to improve matters according to our own dictates, it is wiser and in the long run more humane to let people work things out for themselves, even when you are sure you know better.

NINE

Nature's Classroom

HEADING WEST from Oraibi, I climbed the mesa to Old Oraibi. Unlike foothills, mesas are high flat-top tablelands, the result of erosion of softer rock or soil protected by hard cap rock. From the edge of most of the Hopi mesas there is a vertical drop ranging from one hundred to a thousand or more feet. Mesas are impressive. They were easily defended against enemies and the Hopi children soon learn to avoid the edge.

If it hadn't rained recently, the steep grade from New Oraibi to Old Oraibi would be negotiable, and everything from there on to Hotevilla would be clear sailing. Unlike most reservation roads, which attacked the mesas at an angle, this one approached head-on starting from opposite Lorenzo's store. The grade was flat and it was like taking off in a small plane from a dirt strip, the houses flashing by on either side as the car gathered the momentum needed to reach the top. The grade increased logarithmically. Just below the rim, the car's hood was actually aimed toward the blue sky above, then just at the point where power, momentum, and traction were simultaneously giving out, the road hooked hard to the south on a new, barely negotiable, but more level tack, passing a burned-out church on the left. The church, which had dominated the skyline from below, proved to be only a tiny chapel. Level only for a few feet, the road then curved upward again, through the trash mound I mentioned earlier of ashes, bones, and potsherds dating from the ninth or tenth century A.D.

Passing the village of Old Oraibi on the right, the road climbed a bit farther to the top of the Wingate sandstone shelf. After one more grade, winding in and out between remnants of eroding formations, past springs and petroglyphs, the road climbed gradually to the dune-studded mesa top.

Skirting through and around sand dunes, past Hopi orchards and the new day school, I would soon come on the village of Hotevilla. Dogs and naked Hopi children would erupt from the village. The children were great show-offs, jumping up and down, waving their arms and yelling. The dogs, encouraged by the children, would dash along, stiff bristles of black hair raised, barking and snapping at the car's front wheels. Curving around the northern edge of Hotevilla, the twin ruts of the road dove over the edge of the mesa, and a merciful silence would rush in, filling the void left by my canine pursuers.

On my way to the Dinnebito wash on a road winding quietly through sand dunes spotted with fields, I would admire the way the Hopi had adapted their agriculture to the harsh country. Miniature brush screens placed in the sand to windward kept vines and creeping plants such as beans from being tangled by the wind. There was no wasted effort, just the simple use of water trapped in the sand, and there was no one explaining desert horticulture and saying, "See how we figured things out," either. At the arroyo crossing, the road plunged over the edge of the bank and down to the bottom, which was sandy and difficult to negotiate even when dry, and almost impossible when wet. The far side was steep and rutted and could be climbed only if I had enough momentum. If the first try didn't get me over the top, I had to put the car in reverse, back down again—being careful to stay in the ruts—into the sandy bottom of the wash until I reached a place allowing enough room for a fresh run. Technique was crucial. Too little power and the car foundered; too much and the wheels bounced and dug in.

The reservation was yet to be adapted to automobiles. Only one

Navajo had a car (a Model-T Ford); the rest had wagons pulled by horses and mules.

Getting the car stuck and digging it out were as much a part of living on the reservation as getting up and having breakfast. To me the process was a metaphor for life. The newcomers, not familiar with the reservation, would get angry and frustrated on finding themselves stuck in the mud, mired down in a sand dune or hung up on a high center. There would be a great gnashing of teeth, swearing, surveying the situation, slamming of car doors, spinning the wheels—all of which only made things worse. Somehow, if you knew how to drive, things like this were not supposed to happen. Then they would curse the reservation. What kind of a country was this with no roads anyway? The status of the male ego was at stake. Then reality and along with it reason would begin to seep in. There they were, all four wheels mired to the hubcaps in mud. How were they going to get out? There was nobody around to pull them out. What were they going to do? After a day or so they might start walking back along the road from the direction they had come from. Or someone might come along and actually be able to help.

But for the rest of us it was a different story. The best of us got stuck and there was no stigma attached. Gone was the ego involvement. Driving on the reservation was an *acquired* skill and required judgments as to which road to take *before* starting out by taking into account distance, conditions, and risk: twenty miles of sand dunes from Moencopi to be climbed on the way to Oraibi, slopes that while not quite vertical were close enough to give that impression, one-car-width passages through Blue Canyon from Red Lake to the Tuba City road with nothing but vertical cliffs on each side. A storm on Black Mesa could fill that canyon to a depth of fifty feet, and there was no way out. Colorful, spectacular, and incredibly dramatic as it was, I never felt comfortable driving through Blue Canyon. Pitfalls by the dozen awaited the uninformed or the unwary traveler, the most common of which were flooding arroyos.

Then there was just your plain old run-of-the-mill slop and goo: eighty miles of mud from Oraibi to Winslow and the greasy slope up to Hano on the first mesa. Ordinary mudholes were negotiated by stepping on the gas and maintaining momentum—driving just a hair below take-off speed. I slipped and slid and bounced and prayed (we all prayed in our own way, to our own gods) that the mud wouldn't be so deep as to hang the car up on a high center. The main problem on a drive through the Dinnebito flats—where I seemed to spend most of my time—was that there was seldom enough distance *between* mudholes to achieve the necessary momentum to get through them. This configuration of too many mudholes too close together came home to me with a vengeance one week following an extra-heavy rainstorm. The mesas and sand dune slopes had not been seriously affected; in fact, the dunes were easier to negotiate following such a rain, because damp sand is more consolidated and stable than dry sand. But reservation clay was something else again. There was no problem negotiating the Dinnebito wash; the steep bank had also dried out enough for me to get over the top, but when I reached level ground, there I was with my car immobilized—all four wheels mired in a sea of mud. Digging out took two hours. Thirty minutes later I was stuck again, this time really stuck—in a hundred-yard stretch of soft clay with no bottom.

Realizing that it was impossible to traverse the three to five miles of flats to reach the welcome dryness of high ground, I got out and walked to my nearest job. This pattern of getting stuck, digging out, and then walking was repeated for the rest of the week. I finally ended up walking the sixteen miles home to Oraibi where I was sharing a house with Bert Cronin, another foreman. Mud was everywhere and the only sensible thing to do was to allow time for the mud to dry out, so I could get Bert to drive me out to where my car was stuck in the flat on the Dinnebito plain.

At the time of this writing, there is considerable interest in the *experience of place*. In essence the experience of place is one of those things that everyone recognizes but few take the trouble either to analyze or describe. It is easy to comprehend that the plains of Nebraska, the buildings of Times Square and the Toshugo Shrine at Nikko produce different experiences that are the result of one's being there. There are different types of places, some of them extraordinarily subtle in their influence. The reservation taught me

—without my even knowing that it was happening—my first lessons in the experience of this second, more subtle kind of place. Every part of the reservation was different in important ways. The country itself forced me to learn things I could not have learned in any other way. My life was bringing me back into contact with the world as it really is, not as it has been altered by human beings to make life easier, and this left me with a deep respect for nature and what it can do. To me, today, the possibility of the greenhouse effect is especially real, and part of the reality can be traced to my experiences on a more modest scale on the reservation when there were no roads and I was really at the mercy of the environment.

I said earlier, getting stuck can be a metaphor for life. The basic lesson the reservation had for all of us who lived there concerned the things one must know, the skills one must have and the character traits that are essential, in order to get around. I learned that if there was a dirty, difficult, complex, crucial job to do (such as getting a car moving again once it has become mired up to the hubcaps in mud), one should forgo the temptation of a quick fix, avoid shortcuts, roll up one's sleeves (figuratively or literally), take a deep breath, and do what needed to be done. One must tackle the job with determination and without reservations and do it properly, which might involve anything from removing the entire front end of a car—which I did once—in order to replace a broken cross member in the frame, to digging out muddy ruts for several hundred feet and filling them with sand (carried in a Stetson hat from a nearby sand dune), so that when the car's wheels have been raised and are sitting on sand packed into the ruts under the wheels you won't get stuck again twenty feet down the road. When you are finished with your three hours of work, you will know that you are really free.

For the eighty-mile winter trip from Oraibi to Winslow on the main road, which had turned with the season from dust and sand to mud, slush, and slime, chains would be combined with rope wrapped around all four wheels. Snow tires weren't invented until a few years later and were a great step forward. Simply being able to drive on hard pavement after grinding through eighty miles of mud was a true luxury. Once I was on the hard road I *knew* I was going to get there, but until then . . . . ! I often saw abandoned cars sitting like beached hulks of abandoned ships at low tide less than a quarter of a mile from the highway. That quarter of a mile might as well have been a hundred.

Discipline, willingness to tackle an essentially dirty, difficult job requiring perseverance, and, in some cases, raw courage and a willingness to gamble eventually became an integral part of my personality. That was the gift of the country.

The second lesson I learned had to do with arroyos. Years later, when I no longer lived on the reservation, I found I could cover distances in three hours that had taken as many days in the 1930s! (That is, if the washes weren't running.) Now paved roads and bridges whisk you through "Indian country" with a tempo so characteristic of our speeded-up world. And while I never thought of bridges as agents of change, that is what they are.

The Indians say that the white man suffers from the time disease; he's always in a hurry. The Weepo and the Oraibi washes would cure that disease in a jiffy. A flood one-third of a mile across and ten to fifteen feet deep would rush by, carving out large chunks of bank which would fall away with a tremendous *plop*. The physical event was almost more than the mind could encompass. Like it or not, sooner or later one came to terms with nature—the impressive, powerful, don't-mess-with-me side. The difference between then and now is that then the air was still pure and clean and human beings had not yet learned how to "harness" the atom, pollute the oceans, and dissolve half the ozone layer with propellants from aerosol cans. The barely perceptible process of pollution was just beginning. Our people (those who lived in cities) had not learned to respect nature, only to "conquer" it. Sitting on the bank of a big wash for two days waiting for the water to stop running provides time to think, as well as to observe the reactions of any others who might be there too. During snake dance time, businessmen and tourists, several of whom could be counted on to fancy themselves as big shots accustomed to pushing both people and nature around, would rant and rave, looking for someone to blame and wanting to know where the "river" came out, as though that made any difference. There on the side of the big wash they were out of place and looked foolish. But then foolishness did not begin and end with the treatment accorded nature but could be found (along with solutions) in our treatment of each other. For as I learned from a remarkable man, some of the rarely challenged, most respected, least examined, taken-for-granted activities people engage in can be deleterious to others and stupid as well.

There was just a hint of fall in the air as I climbed the wooden steps to the screened porch outside Lorenzo's office. It was my second year on the reservation and I was beginning to feel at home. Lorenzo was not in the office, so I went through his bedroom into the kitchen where I could hear gales of raucous laughter. Lorenzo and three people I had not seen before were sitting at the table deeply immersed in an intense, animated conversation. I was introduced to two attractive women, Dr. Sophie Aberle and Dr. Lucille Farquhar, and a man who said, "Just call me Shine." I never knew him by any name other than Shine Smith. Listening to him talk and watching him move, it was hard to believe that Shine, single and about forty-five years old, had ever been a missionary. Originally from the Deep South, he had an active, mobile face reminiscent of the French actor Fernandel, red hair, a prominent nose, and a full-lipped mouth that was seldom still. There was a fourth member of the party—a gibbon locked up in the visitors' new 1934 Ford V-8 sedan. I would meet the gibbon later. In no time at all, we were talking all at once and the conversation bounced around like the ball in a handball court. From the first it was obvious that Shine was a reservation character and was as much a part of the country as the mesas and washes. Shine's home base was Tuba City—a regional administrative center fifty miles west of Oraibi—which included the usual administration building, a large boarding school, a hospital, and shops.

Getting from Tuba to Oraibi could take the better part of a day. Shine explained, "I met these two pretty doctors at the hospital in Tuba. I didn't know doctors could be so pretty. I never met a pretty doctor before. Yuk, yuk. They were asking me how to get to Hotevilla where they were going to run some tests on the Hopi schoolchildren. I just knew these pretty little doctors couldn't make it on their own up those sand dunes or through Blue Canyon, so I came along just to help and look out for them. Yuk, yuk."[1]

Sophie Aberle was a close associate of John Collier's; she taught pathology at Yale, and was later superintendent of the Central Pueblo Agency in Albuquerque. She was auburn-haired, trim, and unusually attractive; all business charm over a political core.

Lucille Farquhar, from New Orleans, was one of Sophie's students. She did her best to explain that she was not a doctor yet because she hadn't finished her medical training, but to us laymen, she was always Dr. Farquhar. Even as a very young woman in blue jeans, she exuded elegance, sensitivity, and style.

Their study had to do with maturation rates in different ethnic groups, with controls for diet and sex. The two women, because they were on official business, were billeted in one of the school buildings and scheduled to eat their meals with Dr. and Mrs. Jones—he was a worn-out civil servant spending his days waiting for retirement, whose only interest was in hunting ducks. But this arrangement only lasted one night. The next day there was a knock on Lorenzo's office door and a desperate Lucille entered with Sophie on her heels. She used the direct approach, without preliminaries. "Mr. Hubbell, you simply have to let us eat with you. We cannot go on where we are. I don't care what adjustments you have to make or what you want us to do." Lorenzo, of course, took it for granted that anyone who wanted to stay with him could and would. Apart from Elizabeth White's place (a Hopi woman, she took in an occasional tourist) there were no accommodations on the reservation.

I could see the twinkle in Lorenzo's eye and hear the amusement in his gravelly voice. He knew that Lucille was a lady and that this brushing aside of protocol must have been the by-product of desperation, requiring great courage on her part. Replying with mock deference and humility, he said, "You must understand we're just a bunch of rough, crude men. I don't know how you would put up with us." Lucille persisted. "You don't understand. You're not just crude men—that's the whole point. You're . . . you're . . . well, I don't know how to say it, but you can't leave us where we are."

There were several facets to the problem confronting Lucille.

She came out of one tradition—the eastern and southern gentry—and there she was dealing daily with another bureaucratic, narrow, and very different, but equally real tradition. The country too was a shock—it wasn't just that it was dry and barren and not green and lush as she was used to, but that it was so goddamned *real.* Its presence penetrated one's very pores. It made its own alien statement. She needed some way of reassuring herself that there was still wit and intelligence in this world and not just people who had been ground down and estranged like the doctor and his wife. At Hubbell's there was Shine, with his crazy oddball humor and all his experiences, and Lorenzo with his international reputation (people came from all over the world to visit him). And then there was me, out of a similar tradition, who was articulate, alive, responsive, and, by then, who actually knew something about the Hopi and the Navajo. That was the core to which one added any number of unexpected guests. A typical cross section might include truck drivers from Winslow, one of Lorenzo's cousins from St. Johns, Arizona, a tourist driving through on his way to the Grand Canyon, and even at times people like Mrs. Ickes, wife of Secretary Ickes, Oliver La Farge, author of *Laughing Boy,* Dr. Youngblood from Washington, who had developed a new way of grading wool that made it possible to improve the quality, or a French writer from Paris who would later send Lorenzo an entire "Société" Roquefort cheese, which he would immediately put into mason jars (after removing the foil wrapping) so that he could eat it out of the jar by ladling it with a spoon. What put the twinkle in Lorenzo's eye was that no one had made such an occasion out of joining us "crude men." To us it was a wonderful compliment.

That night Sophie and Lucille joined us. From then on they ate their meals in our humble surroundings, cooked by Lorenzo or another of us. The addition of these special guests was a welcome one and it provided Shine with a foil.

Each morning after breakfast, Shine and the doctors and the gibbon would take off for the school between Bacabi and Hotevilla. Shine carried a little piece of wood, on one side of which he had written the Hopi words for "Piss in this bottle." On the other side he had inscribed, "Not enough, try again." The school matrons obtained the required urine samples from the girls. There were also blood tests and the usual medical questions about height, weight, age, pulse rate, blood pressure, and so forth. Today the examinations they made would seem routine. At the time they were unusually complete.

Sophie knew that Native American schoolchildren tended to be shy, bashful, and withdrawn until a person was known to them. The shock of being forcibly removed from their families, the unfamiliar surroundings, the incredible cultural gap, and the force and effect of "deficit thinking" made most Indian children distrustful of white strangers. In planning their research, it was necessary for the doctors to find a powerful compensatory device which would provide entree into the school community without too much loss of time. They took great pride in having successfully raised their gibbon in captivity. Attention-getting and unusual, the gibbon was a social tool and an elegant solution to a difficult problem. Somehow the two women had managed to break the gibbon of the habit of making the characteristic call of his species, which is a both loud and rapid "whoop whoop, whoop, whoop, whoop," getting increasingly higher in pitch with each whoop. When the gibbon was excited or threatened, he would still whoop, but in general, he performed his function of captivating the children in an extraordinary manner. They all wanted to touch and pet him, to which he adjusted remarkably well.

Spending their lives in trees in the natural state, gibbons must hang from the branch of a tree in order to defecate. Since most of the Hopi reservation was treeless, we soon became adept at improvising suitable substitutes for branches, such as the luggage rack on the back of Lucille's car. The gibbon always knew what these mock branches were for and dutifully hung from whatever we could come up with by latching on with his hands, pulling his legs up to his chest, and performing—a solution which could be counted on to amuse any one who was around.

Originally a Protestant, Shine had been sent by his missionary board to Chinle, Arizona, to convert the "heathen" Navajos to its version of Christianity. Schooled in the methods of the times, Shine would see a Navajo, ride up to him, and start reading the

Bible in English. Polite as well as tolerant, the Navajo would stand still and listen until Shine was finished—not understanding a word he had said. No one had thought to tell Shine that if he wanted to communicate to people he must use their language. Perhaps the missionary board had thought that the Word would transcend language barriers. Shine set about learning Navajo and, in the process, began to learn all sorts of other things about the Navajo mind (demonstrating the linguist Edward Sapir's thesis of the intimate relationship between a people's language and the way they structure the world. Sapir maintained that language not only expresses thought, but *is* thought). The undoing of the missionary in Shine and the beginning of his growth as a human being began in earnest when he learned to speak Navajo. Somehow the Word didn't sound quite the same or mean the same things in Navajo as it did in English.

Shine had first been quartered in a small sandstone house across the road from the Catholic mission in Chinle. Unique and not fitting into anybody's mold, Shine was not about to be restrained by artificial beliefs and dogmas. His freedom of spirit manifested itself almost from the moment he arrived on the reservation. Stepping out on his front stoop one night for a breath of evening air, he looked around at the beautiful desert scene. Scanning the landscape, what should he see but the competition, in the form of a Catholic priest sitting across the road less than one hundred feet from his doorstep. But this was more than just a priest, he was another human being and one of the few within a hundred miles to whom Shine could talk in his own language. Shine crossed the road, introduced himself, and settled down to the business of making friends. Soon the evening visits became an important part of his daily routine. Shine learned practical insights into Navajo culture while he was soaking up the language from anyone who could help him learn it. These insights, his language ability, and his engaging, gregarious personality began to produce results. What had been a backwater to his own particular sect of fundamentalism gradually grew into a prosperous mission. Shine knew he was successful and, taking pride in what he had accomplished, began to feel good about his work for the Lord.

Once he had settled into the business of saving souls, it was not long until Shine was asked to attend the regional congress held in Flagstaff, Arizona, a city that sat nestled at the foot of San Francisco Mountains, about four days' ride on a good horse. Arriving in Flagstaff, he picked up a program on his way to the conference hall and noted with pride that his name was on the agenda. Not bad for a young missionary just starting out. He sat impatiently through the usual series of reports and bureaucratic trivia until his name came up. Leaning back in pleased anticipation of the recognition of his success, he was brought upright in his seat by quite a different message from the podium. Instead of being commended, he was about to be censured! Shine could hardly believe his ears. He was being charged with consorting with a Catholic priest and, from this one fact, all sorts of other inferences were drawn concerning his faith and the purity of his commitment to doctrine. The list of charges was a long one and included distortions about his sermons, which were now in Navajo and therefore open to suspicion because the other missionaries couldn't understand them. It was clear that Shine was in league with the devil; otherwise, why didn't he preach in English? As Shine explained it, the full impact of what was *really* happening came crashing through his defenses like a Mack truck. In a flash of insight he saw it all. For the first time he understood what this missionary business was all about. Rising in indignation, his usual good nature drained away, he shouted so all could hear, "You are all a bunch of narrow-minded sons of bitches. I quit!" Shine strode out through the stunned silence, went to the stable where he had left his horse, saddled it, and headed northeast back to the reservation, still seething.

Despite his resignation as a missionary, Shine was still a holy man. But from then on his purpose was to learn from the Navajos the best of their philosophy and theology, and he devoted his life to teaching them to live according to the best dictates of their *own* system of values. I doubt that God objected but of course the Church in its many forms did.

Working with the Navajos is not difficult once they know you. So it was not difficult for Shine even with his reputedly atrocious

Navajo to make a promising beginning in the mastery of Navajo ethics.

To support his work, Shine filled an important slot in the social ecology of the reservation as the universal spare part in the reservation machine. If a trader fell ill, Shine would run the store until the trader got well. At one time or another, he had held all positions at the Tuba City agency headquarters except superintendent and doctor. It was quite normal that he would get into midwifery, as well as assisting medicine men. For years he had a collection of old touring cars: Packards, Buicks, Cadillacs, Dodges, and Studebakers —anything he could wheedle from anyone. Each car could carry up to ten Navajo schoolchildren. They were used for going to the Museum of Northern Arizona in Flagstaff, to the Grand Canyon, to Phoenix for athletic events, to anything that might interest and educate the children. The agency motor pool mechanics kept the cars running on their own time. Condemned tires provided rubber for Shine's wheels, and somehow there was always gasoline and oil. Today we would call Shine a facilitator, but then he was just Shine being Shine.

Shine was one of the most remarkable human beings I have ever met—a strange and fortunate amalgam of personality, dedication, commitment, intelligence, and spirituality, in a setting that provided creative outlets for his talents. He was one of the few rare missionaries I have met who lived up to the Christian ideal. Rather than being rooted in some external system of values, his drive to help others in a positive way was an integral part of his makeup, more like his heart or his liver than a spinoff from the Scriptures. Some people are just that way. Like several people who have influenced my life, he had an oddball idealism I couldn't help but admire. He was a free spirit, totally unafraid, unanxious, unbound by the needs for status, recognition, convention, or approval of others. There are not too many of those in the world.

Part III

Transitions

1935–1949

TEN

The Hispanics

IT WAS BOUND TO HAPPEN: early in the spring of 1935, a letter from Keams Canyon arrived, stating that per Executive Order XYZ I had been "riffed," a term familiar to thousands of government employees. It was time, anyway. That last summer Lucille Farquhar (who could see the disparity between the person I could become and what I was doing) had done her best to persuade me to give up my job and return to college at Yale. The problem, of course, was how to finance such a wild and wonderful notion. No one before had ever given me the idea that I was really worth educating. But out of the blue there appeared someone who not only cared, but really believed that I was wasting my time building dams for the Indian Service.

I was too close to it all, and not yet aware that there was pattern and design to my life, that even disasters (such as when my mother left us for a bohemian life in Paris with Heinz Warneke), while devastating at the time, were actually blessings in disguise. My intuition told me that I should stick with my Indian Service work a while longer and that for the time being my life was still in the hands of others.

One of these "others" was Elizabeth Boyd White Andrews Van

Cleve, a painter and authority on Spanish colonial art. She had shortened her name to E.Boyd, pronounced as one word. Puckish, tanned, pug-nosed, compactly built, well endowed, slightly steatopygic, with short straight reddish brown hair cut like a man's, she had a way of lighting up whenever she saw someone she liked; her face darkened when she was confronted with someone she didn't like. You always knew where you stood with E.Boyd. She ran a dude ranch for her husband—frequented by painters and writers—in Pojoaque, a village north of Santa Fe. We were both members of a loose-knit group of intellectuals that made up the core of Santa Fe's bohemian crowd and used to see each other from time to time over a period of years.

That winter I had rented a small house from a Hopi outside Hotevilla when a telegram arrived from E.Boyd announcing that Van, her second husband, wanted a divorce (very easy and quick in New Mexico then) and that she planned on joining me on the reservation! The last thing in the world I had in mind at the time was to get mixed up permanently with a woman. If I didn't take her in, where was she to stay and who would support her? I might know about dams and cars and Hopis but I was hardly out of kindergarten when it came to knowing how to deal with the opposite sex. Once hooked, I was putty in women's hands. Not knowing what else to do about E.Boyd, I picked her up in Santa Fe that weekend. Even I, who was living with the minimum of material goods, was somewhat shocked when I learned that her worldly belongings consisted of a well-worn man's fedora hat, a pair of blue denim culottes, a plaid cotton shirt, cowboy boots, ground gripper shoes, and a denim jacket. Then there was the livestock: two Airedales, a Seelyham terrier and two horses (these were all to come later). She was traveling light.

As a child, E.Boyd had lived on the Philadelphia Main Line, studied painting at the Pennsylvania Academy of Fine Arts, and continued her training at the Académie de la Grande Chaumière in Paris in the 1920s, where she was with her first husband, who also painted. Other than with painting and literature, she had been told all her life that in practical matters, she was essentially incompetent. Part of this crazy notion could be traced to projective identification, first by her mother and second by the men around her, most of whom, having been born to wealth, had never worked at anything, nor did they even know how to fix or repair the simplest household gadgets. I could sympathize with E.Boyd, except that my handicap was more the result of neglect than conscious putdown. Competence is often a state of mind and has little to do with what one can do or how well one can do it. Actually, when it came to getting along with and understanding the Indians, getting around the country, fixing cars when they broke down, building dams—in everything but surviving in the bureaucracy—I was as competent as many of the men on the reservation and significantly more competent than some I had met. What I lacked was social competence and the ability to feign it. Nevertheless, and in spite of my own diffidence, I did manage to provide E.Boyd, through encouragement and support, with some feeling that she had skills, intelligence, and experience.

Highly intelligent, strong-willed, rebellious, unconventional (she even outdid Mabel Dodge Luhan in that department), talented, with an unusually sophisticated taste in literature and good food, she was—in spite of her masculine protest facade—deeply sensuous. Direct, outspoken, and lacking in the traits normally associated with women of her period, she seldom put herself out to smooth things over. Liberated in her views, she had developed an unerring eye for the best in just about everything. She did pretty much as she pleased and to hell with anyone who didn't like it. A dynamic, thoughtful conversationalist, she used to regale me with tales of Newport, Rhode Island, where her first husband (who managed to dissolve himself in alcohol) grew up. Their lifestyle encouraged in her a penchant for hard liquor and for sex with those who touched some part of her complex and talented makeup. In many ways and in spite of the age difference (she was ten years older than I), we were oddly suited to one another.

If there had been children our marriage might have lasted. But there were other obstacles to a lifetime relationship: an almost total lack of ambition for either of us (she was perfectly content with a hand-to-mouth existence as long as we were left alone and had the minimum to live on), and an absence of any political sense. Our life was for the most part marginal, which she didn't mind as long as she could live in New Mexico. Her telegram asking to be taken in was entirely consistent with her mind-set at the time.

She moved in with me, into the house outside Hotevilla. Her horses, Bobby and Siki, were pastured outside Santa Fe, awaiting arrangements to be moved. Taking leave later that summer, the two of us rode them and Mormon, a wonderful horse I had bought, out to the reservation. Saddling Siki and Mormon and packing Bobby with our gear, we rode across the land now occupied by the Los Alamos National Laboratory, due west across the Jemez Mountains and the high desert plateau separating the Jemez from the Chuska Mountains north of Gallup, New Mexico, and the Defiance plateau to the west, on out to the Hopi country. It was not an easy trip. The best part was in the Jemez where grass and water were abundant for the horses, and the temperature was cool enough for the Airedales. The rest of the trip was primarily a matter of settling into a new rhythm established by the horses as they walked. Even the normally frisky Airedales settled in behind the horses and conserved their energy. (The Seelyham was left in a kennel in Santa Fe; she never would have made it on those short legs.) Running around in the forest mornings and evenings as they were wont to do was one thing, but a daily grind of twenty-five miles was something else.

E.Boyd had taken to horse culture late in life; I had lived with it from the age of ten. From the perspective of years, it is possible to realize how unusual and rare our relationship was on that trip. There were stresses but not in us. We had turned back the clock a hundred years so that stress came primarily from the environment we were coping with, such as when an incredible razorback ridge formed by an upturned layer of cap rock north of Gallup blocked our progress. Usually I would lead Bobby, a cross between an Arab and a Barb, who was a descendant of the tiny herd brought to the New World by the Spanish. But here the terrain was so rough that it was out of the question to lead him. I let him have his head and soon discovered that when we got into what appeared to be impossible situations, Bobby could be depended on to find a way out. He knew better than I did how to get around that impossible terrain.

That winter I was assigned to Piñon. We lived in a shack made from the boards left over from the cement forms used to make the sheep dip. We and the horses were on a nearly equal footing (they had the advantage of a thick winter coat). The mud was so bad that it was unrealistic even to try using wheels for transportation. That was when our horses really came into their own. Since Navajos had only horses and wagons, we were in vogue, and my status rose because I had such a good horse. Getting from here to there was not only easy but a pleasure and provided the added benefit of relating me to the country in an entirely different way. Since there were no blacksmiths (the Navajos didn't shoe their horses), I had to shoe my own. All my life I had seen horses shod but I had never paid the kind of attention you do when you are going to have to do something yourself. However, one of E.Boyd's boyfriends had been an expert, so she coached me. Today I no longer have the strength to shoe a horse. However, I can, if the occasion should arise, still coach another person to do so.

When the riff notice came, Lorenzo loaned me a truck and driver to get the horses to Santa Fe, where I was able to rent a house in the midst of a Hispanic family settlement above the reservoir that even had a corral for the horses. We paid nine dollars a month for three rooms. No light, water, electricity, or plumbing, just like the reservation! It was lucky that we had already become adjusted to living like our Hispanic neighbors, because the times were hard.

As was the case so many times in my life before, my career as an anthropologist has been served in concrete ways that could never be replaced by book learning alone. Not only was I living in the midst of another culture, but I was in the minority and hence put in the position of having to do things their way. E.Boyd—who had lived for some time with an intelligent, energetic, resourceful, unstable Hispanic man who used to drink and smoke marijuana and beat her in fits of paranoid rage—had accumulated a compendium of firsthand knowledge of the basic Hispanic culture of everyday life. She had not only learned how to calm her man but she also knew how that combination of psychology, sociology, and culture worked as a system at the grass roots. Though I did not think of it that way at the time, I was once again immersed in field work. While my observations had very little to do with any grand theory, they were deeply relevant when I was studying the unstated rules underlying the anthropology of everyday life.

The springtime after we moved, I even built our own house with the help of one of my neighbors. We made the adobe bricks, laid the foundation of cement and fieldstone, laid the floors, did all the carpentry work, built the door, and installed the roof. At first the house was just an idea. As the walls grew each day it began to take on form, but it wasn't until the roof was on that I could see what those spaces were going to be like. Then I knew it was all mine—that I had built it and that we could live in it. The house was no longer a fantasy but real—still requiring work but tangibly there. I learned that there is something about having built one's own house that is so basic, so fundamental, so rooted in the past and in the evolution of species, that it invokes the territorial archetype. Once you have done it, no one can take the experience away from you or in any way diminish the confidence it inspires. Over fifty years later all those skills are pretty much a thing of the past, but the experiences are still vivid, tangible, and deeply significant.

E.Boyd was hired by the WPA artists program and by the Federal Arts Project. She had by then become deeply involved in post-Spanish conquest art—the eighteenth-century *santos* (images of saints called *retablos* and *bultos)* made by local santeros. Working at the New Mexico Museum of Folk Art, E.Boyd later earned a reputation as one of the leading authorities on Spanish colonial art, which had an interesting history.

Following Mexico's liberation from Spain, the supply of religious objects dwindled to a trickle and then stopped. Local santeros filled that particular gap, producing authentic folk art which was thought to be crude and ugly by the Church and particularly by Archbishop Lamy of Willa Cather fame. Most of this art was in the village churches; while it was originally quite beautiful and authentic, many pieces had been repainted by the parishioners with barn paint bought from the local stores as a way of keeping up with the times! The work of the second and third artists (who were not professionals) satisfied only the need to be doing something and to change something.

I used to help E.Boyd restore retablos to their original state by chipping away the hardened oil overlay. One wretched piece owned by a friend, Cady Wells, was about as poor an example as one would find of repainting, so poor in fact that Cady was willing to sacrifice it if necessary to the restoration process, which was still new and virtually unknown. I remember this piece with particular clarity.

I put myself in the frame of mind of a neurosurgeon opening the brain. Placing the wooden tablet on the only table where the light was good, I began by carefully examining the entire surface. The upper right-hand corner seemed to be a good place to begin. Taking a sharp knife with a thin blade, I started by slipping the blade between the original surface and the recent crude oil paint overlay. Lifting off the dried oil paint I looked to see if there was anything left of the original surface underneath. Holding my breath I applied a little pressure to an edge of the rough brown surface. As I had hoped, a chip of paint flew off, revealing another surface underneath. There, waiting to be revealed, was a meticulously executed surface rich in colors and with a pristine freshness, as close as one could imagine to how it must have been when first painted.

I worked my way down from the top, chip by chip so as not to mar the old surface, and my technique proved to be suited to the task at hand. First to be revealed was the background, aged to a rich yellowish color. Then the top of a beautiful figure of a saint gradually appeared with hardly a mark on the old gesso surface. And then the unexpected happened—writing began to appear! I could hardly believe my eyes. It was hard to decipher, but at the end was clearly inscribed:

SANTA BARBARA. Se pinto en el Chamisal
A 21 de Julio de 1830
Ano.
Jose Aragon.

Until that time none of the santos, apart from tree-ring dates of the wood, had been dated, nor had their makers been identified.

Today the works attributable to Jose Aragon are worth tens of thousands of dollars.

There was a symbolism to the entire process of restoring Aragon's retablo that touched my own life deeply because it gave vent to the discovery of a beauty and truth underneath (reminiscent of archaeology) that has been the driving force in my life. Uncovering hidden truths has always been a powerful, though not always recognized, metaphor for life itself, and the process carries with it as much reward as the discovery. The excitement that accompanies the uncovering of a dirt floor that has lain there in its pristine condition for a thousand years is hard to beat. Discovery is preceded by as much as several weeks of backbreaking, hot, dirty, dusty work—shoveling out the fill accumulated during a millennium. Life's beautiful discoveries are not too different. One works and works and puts up with a lot before the underlying patterns begin to appear. And there is very little about it that can be called romantic.

LIVING in a Hispanic family community on Canyon Road put me in close touch with my neighbors. Cultural differences can always be counted on to produce surprises, so it wasn't long before I was confronted once again with an instance where North European logic proved not only useless but counterproductive.

Back in Santa Fe, in my home environment, I labored under the delusion that I understood my neighbors and could communicate with them in reasonably straightforward ways. The situation I am about to relate, when it occurred, was so simple and common that in my unprepared state I was unable to cope. Yet within this capsule of daily life there were hidden patterns illustrative of events on a much larger and more significant scale.

It had been our custom to have our laundry done by the Santa Fe Electric Laundry on Water Street, but this was not the best solution (too much strong bleach, too much starch on the shirts, too many buttons missing, sheets torn, et cetera). So we did what other Anglos invariably did. Thinking that we could help our neighbors by feeding a little cash into their meager economy, we turned to the women (young and old) who were doing laundry all around us. One of the younger women seemed particularly anxious to earn some money. Three days later our laundry was returned, not too well done (you could see she was just beginning) but at least not overstarched.

Expressing pleasure at getting the laundry back so promptly I said, "That looks very fine, Josephine. Now, how much do I owe you for the laundry?" "I don't know. Whatever you want," she said in that singsong intonation so characteristic of the northern New Mexican Hispanics. "Well, let's see what we have here: three shirts, three sets of underwear . . . That would amount to about two-fifty. How about three dollars?" Josephine was hardly enchanted but took the money. Something seemed wrong.

The next evening there was a knock on the door. It was Josephine. Standing with knees straight, shoulders braced, she blurted out, "Inotdothelaundry. Mysisterdothelaundry. Shesaythatnotenough." I knew immediately that it was not her sister who had done the laundry; she was just pretending to be an intermediary—a Hispanic way of resolving difficulties. I replied, "I am really sorry, Josephine. We thought we were doing you a favor by giving you the laundry. After all we paid you more than the laundry downtown. I can't understand why your sister is not satisfied." Again Josephine said, "Inotdothelaundry. Mysisterdothelaundry. Shesaythatnotenough." "Well, how much does she want then?" I asked. "Whatever you think." Searching desperately for a figure that was outrageous but still within the bounds of our own meager budget, I said, "Would five dollars be enough? That is double what they would charge me downtown. Here is two dollars more. With the three dollars I gave you yesterday that makes five dollars altogether."

Five 1930s dollars was highway robbery. But what could I do? I knew that something was terribly wrong and that I was in the grip of a system I knew nothing about. I was left with the feeling that I had been had. Obviously, however, the girl felt justified in charging me whatever she could get.

I felt anxious, angry, helpless, and frustrated. Now, with fifty more years of experience in the multiple traps life sets for the unwary traveler, I can see how pattern differences of this sort are at the crux of smooth or rough sailing in the sea of interethnic encounters all over the world. The pattern of this imbroglio was of a type that could break up marriages, and on a larger scale can cause strikes and ultimately lead to wars.

What was far from clear, despite my full awareness that Josephine and I were bogged down in a cultural morass, was the question of culture itself. The aspect of culture I was facing had not been described in any of the anthropology books I had read.

An important part of the answer came when least expected, seventeen years later and more than a third of the way around the globe. An old hand in Beirut was telling recent arrivals how to avoid being "cheated" by the taxi drivers. He said, "When you take a cab in Beirut there are certain rules you must follow. Otherwise you get stung and there isn't anything you can do. We have all been stung, which is why I am telling you about it. It is crucially important for you to know that if you and the driver haven't agreed on the price of the ride beforehand, the driver can charge you anything he likes. It doesn't matter how much the usual fare is. The sky is the limit. He can charge as much as he thinks he can get from you."

Flash. It hit me. This was one of those big, deep, unanalyzed cultural differences between the Europeans and the Arab peoples. The taxi driver case was visible, so blatant that people were able to decode the basic pattern and, in so doing, transmit it to others. The experience triggered two sets of memories of events in distant places and times: Arab bargaining patterns in Cairo and Damascus and similar patterns in New Mexico seventeen years earlier, such as the laundry transaction with Josephine.

All this was centered on *patterns*, the product of a different culture with a different time system, different bargaining customs, different loyalties, and different sets of relationships and expectations. In Egypt I had encountered bargaining patterns in the markets which, while confounding my fellow countrymen, were nevertheless identical in form to those I encountered in New Mexico in the 1920s while buying hay from Hispanic farmers in the Pojoaque Valley. Obviously, the eight hundred years the Moors spent in

Spain had left an indelible imprint on Spanish culture and hence on the culture the Spanish brought with them to the new world.

Neither the Anglos nor the Hispanics were aware of the pattern differences, only that at times the others were difficult to deal with and sometimes impossible to understand. Each side of course used these instances as reinforcement for existing prejudices and stereotypes.

That which differentiates the Arab Mediterranean pattern from its European counterpart is a special kind of "price as language," entailing up-to-the-minute knowledge of the market, social networks, psychology, and even the ability to read the pupillary reflex. Instead of splitting the difference—as is common in the United States and Northern Europe—between the asking price and the selling price, the Arab pattern is based on several prices all of which *communicate* how the seller or buyer *feels* about the transaction. A selling price that is too much above the market indicates the merchant doesn't really want to do business with you. So that in New Mexico if we found a farmer whose price was too high we would know that he simply wasn't ready to sell yet, or, at times, that he didn't even want us to come back. In the United States, in areas where Anglo culture predominates, the buyer depends on the seller to be reasonable by sticking to some approximation of the market price.

As far as Josephine was concerned, since I had not stipulated a price in advance, she felt she had virtually unlimited heights to which she could aspire. The implications of a psychology of this sort are enormous, producing people who can vacillate from hard realism to unrealistic fantasies and then hold others responsible for not fulfilling the fantasy. This pattern, like that of the Navajos I encountered earlier, is incompatible with Aristotelian logic. It also accentuates the feeling part of the personality as contrasted with the thinking part.

It was this "Inotdothelaundry. Mysisterdothelaundry. Shesaythatnotenough" syndrome and the time it took me to solve the puzzle which reinforced my commitment to do what I could to aid in the process of straightening out the tangled web of intercultural relations in which we all are stuck.

E.Boyd and I lived in that little house I built above the reservoir throughout my earning of three degrees and my entry into the life of a professional anthropologist. The house was so simple and basic that few of our friends and associates could accept our living under such primitive conditions. Yet for Depression times without money, it made sense: light and heat for the year, twenty dollars; county taxes, eighty-five cents! We could leave and shut the place up and find it intact on our return months later.

In the Southwest archaeology was popular; it was one of the few fields in which one could remain gainfully employed, even during bad times. Cultural anthropology was virtually unknown in the 1930s. Therefore, I studied what everyone else was studying and became an archaeologist and later a dendrochronologist (a specialist in tree-ring dating). Both these fields demanded the ability to make the most of minimal clues. To be successful or creative one needed a feeling for pattern as well as a willingness to work with the smallest of details, all of which fit my particular cast of mind. All unknowingly, I was following in the footsteps of several of the field's leaders who had started as archaeologists and later switched to ethnology and cultural anthropology.

Living without extended family and connections, young, restless, ambitious, wanting to make something of myself, full of energy, socially unskillful, lonely, perched on the bare fringes of life with a brain that wouldn't stop, there were times when it seemed as though I was facing impossible odds and would end up as nothing but a marginal misfit. What kept me going was that underneath, there was a tiny voice that kept saying if I could stick it out, things would eventually improve. That was the voice of the self, or to some, the soul.

MY PH.D. FROM COLUMBIA UNIVERSITY was awarded just in time to allow me to volunteer as a private for service in World War II. Armies around the world all have their specific cultural overtones but they also have much in common. Up to this time I had been able to get away with being diffident and insecure. The army at first was a monstrous overwhelming unknown, but like most others

I adjusted. The big hurdle was learning to do things the army way. The stress of the war, separation, and the army were too much for my marriage to E.Boyd. We were divorced before I sailed for Europe.

ELEVEN

Army Life

MY ARMY EXPERIENCE was one of challenges and obstacles. As an inductee into the army as a private it wasn't necessary to be Einstein to catch on to the fact that, for the present, we were simply being processed and classified, like goods on a loading dock. We would meet the real army later, following assignment to different branches of the service where basic training occurred and the classification process continued. Those who have been there know all too well the old "hurry up and wait" syndrome, a combination of order and chaos. There is one image from my first days in the army that remains with me still: that of a small wiry cowboy rapidly descending into catatonia, standing naked and mute, insulated from the milling mob of boisterous recruits by a small circle of space as we awaited our turn during one of the many mass physical examinations. There he was, body twisted and scarred, a visible record of the hazards of his profession. He had been caught in the web of the draft, lugged unwillingly into the forced proximity of strangers, and forced to stand naked in front of people he had never seen before. The cowboy hat was gone, but I could see the sharp line where the sunburn stopped in the middle of his forehead. Red face, neck, and hands were sharply demarcated by a line separating his public person from the pale skin of his private, hitherto covered body. He looked humiliated and exposed. I feared he would never make it. The adjustment would be too violent and the transition too great. Here was a man who thought nothing of taming the wildest bronco or confronting a bear in a scrub oak thicket. But by standing naked, not just the body but the soul was exposed. I had known others like him and how they felt about the privacy of the body, but I have seldom seen anyone so totally bereft of the familiar supporting structures of his former, and only other life.

I could feel his deep panic in my bones. The bond between us was not so much a matter of externals but a consequence of what was going on inside us. We were metaphors for what would happen to most of the men in that room. All of us would eventually be exposed to others with all of our carefully hidden weaknesses. I suppose that's why the image of the cowboy has never left me. He symbolized the transition from civilian to army experience: trashing the past by stripping us to the bone, beating the civilian out of us so that it could be replaced by grist for this new and alien mill.

Trucks full of men roaring around, whistles blowing, sergeants screaming: "Fall in." "Fall out." "All of you with high school educations take one step forward. All of you with a college education take two steps forward. All of you with college educations pick up cigarette butts. All of you with high school educations pick up matches. And you ignorant bastards with no education, you watch and see how it's done!" We were experiencing a severe case of culture shock, and no wonder. We survived. At least most did.

It did, however, take a while to become accustomed to the routines and the army's system of communicating. The sergeant's impudent, audacious, but relaxed display of raw power was effective but, until you got used to it, offensive. I later concluded that these men comprised a group of unruly, recalcitrant goldbricks, and were for the most part from outfits where nobody would have them. If they had been worth anything they wouldn't have been assigned to duty in a reception center.

Endowed with a built-in distrust of bureaucracies, I was slow in comprehending that behind all this apparent confusion and palpable roughness lay an essentially simple, highly pragmatic scheme.

All the army wanted of any of us was to accept that home and civilian life were over. *We were in the ARMY*, and it was up to us recruits to adjust to doing things the army way. That nobody gave a damn how we felt came as a shock. Yet that was the very message the army needed to get across early in the game; otherwise, all that followed would be more difficult to teach and to learn.

In spite of this unpromising beginning, I learned to have great respect for the army and for how it could take raw civilians and turn them into soldiers in a matter of months. It was a while, however, before I was able to loosen the grip that diffidence had on me and to overcome my dislike of being yelled at. Much to my surprise, in the end the total experience made me over. I was given a whole new life. How do I explain it? *The army made me behave in new and different ways* and, as I later learned from the transactional psychologists, when you change behavior you change perceptions!

The most successful group, when it came to holding on to their own values and being least affected by the army as an institution, were the doctors. This may have been because they simply had their thing to do, they knew how to do it, and were intolerant of interference from unit commanders or anyone else. In general they were damn good. A neat, smart old doctor explained to me something I had been slow to catch on to—the notion that behind all the army's male macho persona was another, nearly invisible and seldom stated policy: it wanted me to do well; in fact, the army wanted the best for me and from me. It was a kind of epiphany.

The lessons kept rolling in like the surf during a storm. They came fast, one on top of the other, breaking over me, and I could hardly keep my head above water long enough to catch my breath. In Officers Candidate School when I was feeling both sorry for and unsure of myself, it was a doctor who told me, in a matter-of-fact way, that either I had it or I didn't, it made no difference to him or to anyone else, and it was up to me to decide which it would be. There are times when straight talk can be therapeutic.

In OCS I suffered from stage fright. Being awkward and not too well coordinated, I was terrified of failure whenever I had to drill troops. Why the men put up with me I will never know. But when it seemed that I was failing I found an answer, a second chance:

special training—for the inept—who were thought to be worthy of special attention from "tactical" officers who did the training, one for every six to eight of us. They were extra rough, but they were good. I learned to drill troops with the best of them, and to project my voice so that a thousand or more men could hear my commands.

None of this happened overnight, but the army kept pounding. In the end I was commissioned a second lieutenant in the Army Engineers and got to wear those little castles on my lapels, castles which I had earned and of which I was proud.

The transition from scholar to soldier involved a sort of alchemy—from pottery to steel. The reservation experience was no help; in fact it was just the opposite. There I was conditioned to use my authority with subtlety and finesse, to use my intuition and all my senses to keep a finger on the emotional tone of others. Subtlety, finesse, and emotional tone had no place in the army.

When the army doesn't know what to do with people they send them to school. I was posted to the Holabird Ordnance Depot at Fort Holabird, Maryland, outside Baltimore. At Holabird, I was assigned to a course in automotive maintenance. At least I wouldn't get blown up learning to deactivate bombs and land mines, which was the other specialty taught at Holabird. The army was still in the process of making up its mind about me and was stalling until it had something.

This part of the army was a breeze. Not only did I have a good start on the basics, but I was able to learn new troubleshooting techniques. There was a whole new specialty to learn about: heavy equipment, which included road scrapers and D-6 caterpillar tractors, air compressors, drag lines (big scoops attached to a crane), pile drivers, and crane shovels. Free from stress for the first time in over a year, I had fun for a change, and I actually got to run a heavy-equipment school for a while after I was assigned to my regiment.

Following the sojourn in "Ballmer" I was assigned to the 1543rd Engineer General Service Regiment at Camp Swift, Texas. This was a black regiment, the residue of three battalions trained to defend airfields with 50-caliber machine guns mounted on half-tracks. Since anyone with an engineering background had been shipped out to other *engineer* outfits, we were starting from scratch with a minimum of trained talent to carry out our mission. We had a succession of five colonels, with each managing to get himself transferred out. Shortly before shipment to our port of embarkation, a full colonel, Frederick M. Henry, West Point no less, arrived. Born in the army (in the Philippines while his father commanded a regiment of black troops), it was some time before he could accept the fact that he had been assigned to command a black regiment.

Colonel Henry was a complex, gifted, erratic, demanding, narcissistic man, used to having things his way, and it was a while before I learned to read him as he really was. We called him Freddy, but never to his face.

Working with and for him, I learned about the "army inside the army," where permanent rank was the only yardstick as to who could do what to whom. The army inside the army operated according to its own informal code, which was read and understood only by those who belonged.[1] In contrast to this United States Army (Freddy's army), our civilian army—the Army of the United States (AUS)—was a technical institution run bureaucratically. Freddy's army, like good jazz or professional basketball, was orchestrated from the inside.

I found myself caught between these two diametrically different ways of running things (the informal and the technical). As a result I was in a perpetual sweat of fear that something Freddy had done would not be understood at AUS headquarters. But Freddy always seemed to know the score. Although he flagrantly violated orders, no one laid a glove on him.

During the Normandy campaign, we were all crowded together in a tiny section of Normandy surrounded by the Germans. We camped in open fields surrounded by hedgerows just above Omaha Beach, north of Bayeux. One day in the midst of the campaign, Freddy called me to his tent and told me to get General Clay on the phone. Clay was the commanding general of the Normandy base section with headquarters in Cherbourg, where I had first set foot on French soil as a child shortly after the end of World War I.

Colonel Henry's decision to call Clay followed a decisive battle at St. Lô when our army managed to break through the German lines and in so doing completely redefined everything. Now we could breathe for a while and with the German Army on the run it was possible to think of life as it was before and could be again. Regular communication had yet to be established. Units were connected to each other by an ever-increasing number of field lines gathered together in bundles supported by hedgerows up to eighteen or more inches in diameter. To reach Cherbourg from Omaha Beach —a distance of about a hundred kilometers—it was necessary to go through field unit switchboards at Isigny, Carentan, St. Mère Eglise and Valognes, to name just a few of the links in that sketchily charted network. With each switchboard the signal became weaker. Three switchboards was about the maximum for clear conversation and, for Colonel Henry's call, there were six. With my heart in my throat, I picked up my phone and cranked the handle of a small magneto to ring the bell at the next switchboard. All the while I was doubtful about the propriety of such a call. Should we make the connection, would Lieutenant General Clay even know who Colonel Henry was? Who were we, a mere engineering general service regiment, to be calling a lieutenant general without going through channels? And if so, how would the general with his busy schedule of important matters take such an interruption, just to speak to a mere colonel? The whole army system was set up to prevent occurrences like this. Certainly our unit was far from strategic and barely figured in the general's plans. What could Freddy have to talk to him about anyway?

Despite my fears the connection finally went through. The barely audible voice at the other end of the line inquired as to who wanted to speak to the general. "Colonel Fred M. Henry, sir." After a short silence the voice said, "Put Colonel Henry on the line. General Clay will speak to him." "Sir! General Clay is on the line." Then out of the blue I heard Freddy as he yelled at the top of his voice, "Lucius? What are we supposed to do about these men?" "What's this about, Freddy?" the general asked. "You've got all the goddamn towns off-limits," was Freddy's answer. The next day a general order was issued: as of that date troops could legally visit French towns for the first time.

I was impressed. But where was all the "General, sir . . ." military courtesy?

Another time there were *secret* orders for Colonel Henry to move the regiment immediately. The urgency was indicated by the fact that instead of normal enlisted courier, the orders were delivered by a captain.

Freddy peremptorily tossed the orders into the fire, saying, "Some damn *fool* wrote this!"

Not having seen the orders, I didn't even know where we were headed and knew better than to ask. If I had known, I could have set in motion procedures to get the move under way—assembling route maps and orders for who was to leave, when, and in what order. I kept asking myself, "What was it about that order that set the colonel off? What did he see that the rest of us would have missed?" I never did get the answer. But half a day later, when we should have already been on the way, the same captain appeared in a cloud of dust. Getting off his motorcycle, he heaved a sigh of relief, wiped his brow and exclaimed, "Thank God, you're still here," as he handed me a new set of orders. Freddy's only comment when I handed him the orders was, "That's more like it. We move to Fecamp outside Le Havre. You'd better take off and find us a chateau to stay in. And find out who's in command up there while you're at it."

Continuing to wonder, I took off. It was obvious that the two different systems (that of the regulars—Colonel Henry and friends—and that of the AUS civilians in uniform) had somehow managed to mesh. This part of my army experience helped me give credence to one of my classifications of culture as a system that functions on three different levels: the formal, the informal, and the technical.

My service with the black troops, while stressful and sometimes difficult and complex, turned out to be another blessing in disguise. Relations between the white officers and our men often left much to be desired. Some officers were prejudiced to begin with, and some became more so with time. Freddy was the worst of all when it came to unvarnished, shameless, blatant prejudice. Fortunately our men, like the Navajos on the reservation, were extraordinarily patient. They were also gifted at handling the realities of army life. I found myself dealing with yet a third army culture: the culture of our black troops.

When I first joined the regiment I was assigned to the motor pool and, in addition, ran a heavy equipment school where the men were taught to operate all the different machinery and tools used by construction engineers. Both jobs were interesting but lacked challenge.

When Freddy arrived, he asked to see all of the officers' 66-1's (the pink cards with all the information on assignments, civilian skills, education, technical training, and so on). Clearly he wanted to see what men he had and what they were doing.

Shortly thereafter I was pulled out of the motor pool and assigned to regimental headquarters as orientation officer. In the 1940s there was no television, army units were segregated, as were the majority of schools in the United States, and the knowledge base of the average white soldier was different from and more comprehensive than that of many blacks. Some of our men didn't know what an ocean was, or what it would be like to be on an ocean liner (troop ship). I designed an orientation program which went into detail as to exactly what was going to happen to the individual soldier, from the time the regiment began preparation for departure for the port of embarkation until everyone was actually on board and berthed on a troop ship. I realized that the orientation materials the army provided for white troops left something to be desired, so with trepidation because of limited resources available to me, I set about designing a program which would fit the needs of our own troops. What we produced was not as slick as what had been sent to us for white troops, but it worked. (We didn't lose a man between Texas and Europe, which was a record better than that of many white outfits; no one went AWOL.) Perhaps it was the troops' discovery that someone cared that counted.

The adjutant is the administrative hub of the regiment, a sort of superexecutive officer for administration. It is a difficult and thankless job. Our adjutant was a hysterical man who had the unfortunate habit of screaming when the orders he had written, like errant chickens, came home to roost. At best he was an insensitive, not-too-bright martinet. When things didn't go well, he came unglued. Orders had to be written amending orders that amended orders. If there is such a thing as digging one's own grave with a pen and a typewriter Captain Pendejo-y-Cabron managed to accomplish that rare feat.[2]

When orders arrived moving the regiment to our port of embarkation, Colonel Henry, knowing that a lot of complex paperwork lay ahead and foreseeing a morass of errors if Cabron wasn't relieved, cut through normal standard operating procedures. He figured that even if I was only a second lieutenant, my Ph.D. did stand for something, including the fact that I was accustomed to paying attention to the details of written material. Gambling on the chance that I could straighten things out, he made me regimental adjutant in Cabron's place. My own lack of knowledge of the army kept me from realizing how unique this man was in taking such a chance with an inexperienced officer. Colonel Henry apparently saw in me something that others had missed.

My more predictable, less volatile, steady hand had a calming effect on my personnel. Acting on the notion that it might not be a bad idea to explain a few things to my small crew of clerks and sergeants, I began by reminding them that they must never forget that behind each piece of paper, each name and each number, there was a human being and a human situation. I stressed that they must think about that situation before they took any action.

My rudimentary management skills would never have been effective if it hadn't been for my regimental sergeant, Major La Mond. What struck me first about La Mond was the color of his skin (jet black) and his size (next to him a linebacker looked small). An ex-schoolteacher with a sad expression, he towered over everyone and could quietly and unobtrusively chew ass with a precision and skill unequaled by that of any of the past masters in my experience, in or out of the army. I let La Mond run the office. If La Mond had a suggestion, I listened, and I almost always went along. Apart from my little talk on not forgetting about the human beings behind each piece of paper, I wouldn't have dreamed of interfering.

It wasn't until our regiment was irrevocably berthed on the USS *Brazil* and in convoy on our way to England that the colonel called me into his suite to brief me on my new job. There was much more that I would be responsible for than I had guessed: administering our outfit was just part of it. Freddy organized the regiment as though it were a brigade or a division and I was his deputy. My job was to run the regiment while he took care of more important strategic matters. He even explained how when something needed to be done, I didn't have to come to discuss it with him but simply say that he had ordered it. My job was to take care of the matter and he would back me up.

All armies have much in common, such as *a completely separate identity from the civilian population*, wastefulness, centralized hierarchies, and emphasis on discipline, yet armies are still distillates of the essential elements of the culture from which they spring. Armies are staffed by people representing every shade of regional, class, occupational, and ethnic distinctions. Therefore the army is one of the best places imaginable to learn about one's own culture. Much of what I know of American culture was learned in the army. It was this fact, coupled with the good fortune of having been assigned to black troops for four years that cast the die in my switching from archaeology to cultural anthropology as my primary field (which might have happened anyway because I had always found my crews more interesting and more engaging than the past they were digging up).

Freddy was with us until he ran afoul of an old enemy, a general. A ten-day assignment of our regiment to that general's base section put Freddy under his command. Freddy's solution was typically simple and direct. Taking no chances, he simply removed himself to Paris and paid a visit to his friend General Moore, chief of all engineer troops in the European theater. Returning the next day, Freddy packed his gear, told us he had been ordered back to the United States where he would be in charge of the Mississippi River, climbed into his command car and drove off.[3] When writing my periodic efficiency report, Freddy gave me his usual Superior rating and noted for the record in his recommendation for my promotion to captain that he considered me an "intelligent as well an exacting and demanding officer." I hadn't thought of myself as exacting and demanding, in fact, almost the opposite. He was correct in his assessment, however; it was the situation and the army that had made me over in the army's own image.

The 1543rd made all five campaigns in Europe and then was shipped to the Pacific theater of operations under General MacArthur, affording me the opportunity to observe the effect of MacArthur's command as contrasted to that of other generals our regiment had served under. I had noted the subtle and sometimes not so subtle effect of the commanding general on the troops. When it comes to a theater of operation there are multiple layers separating the man at the top and the soldier in the field. Beginning at the bottom one progresses up the chain of command from platoon to company to battalion to regiment, brigade, division, corps, army, army group, theater. Because the contrast between Eisenhower and MacArthur was so great, the effect of the theater commander down through all those layers caught my attention. Officers who were serving in both headquarters led me to believe that Eisenhower was genuinely interested in his men. When it came to how our regiment and our troops were treated in the two theaters, the difference was inescapable. Eisenhower simply would not have tolerated the multiple indignities and outrages against black troops that were common in the Philippines.

I rode along in an army jeep with Captain Rogers on the road to Manila from San Fernando La Union on our way back to the States. The two of us discussed our feelings about our experience with the regiment. He was without a doubt the best line officer we had. Athletically thin, of medium height, with regular features and a terse, businesslike way about him, he exuded a quiet capability and self-assurance. While we had never been close, we acknowledged each other's competence. The two of us were also the best rifle shots in the regiment. Rogers was from Texas and had entered the Air Force with the usual prejudices of the white Texans of those times against blacks. We both admitted we would miss the regiment and were somewhat anxious about what awaited us at home. I thought I knew how he really felt about our troops, but I had avoided the subject because I didn't know whether he had come to terms with his prejudices yet. Yet as the conversation progressed it was quite clear that each of us, in his own way, had loved his troops. My four years with the regiment laid the foundation for my later work in race relations and with blacks in a variety of capacities. There was something about their energy that I had become imprinted with, not to mention their warmth of expression and special qualities of friendship.

The longer I worked with them, however, the more convinced I became that, as with the Hopi and Navajo, black culture was not to be seen as a substandard version of white culture, but as a genuine system unto itself with its own rules, patterns, and conventions.

Colonel Henry, like Lorenzo Hubbell before him (though the men were as different as it was possible to be), provided me with insights into how culture at the everyday level worked that I could not have acquired in any other way.

At the time of my enlistment in the army, the Depression had still been very much in process. Jobs were scarce. As I was riding along with Rogers in that jeep looking at the Philippine countryside, I was wondering what it would be like to jump back into that pool again, with all its uncertainties and risks. What would it be like to be a civilian again? Having learned much about how the army worked and having ended up with the responsibility for the regiment, I knew what it was like to have all those lives in one's hands. But what would it be like to have my own life in my hands again?

TWELVE

The Micronesians

WITH NO HOME AND NO JOB, I returned to Columbia University and enrolled in postdoctoral sociology courses, hoping to renew friendships and to be visible in case job openings occurred. Actually this was not a bad strategy. My personality had changed radically as a consequence of my army experience and it was important for my professors to know that I was more competent and more effective as a human being than I had been as a graduate student. It was also necessary to spread the word that I had switched fields so that I would no longer be slotted in as an archaeologist. This was a move which I was glad to make and have never regretted. A cold, dispassionate look at the field, however, showed me that those anthropologists who were moving the field ahead were not in the prestigious research jobs but in teaching and writing. The real advances in our thinking were coming from those men and women who had students. So I would teach. Knowing what I wanted simplified matters.

During my second stint at Columbia, Abram Kardiner, Ruth Benedict (whom I greatly admired), Clyde Kluckhohn, my professor Ralph Linton, Margaret Mead, and others managed to put together an innovative weekly seminar on personality and culture.

Kardiner, the psychoanalyst, analyzed and interpreted cultural descriptions provided by strict Freudians, in some cases a bit overdrawn. Nevertheless, the insights marked the beginning of the bridge between cultural theory and psychoanalytic theory, tying the two into a single new discipline which for some reason has still not fulfilled its potential.

In the meantime, much to my surprise, job interviews were materializing. The war was over, older faculty who had been kept on were retiring, departments were expanding, and a five-year buildup of young people was beating down the doors of universities for a chance to complete their educations and get on with their lives. Deans were out searching for new and promising Ph.D.'s in anthropology. And while I did not think of myself as a superstar, I had confidence in my experience and training. I had job offers from quite respectable institutions such as Reed College and the University of Delaware (which had Du Pont money behind it). I didn't yet see that the country was entering a new age after the Depression, an age of prosperity and even of government grants for anthropological research.

After no little soul-searching and weighing of advantages and disadvantages of various propositions, I accepted the offer of my alma mater, the University of Denver, for an assistant professorship with the promise of the chair of the anthropology department the following year. One reason for choosing Denver was that as department chairman I could design my own program. Even so I knew that I would meet resistance to change; in all academic fields I know of, there are great informal pressures from colleagues to stick to the middle of the road. While I have no objection to the middle of the road when it functions and is consistent with field data—I would have welcomed an opportunity to stick to the middle of the road established by Ruth Benedict—unfortunately everything in the anthropology field had changed direction and it lacked its old coherence. A split had occurred between anthropology and everyday life. Anthropologists were trying to become "respectable," yet respectability doesn't fit a subject as complex as anthropology. Our discipline is too young to be respectable, and the values of any single culture are not to be depended on to define how an entire field should operate throughout the world.

I have never felt comfortable conforming for conformity's sake. As far back as my work with the Hopi and the Navajo in the 1930s there were famous colleagues in the field with whom I used to meet and discuss matters. Even as a student I knew that what I was learning from working with the members of these two cultures as well as what I learned from my black troops was different from what my distinguished colleagues were reporting. I didn't know it at the time, nor even when I started teaching, because what was taking shape in my mind was so radical that there were no models in which to fit it. Yet what I knew was so real and so intense that I had no choice but to do my best to define it. I was seeing the patterns of *everyday life*—what was real and not just what people were telling me about their idealized, or even conventionalized, images of themselves—the part you must know if you are to get along, communicate and get things done. It took years to overcome the subtle institutional pressures (from colleagues, from students who had had a little anthropology, from editors of journals) of the status quo. While I recognized and respected the contributions my colleagues were making, I also needed breathing room to develop my own thinking. This could only be possible in a small university department where I was my own boss. As it turned out, even in that situation there was unimaginable pressure to be conventional in everything.

Shying away from theoretical classroom conventions, I realized that my predilection was clearly toward what was later to be known as applied anthropology. Theory did not interest me unless it was rooted in actual practice in the real world, and I had a deep distrust of "supposins."

All these things were in my head while I was still at Columbia University after the war. It was at this time that I was asked to lecture to John Useem's class at Barnard College. John was a sociologist who had been in the navy and worked in the Pacific where he was part of a team of officers in military government on the islands of Yap and Palau. Our military experiences had given us much in common concerning intercultural relations in the real world. The navy was facing the monumental task of governing Micronesia—an area the size of the United States, formerly governed and occupied by the Japanese—and they needed specialists to help. The navy wanted a quick report with recommendations covering economic, political, and cultural factors to guide them. They also needed a program for development of the area consistent with Micronesia's cultural and economic base. It was an ambitious and daring plan. Since the job would only require three months, after a recommendation from John I signed on. I should be able to complete the work in time before starting my new job in Denver.

Only three months out of the army, I found myself in San Francisco about to board a navy (MATS) transport plane—a "bucket" job with no seats—on my way to Honolulu. Ah! the comforts of life in the military. Today I would gladly trade the cattle cars provided by commercial aviation for the bucket job's open deck and a blanket to roll up in. Our next mode of transportation was a tiny vessel powered by four General Motors diesel engines. Though I had had plenty of experience with the beaches of Normandy in World War II, it was my first experience with an LCI—Landing Craft Infantry—which was designed to sail up on a beach, unload troops, and then pull itself back into the water by means of a huge anchor attached to a massive winch in the stern.

My assignment was Truk, an atoll of islands on which the Japanese had constructed their own version of Pearl Harbor. Once on shore and ensconced in my quarters, I set to work getting acquainted and visiting the islands scattered around in the atoll.

This was my first experience with tropical peoples. Yet, in a way, parts of the area seemed familiar; I was reminded of *Rain*, a play I had seen in my youth (based on W. Somerset Maugham's story "Miss Thompson"). It takes place on a tropical island and is about the relationship between a dour, hard-shell, hellfire-and-damnation fundamentalist preacher and a rather happy-go-lucky, full-of-life prostitute, whose soul the minister is obsessed with saving. It is a battle to the death between cultures and the individual psyche as well as between Venus and Mars. All through the play there was constant tropical rain. It never stopped raining onstage, nor did it seem to on Truk.

The rains eventually let up and were replaced by bright sunshine, which intensified the colors of the tropical fish in the lagoons. It was hard to realize in all the tranquillity that hurricanes played such a part in the psychic structure of these island people. Truk's base was a series of high volcanic islands in the middle of a circular reef which offered protection from the mammoth waves generated by the tropical storms. Nevertheless, the typhoon psychology was part of its people's makeup.

For the next three months, with the simulated rank of commander, I lived in the tropics under conditions familiar to most field anthropologists. It was a fascinating time. I was immediately struck by the contrast between these Pacific Islands people and the Pueblo Indians. With the Pueblos, direct questions of any sort were to be avoided. Questions relating to religion were particularly taboo, and since *everything* had to do with nature and the gods, not much was open for discussion with outsiders. On Truk, however, questions were de rigueur. It was a new experience for me to sit around and talk openly about people's lives, their culture, and the things that they took for granted.

The Trukese were anxious that *all* the correct answers be recorded in my notebooks. As the bulk of the books grew, so did my status. My greatest asset, however, was the friendship of Arty Moses, the atoll chief, a plump, pleasant, highly intelligent "survivor." Arty had what is known in the trade as a high adaptability factor, meaning he could adjust from one culture to another and still function effectively. He had started with the Germans before World War I; they made him a village chief. The Japanese made him chief of half of the atoll, including the major island. Under the Americans, a top rank (atoll chief) was created for Arty. I soon learned that I was filling a strategic spot by facilitating Arty's role as chief of all chiefs in relation to our government. He needed me as much as I needed him, which as an adjunct to our friendship formed a sound operational base for my work.

Possibly because the Americans had just won a world war against the Japanese, the Trukese—who had a tradition of deep and violent warfare themselves—were especially anxious to show how cooperative they could be with us. Whenever it would appear that we were stuck and the people couldn't provide information on a particular institution or practice, a small boy would be sent scampering away only to return some time later with an old man (the local authority) in tow.

For everything in my notebooks there were eventually examples taken from real life. That is, instead of simply asking people to tell me about Trukese culture, I became part and parcel of a series of working administrative relationships at the interface between the two cultures. How this worked is illustrated by our government's obsession with the need to "bring democracy to the Trukese." The instrument chosen to implement this well-intentioned (albeit somewhat chauvinistic) scheme was the military governor's weekly meetings with the fifty or sixty island and village chiefs who ruled the atoll. There were two subchiefs under Arty, and below them one chief for each island inside the atoll barrier reef, as well a chief for each village. The meeting, held in a specially constructed open thatched-roof structure, would be called to order by Commander Prince, military governor. Prince, a genial, easy-going naval officer who was writing a Trukese dictionary, would go through the routine of announcing directives and explaining his plans for the week. A typical agenda would include a short talk on democracy and what the United States government was trying to do, details of construction projects to be implemented, new rules and regulations applying to the Trukese people, services the navy was providing, complaints against chiefs, and so on. Seated on a dais above the chiefs gathered below around a large table, he would then ask for discussion and comments on the points he had just raised. Silence. The chiefs would just sit there. He could never get any of them to express an opinion as to how anyone was feeling about anything the Americans were doing in the process of governing the islands, and since democracy was rooted in free and open discussion of the issues, Commander Prince, being conscientious by nature, could not help but feel frustrated. Yet the chiefs just sat there, saying nothing. When Prince finally unloaded his misgivings onto me, I saw that this was the time and the place to begin fulfilling my mission as adviser to the navy.

Knowing that no society can function without a feedback loop connecting those who must carry out directives and those who pronounce them, I embarked on a series of conversations with Arty. Sitting in his thatched house by the side of a quiet lagoon, we explored the process of where and how information was channeled and how the chiefs maintained contact with their people. It wasn't easy or direct, but after a while the skeleton of a paradigm began to emerge. The Trukese model could not have been more different from the one Prince was used to, the one he took for granted and on which he and other Americans depended to get things done.

On Truk no one could express or display displeasure or disagreement with the chief. "But Arty, how does the chief know when people don't like what he is doing?" I asked.

"It's like this," Arty replied. "Yesterday Commander Prince called me to his office and he asked me about the morning meeting with the chiefs. The chiefs don't like the way the work crews are bossed by the navy crew chiefs. On Truk we work for four hours and we rest for two hours, then we work for two more hours and rest for one hour and then we work for one hour and take the rest of the day off. The navy crew chiefs want us to work for fifty minutes and then take a ten-minute break and to do that every hour. Our people don't like that. It makes them too tired and they spend too much time in the hot sun."

"Can't you explain that to Commander Prince?"

"No, because he is over me and I can't complain to him."

"Well, how is he supposed to know?" I asked in puzzlement.

"For any chief to know what is happening and how the people think, someone who is equal to him but not in his lineage must tell him what the people are saying."

"There is no way for the chief to get it straight from his own people, then. He must depend upon what the Americans call hearsay. Is that right?"

"Yes, that's right. So when I tell you something, you are supposed to tell Commander Prince how I feel."

That very afternoon, since I was seeing Prince anyway, I brought up the subject of work schedules. Prince, departing from his normally mild-mannered self, hit the ceiling. Red-faced and pounding the desk, he said, "Goddamn it! Arty Moses told me to my face only an hour ago that everything was going fine. Who am I supposed to believe, you or him?" I tried to explain that there were two systems for feedback that he should take into account—his and the Trukese's—but I got nowhere. None of it made any sense to Prince. After trying several different approaches and metaphors it became apparent that there was no way I could explain that we were engaged in an exercise of intercultural communication.

Despite amity and respect, I was never able to get through to Prince on this matter. In fact, it was the Indians and the government reservation employees all over again. I could talk to Prince about how the Trukese had a different kinship system from ours and he would appreciate the differences, but when I tried to explain anything having to do with the micropatterns that rule how people think and communicate and that govern day-to-day transactions, I got nowhere. There was a hidden grammar governing how people communicated and related to each other that he was unable to acknowledge.

This hidden grammar was an exact analog to what Yale's linguist Edward Sapir finally settled on after discovering that the grammars on which Indo-European languages were based simply did not apply to the American Indian languages he was studying. It became necessary for him to build from the ground up and from the inside out rather than from the top down and the outside in. Every language and every culture represented a new and original set of problems to be solved.

The Trukese chiefs had advisers—*itongs*. When war broke out, which was frequent in the old days, the itongs were the only ones who could make peace. The itongs were the smart ones, the schemers, and the power behind the chief. But there was also enormous power in the island spirits—power which only the chief could control. Knowing this the people would give "chiefs' feasts" in order to validate the chief's position as intermediary between the people and the power of the island spirits. Although the people quite commonly objected to many of the things that their chiefs did they also accepted the fact that without the chief to intervene in their behalf the power of the island spirits would run amok.

I had seen people walking past Arty's house and ducking their heads as though in prayer. The Trukese were being *sufan* or humble, not just humble in spirit but in a manner and demeanor that was highly specific in posture and stance. The behavioral and attitudinal infrastructure of Trukese society did not provide a fertile soil for transplanted democratic institutions; given the structure of power in Trukese culture, the very core of that culture worked against straightforward communication.

The Trukese history was punctuated by wars that broke out, like the plague, without warning, for reasons of violence, intrigue and death; sex was a highly evolved art, as was revenge, that could be touched off for the most trivial of affronts; incest at the highest levels, sisters who felt compelled to steal the love of their brothers-in-law despite the fact that custom permitted free and easy sexual access to those men with whom they shared a common roof.

Working out the details as well as some of the mechanics of how these patterns worked was a process involving the laborious piecing together of models of the networks of chiefs and their relationships to each other. In a pattern not too dissimilar from the old aristocracy of Europe, these were genuine power networks; it was possible to learn how power was structured. However, the people could not have cared less about the abstractions of power—they only really came alive when the subject turned to sex.

Dreams were an important avenue to the Trukese psyche, and the people used to bring me dreams to interpret. This was not difficult, because the symbolism not only fitted the culture but was apparently tied to archetypal material. What was remarkable was that the dreams, without exception, fit the situation. They were also another communication channel, which the Trukese preferred to use to communicate sensitive or highly personal material.

As time went on and we got to know each other better, I discovered that the Trukese had realistic well-defined ideas concerning the future and the place of their children in that future. They wanted to know whether the Americans would replicate and improve on the Japanese education. Despite my own prejudices as a consequence of the war, there was abundant evidence of the excellence of the Japanese schools and the effectiveness of their efforts to educate the local people. The signs were everywhere: in the schools themselves, in the housing provided to schoolteachers, in the attitudes and stories which the people told me. Also, there were signs that the Japanese, despite American preconceptions, had been excellent administrators of island people.

Why education occupied such a high position on the Trukese list of priorities was puzzling to me. My only explanation is that for human beings, the drive to learn and to expand one's horizons is insatiable and overpowering and that, despite massive assaults on our own children's learning capabilities, the greatest untapped market in the world is the one that satisfies the human need for growth and information.

I began to see that Truk was far from the "island paradise" stereotype, and I am not sure that there ever has been such a place, because people are inevitably confronted with their own dark sides. In spite of tremendous and powerful assets, we humans seem to be stuck with envy, greed, the need for revenge, and all the other liabilities we must face in ourselves. Some peoples are more open to others, some more accepting and more forgiving. All seem to be capable of doing great harm to their brothers and sisters but also of giving great love and support.

The Trukese had the misfortune to be caught in one of America's bureaucratic nets. My report to the navy recommended that since the Trukese had a subsistence economy, and the per capita GNP—if one chose to be absurd enough to apply such a term—when compared to that of the United States was so minuscule (on Truk the daily wage was barely enough to cover the cost of a single pack of cigarettes), it would be unrealistic to try to mesh the two systems. It would make more sense to follow the trail already blazed by the people of the area and encourage continued trading with those neighbors who were at the same economic level. Should this recommendation prove to be unacceptable, it would then be necessary to artificially raise the Trukese standard of living so that they could afford to buy American goods. This would mean subsidizing the natives, which would be demoralizing and which, by creating dependence on the government, would ultimately destroy initiative and have a disastrous effect on all native institutions.

My recommendation that the Trukese stay within the indigenous trading ring might have been implemented if it hadn't been for bureaucratic infighting in Washington over who was to be assigned the administrative responsibilities for the formerly Japanese-mandated territories. The navy had experience in administering Guam in the Pacific. The Department of the Interior was accountable for Indian affairs in the continental United States and had a bureau with that name. Interior won. Naturally no self-respecting bureaucrat would be caught dead following plans and recommendations or studies conducted by his predecessor (even if within the same bureaucracy). None of our recommendations were followed and ultimately the Trukese suffered from too much government, too much largess, too little work, and too little understanding. The result, I am told, is that alcohol has taken its toll. The most up-to-date report on the Federated States of Micronesia indicates eighty percent unemployment with a top-heavy bureaucracy providing what few jobs there are.

I RETURNED TO HONOLULU to transcribe my field notes and draft my final report, facing a five-week deadline to be in Denver in time to start teaching. Without the help of an unusually well organized and talented young woman who applied for a job as my research assistant, I never would have made the deadline. Nor would I have been able to accomplish a fraction of what I have in the course of our life together. Without her help and cooperation, my life would have been different and much less rewarding.

Mildred Ellis Reed had studied with John Useem at Barnard College. Mildy was just out of college and in Honolulu with her mother and brother and Coy Metts, a friend from school whose family were both army and navy. She soon tired of beach life. Knowing her former professor was in Honolulu, she tracked him down to ask for a job. Useem knew I was in sore need of help, and did me one of the greatest favors in my life when he dropped by my office with Mildy in tow. I was introduced to a slight, smiling young woman with an eager intense face that reached out to people. There was none of that holding back or any of the aloofness one sometimes sees in young people educated in eastern private schools. Useem explained that Mildred Reed had been one of his best students and that he could recommend her highly. I asked if she could start to work immediately. Yes, she could start the next day.

Turning up at 8:30, she began immediately; not waiting to be told what to do, she took charge of my six Nisei secretaries. To four of them she parceled out notebooks full of my field notes to be transcribed while I dictated to the other two. I had never seen anything like it. Mildy arranged it so that the office and its staff were organized around accomplishing two tasks: editing and transcribing the field records and writing a report to conform to the navy's expectations and requirements. The typists worked in relays, taking dictation and producing rough copy, which the two of us proofed and corrected each night. Our Hawaiian experience both defined and adumbrated a pattern which would be repeated many times in our lifetime, the only difference being that in time she was writing her own material as well as co-authoring books and articles with me.

As has happened many times before and since, fate stepped in with a helping hand when least expected. This time it was in the form of a friendly navy lieutenant who, just before I left the Truk atoll, had said, "You will be needing a car when you get to Honolulu. Mine isn't being used and I would be glad to have it driven." The car was a 1937 65-horsepower blue Ford two-door sedan, which I called Betsy. Without Betsy to get us around, back and forth from the Moana Hotel and the Bishop Museum, it would have been a very different story. After work Mildy and I would climb into Betsy and drive to one of the many officers' clubs on the island with our notes and rough copy, eat dinner, and then correct copy for the next day's work. At ten o'clock we would stop working and dance awhile, and then drive to the nearest beach and park under the palm trees in that moist warm tropical air. From time to time we would join other members of our crew at Trader Vic's or another restaurant with a reputation for good food. Mildy turned out to be an enthusiastic gourmet, an almost sure sign of a sensualist. One day, looking for a lunch place not too far from the Bishop Museum, I spotted a most unprepossessing Chinese restaurant with whitewashed windows; squads of workmen, obviously Chinese, would troop inside, emerging thirty minutes later only to be replaced by another shift. I said, "There must be something worth eating there; otherwise, it wouldn't be so popular. Also the price must be right." Squeezing in between two of the phalanxes of workmen, Mildy and I found a free booth. We were the only Caucasians in the place, and the proprietor, a nice intelligent man, served us personally. Despite the workingman's ambiance with raw wood tables and unpainted wood walls, the food was first rate. Other days I would buy sandwiches and we would drive up the mountain behind the museum, where we could sit on the grass and look out at the Pacific.

Mildy's early life couldn't have been more different from my own. Her parents were conventional by almost any standard, well placed socially and far from interested in intellectual matters. When her father thought she should be outside playing, she would put her bicycle up on its stand and pedal while reading a book. Outgoing, gregarious, oriented toward people, energetic, quick of mind, she had a nimble wit and was fun to be with—*and*, for better or worse, her zeal for work was equal to my own. She had been born in Pittsburgh, where her father's family had owned a newspaper, the *Post-Gazette*. She attended Ashley Hall in Charleston, South Carolina, and graduated from Barnard in sociology and anthropology.

With her wit, class, intelligence, energy, social competence, and cheerful, generous nature, she reminded me of the girls I had met at dancing and grade school in St. Louis. Time and experience proved her to have a strong mothering instinct, which she applied far beyond the boundaries of our own family, and a deep sense of social justice and responsibility for community affairs. She was well read with good taste in literature, and with the exception of how our minds worked we were well matched. One of the many things she did was to reintroduce me to my own culture, coaching me until I got it right. Neither the cowboys nor the artists had been suitable models for the life I was going to be living.

Although it took me a long time to realize it, my life has always had a kind of magic quality to it. Admittedly there were tough times but even these provided the very kind of experience or expertise I would need later. Usually I only recognized this process after it was over. It was as though I were being led down a preordained path.

Having returned from the field with nothing but navy summer uniforms, I needed to upgrade my wardrobe to something more suitable for civilian life. Since Mildy was well brought up and knowledgeable about clothes and fashion, I asked her to join me while I shopped for some clothes. At that time, which was just after we had started working together, we had not even so much as held hands or expressed any feelings for each other, other than those dictated by custom between professional colleagues. Yet as I was trying on a gray worsted suit (she was being absolutely no help whatever) I heard myself saying, "You might as well get used to this, because you are going to be doing it for a long, long time!"

Four months later, we were married.

THIRTEEN

Academia: University of Denver

AFTER GRADUATING from the University of Denver in 1936, I felt I knew Denver reasonably well. But I was soon forced to accept the fact that my view of the city was seriously skewed; for one thing, I knew practically nothing of Denver's ethnic situation at that time.

Three different events conspired to land me in the middle of what proved to be an interethnic crisis of major proportions: my army experience with black troops in three different theaters of operation; the need to have something real for students to work on; and the demise of the Stapleton political regime in Denver that had ended with the election of a new reform mayor, Quigg Newton.

Visiting Quigg's office one day to see what would be done about the ethnic crisis, a colleague and I were told that there was to be a Mayor's Committee on Human Relations composed mostly of members of different professional organizations such as the Urban League and the Anti-Defamation League of B'nai B'rith, as well as several religious organizations. It sounded political and therefore not too promising, but it was the only game in town so the two of us joined up. It didn't take long before the wraps so carefully kept in place over the years began to come off, exposing such ghastly situations as those in which blacks and Hispanics were picked up alive and healthy by the police and arrived at the police station beaten half to death. The politicians as well as the professionals in the Anti-Defamation League and the Urban League were familiar with the situation but they also "knew" that nothing could be done about it. We academicians didn't know that nothing could be done.

First on our committee's list was to assess the damage by gathering as much information as possible from all affected quarters. Fifteen of us of many races and persuasions took our seats around the large conference table in the mayor's suite and divided up the work. It was apparent from the beginning that there was an immediate need for foot soldiers to gather data. Without our students, who were given laboratory credit in social science classes, nothing of significance could have been done. With energy, enthusiasm, deep commitment, resourcefulness, and ingenuity, the students began doing research. Every business in the city regardless of size was surveyed, not by questionnaires (which are so popular these days), but by a personal visit. Every business owner was interviewed, even if it meant coming back time and again and developing clever strategies for catching them at work. Employees were interviewed either on or off the premises depending upon how much interference there was from management. Lacking the luxury of time to train our student researchers properly, we spent what time there was in explaining the situation and what our objectives were, which may have been the best training in the long run. Our weekly staff meetings revealed that the students, left to work things out for themselves, managed to keep our principal goals in mind, maintain objectivity and fairness, and never lose sight that it was the state of discrimination and equal opportunity that was being investigated.

Neighborhoods in all parts of the city were canvassed for the views and sentiments of their inhabitants. If it was a white neighborhood, how did the people feel about selling a home to a black or Hispanic family? If the neighborhood was mixed, how were things going and how were disputes handled? It was at this point that we first learned of an incredibly effective system of *informal* leadership that was firmly entrenched in many of the neighborhoods. The people spoke of "Little Joes" whose advice was taken in all situations ranging from the strictly personal to larger matters affecting the neighborhood, including voting. The Yale political scientist Harold Lasswell had identified a similar pattern elsewhere in the United States and I was to learn later of a comparable pattern of informal leadership on the high western plains in dust bowl days—farmers without whose help the basic situation leading to the dust bowl never could have been corrected. In Denver the name came from the people. On the plains they didn't have a name, so the Department of Agriculture called them "Johns and Marys."

The Little Joes represent an interesting phenomenon, as critical ingredients in the process of change. They were grass-roots constituents of an element in American culture that had been largely overlooked—the informal neighborhood opinion leaders. Their power was and is enormous, and like truly powerful people who draw their power from inside themselves and not from the outside, they made little of it. They weren't beholden to anybody. Their position went unrecognized, except at the grass roots.

My job as a member of the mayor's committee was to interview the heads of all city departments, including the police and the judiciary. Police brutality was so rampant that even today I have trouble writing about it. The Social Services Department, since it was closer to reality, was the *only* department where equal opportunity seemed to have a chance.

It is frequently the least expected abrogations of the spirit of democracy that prove to be most persuasive and potent. In Denver it was the fact that if you were Jewish you were not entitled to a locker in the city-owned golf clubs, nor were Jews eligible to play in city golf tournaments. The general public could become outraged with the injustice of this kind of exclusion, which affected "respectable" citizens, but not with what was happening to minorities on the streets or in the patrol wagons on the way to the police station.

Appointments with the heads of city departments were made for me by the mayor's office, with requests for full and candid cooperation. What I wanted to assess was the degree of resistance within each department toward equal opportunity. Would minorities be discriminated against when applying for a job? What were the chances for promotion and the use of their talents on the job? Or would they end up like the black elevator operator at Barnard College, who had a Ph.D.?

In the forties this was heady stuff. People could be counted on to say the right thing, but would they move things along, or would they silently put roadblocks in the way when our backs were turned?

Given the fact that I could expect stereotyped responses, I did two things. First, I dressed as any conventional businessman in Denver would dress (suit, white shirt, tie, shined black shoes) and second, I centered my attention on what are now called nonverbal cues: Was I expected? How was I announced and treated by the secretaries? Was I kept waiting? If so, how long? In the course of the interview, how were interruptions handled? Did the interviewee lunge for the phone if it rang or did he let it ring? And if it kept ringing, did he pick it up reluctantly? Did his presentation show that he had thought about the situation and what he would have to do to implement any plan the committee recommended?

The results were extraordinary. As predicted, everyone said the right thing. Waiting times in the outer office ran from a minimum of five minutes up to an hour for my interview with the chief of police. In most instances there was a decided coolness in the air, a kind of intellectual foot dragging. The police chief had failed to record my appointment on his calendar. When he finally emerged from his lair it was with a bureaucratic, bullying attitude. His opening remark was, "What can I do for you, Bud?" That interview didn't go well; the wait, coupled with the other cues, made the interview pro forma at best.

Prior to meeting with the heads of the city departments, I mentally reviewed how I should organize my interviews in such a way as to get at their true attitudes. In doing this I decided to make use of the only available model, one with proven success in penetrating the barriers erected by the conscious self—the so-called Freudian error, or slip of the tongue or pen. The basic principle behind the error is that if the difference between what people say and what they really feel is too great, the underlying attitude will reveal itself via a slip of the tongue or the equivalent in behavior that would provide clues as to my respondents' real feelings. So I looked for how interruptions were handled (were they welcome or not?). The time I was kept waiting in the anteroom proved to be a consistently reliable indicator of the basic attitude toward equal opportunity of the department head I was interviewing. If the "unconscious" indicators consistently pointed in one direction, especially if combined with a little judicious questioning of employees who were in a position to know the score, I would then be able to give a valid opinion that had predictive value to it. Why? Because everything I knew about this process told me that data rooted in the unconscious, since it was out of range of the manipulations of the ego, was far more reliable as an indicator of where an individual stood than anything he or she might say out loud. This knowledge was a tiny straw in the wind of my career, pointing my way to later work in the field of nonverbal communication.

I assumed that public opinion practitioners might be interested in attitudes and would want to improve their discipline, so I wrote a paper on the results of my interviews, "The Freudian Error as an Aid to Determining Attitudes." None of the public opinion journals in the United States would publish it. *The Journal of International Public Opinion Research* in Mexico finally took it. The problem with my approach to polling was that there was no way to attach a number to it. You could count opinions but not basic core attitudes, some of which were out of awareness.

A significant body of data was generated by students. For example, an ex–army nurse from the South, a short, dumpy woman, not the kind to attract attention, had until then failed to participate in our normally active and open class discussions. Finally she started telling her story, about the changes that had taken place in her attitudes while she was nursing seriously wounded and critically ill patients at a large army hospital during the war. She had been raised with a deep and abiding prejudice against blacks, but she covered her feelings with the professional demeanor of a head nurse. No one had ever told her it was wrong to feel prejudiced toward one class of human being and to discriminate, or that racial prejudice might even conflict with good nursing practice. But one day, with no warning, there was a complete flip-flop inside her. Something about the suffering of the men had gotten through to her. "Suffering was independent of skin color," she said. From that time on her patients were all the same, fellow human beings in pain needing everything she could give them, including her loving care. It was the greatest discovery of her life.

I had been operating under a system of beliefs dating back through Thomas Aquinas to Socrates and Plato, all of whom held that reason was king and that if the proper arguments were used it was possible to change people's minds, hearts, and souls. Yet there was little in the actual performance of human beings to support this notion. Certainly my experiences with the Indian Service and with the navy on Truk had failed to do this. What I had been lacking was a model of how people changed, when and if they changed at all. My nurse friend had changed from the inside out, but I had been taught that changes are accomplished from the outside in, an assumption reinforced by everything in the institutions with which I was associated.

In drafting my report I was faced with the inescapable conclusion that, given the tenor of the times, there was no way I could be optimistic concerning the future of fair employment practices in the city of Denver. I did note one thing before publication of the preliminary report. The professionals—those who headed up major minority organizations, as well as the heads of various religious organizations concerned with interethnic matters—were all much more interested in the meager public opinion survey data produced by the National Opinion Research Center at Denver University than they were in the data produced by the students on what was actually happening. In this sense they were more clued in to the core of American culture than I was. Since then polls have become endemic and the importance of "image"—independent of character or effectiveness—has become an embedded feature of American culture.

The reception accorded the report of the Mayor's Committee on Human Relations (over four hundred pages long) was both enlightening and frightening. In the report we not only described our findings but suggested programs for dealing with them. One of these suggestions was to ban unsigned hate literature, and we named some of the more notorious hatemongers, including an evangelical preacher, all of whom had previously been identified and labeled by national magazines such as *Time*.

The press had a field day with our report. There was a tremendous uproar and for weeks the committee took a beating. Every day there was something new as interested parties jumped on the bandwagon. Innocents that we were, we had given them a ready-made present—a means for creating controversy and building circulation. Much to our surprise, even the Jewish press denounced the report, presumably for fear of alienating advertisers—this in a city where anti-Semitism was rampant. We were attacked by everyone who had anything to gain from maintaining the status quo. Denver's image was on the line. Headlines of the size reserved for announcing war screamed, PREJUDICE RAMPANT IN DENVER: MAYOR'S COMMITTEE ATTACKS ALL DEPARTMENTS. We had expected something a little like this from the extreme right wing press, but we were fair game for all, even the minority presses.

We had also assumed, having uncovered a shocking situation, that something would be done to correct it. Instead our report was used as an opportunity to do the opposite.

One thing was quite clear. None of us committee members knew our own culture, particularly that side of culture having to do with politics. We academicians were babes in the woods and had been made fools of; in fact, we had become tools in the hands of the very people who were responsible for the awful conditions described in the report.

Through all of this experience I began to sense strong undercurrents pushing people this way and that way, forces over which they had no control, almost like an immense cultural unconscious. It did little good to question people because no one seemed able to describe how the system really worked.

Our big mistake in Denver had been publishing our report in the naive assumption that the press would treat it fairly. We had misjudged completely how to present to Denver the fact that it had a massive problem and that Denver itself was going to have to do something about it. What was interesting was that the mayor and the people around him were quite naturally upset by all the commotion as well as by our naïveté in the way in which we handled our report. They wondered why we had been so inept as to reveal the nature of the disease in such explicit terms. What did we want to do? Get Quigg Newton thrown out of office?

The committee had assumed that the press was fair and impartial. Palmer Hoyt, publisher of the *Denver Post*, had a national reputation as a straight shooter who would report the truth. And we had built our strategy on that assumption. We assumed that, if we held nothing back and made all the information available to the media, the story would carry itself without undue distortion. It didn't happen; eye-catching and inflammatory quotes were torn out of context. All of the racist rabble-rousers were interviewed and their opinions broadcast by newspaper and radio. The press likes a fight. Fights are dramatic and help to sell newspapers.

In Denver I found myself confronting an entire *silent* dimension of culture which had been overlooked or ignored, almost as though there were a conspiracy to keep it hidden, a dimension which was just as inaccessible to reason as a totally foreign culture would have been. Anthropologists such as Linton and Kluckhohn had spoken of manifest and latent culture. To me, the latent, tacit culture was clearly the real one, whereas the manifest culture, like the persona of the Greek actor, was simply a mask, a carved and painted thing, an artifice created to fit a particular culturally defined status or situational behavior. Nevertheless, people treated the artificial as the real, turning their backs on the authenticity underneath!

There were two big lessons for me in Denver. The first was my experience on the Mayor's Committee on Human Relations; the second had to do with teaching and how to present a living anthropology to students. When I first started teaching I was full of how the world could be a better place if people only knew more about the importance of cultural differences. What was real to *me*, however, did not always come across as real to others. How to teach what I knew was the question. I felt anxious and was eager to do it right.

Armed with carefully prepared notes, I took my position at the head of my first class and started lecturing. The students' eyes, which had been alive and alert a moment before, began to glaze over. Beginning in the back of the room, the freeze moved forward. Desperate to save myself, I thought back to my own days in graduate school. Even then I had an advantage: I already knew what Indian life was like. I also knew that my students in Denver had not been to the field, and had no way of relating what I was telling them in class to reality.

Abandoning my carefully prepared notes and noting that almost three-fourths of my students were veterans, I began using real-life examples lifted directly from the army and the navy. I did this because the abstractions of life as refined by social scientists are just that—abstractions which inevitably take a great deal for granted and have little link to real life. What the students needed were tangible links between theory and practice; since the life of any army reflects civilian life, I was in the best position possible to provide the links the students needed to make my subject come alive.

From the moment I began to focus my attention on the students and to teach from real life, the classes began to be fun. The real problem was overcoming my anxiety brought on by using less than fully structured linear lesson plans. I knew the arguments well: "If it isn't linear and organized in advance, how do you know the students are going to get it all?" "If you don't know what you are going to discuss before you get to class, how can you possibly get up there and run a class?" But I discovered much more order hidden in the students' heads than I had imagined. My job was to discover that order and work with it and not against it, which called for full student participation in everything we were doing. In the end the students proved to be so alive, so active and inquiring, that I realized that, as with the Navajos and my troops in the army, our lives were bound together in some mysterious way by an alchemy which I accepted but did not fully understand. Part of what was happening was that we were getting around the "us-them" syndrome.

. . . .

THE MATERIAL I PRESENTED seemed at first to be much less linear than I would have wished—that is, until I had done it for a while. The University of Denver was, from the point of view of rank and prestige, hardly an auspicious place to begin a career. The work load was unconscionably heavy, and the administration, as is common in academia, manipulated and exploited the faculty. In a word we were underpaid and overworked, a situation which I learned is unfortunately all too common.

However, the great advantage of the job was that I was free to experiment and to develop not only new techniques but new material more consistent with what I had learned in the field—on the reservation, in the army, on Truk. I felt fortunate that I was able to adapt my teaching to my students' needs, which I could not have done in a more conventional department. What I could not have predicted was that I could teach pretty much the material I would have covered using the old method of instruction, except that the rhythm and order of presentation were more compatible with the rhythm and mood of the class.

My teaching experience went to the very roots of my profession. By laying myself open as I did by breaking with tradition, I was facing a chasm between what people were saying and what they were doing. This third major exposure to the hidden rules of culture shook me. It set me apart. I was seeing things that were definitely there but were unexplored, and in a way seemed taboo. The shaking, however, had a positive side because it brought into question how I had been relating to the world myself and provided an added incentive to learn more about my psychological side so that I could begin to understand other people better. I was still under the power of the delusion that social science could save the world.

I set out to make the acquaintance of some of the dynamic psychiatrists who were just beginning to make their thinking felt in America—people such as Erich Fromm and Karen Horney. Their insights had proven in the past to be helpful and relevant to what I had been trying to accomplish. I needed to know more, so I contacted Erich Fromm. We arranged to meet shortly on my next visit to New York. A short, intense, sensual man, with an inherently scholarly air about him, Fromm greeted Mildy and me at the door to his apartment on the West Side in New York. Polite, somewhat formal, and abrupt at first, he reminded me of Mrs. Jensen, who had run the boardinghouse in Santa Fe. But it didn't take long until we were, in a Germanic way, on the way to becoming friends.

As our visit was drawing to a close, he managed to talk me into visiting Bennington College in Vermont, where he taught and where there was an opening for an anthropologist. It has been my experience that the greatness of those who work in the intellectual realm is, unlike the ones who espouse power, proportional to their availability to colleagues. Fromm was no exception to this rule.

My subsequent visit to Bennington provided me with an opportunity to meet faculty members and staff. An added attraction to Bennington was that I would have an opportunity to get better acquainted with Fromm. In 1948 I applied for and got the job, and Mildy and I moved to Vermont.

FOURTEEN

Academia: Bennington College

WHEN IT COMES to job satisfaction, quality of life, and peace of mind, the importance of living quarters and work spaces are frequently overlooked. At Bennington we had a brand-new bright and shiny two-story house in an orchard a short distance from the college. There were two rooms and a bath upstairs, a living room, study, and modern kitchen downstairs and even a garage for the car. I had never felt so opulent or so fortunate.

An added advantage of moving to Vermont was that instead of two thousand miles separating me from the rest of my family, the distance was now a mere two hundred or less. There was my Aunt Delight in Andover, my father and brother in New York City, my mother and Heinz in either Washington, D.C., or on their farm in East Haddam, Connecticut, as well as one sister and her husband and children in Greenwich. Then there was Priscilla—to whom I was closest—and her husband on the outskirts of Guilford, Connecticut. There were so many Halls in Bennington that I had to spell out my middle name (Twitchell) before the telephone company would list my name in the Bennington directory.

At Denver we had lived in one-half of a single Quonset hut (those corrugated steel houses that look like a culvert sliced down the middle). Our usable space was about 270 square feet and we were lucky because I was entitled to this veteran's housing. Other faculty members lived in trailers and had to go outside in thirty degrees below zero weather to bathe and use the toilet. At least we had indoor plumbing. Bennington was a vast step up in our life-style.

We found the faculty at Bennington not only stimulating and talented but people with whom we could be friends. The proximity to New York City was a distinct advantage, and a brand-new house in an apple orchard almost more than we could have dreamed of. My friendship with Erich Fromm was one of the highlights of a rich and varied life and paved the way for my future work with the psychiatrists that Harry Stack Sullivan had pulled together in Washington under the umbrella of the Washington School of Psychiatry.[1]

Erich Fromm was our best friend and our closest relationship with those in the Bennington community. No matter how often we met, I never lost a sense of awe at his ability to formulate problems in his head, evaluate them, and come up with a well-reasoned judgment. At some point in his university training his classmates had started calling him "the Brain." I was always struck not only by the impact of his mind, but also by his deep humanity. Psychiatrists often give the impression of reading one's mind and finding all sorts of character flaws; there was none of this in Fromm.

Erich's psychoanalytic practice kept him in New York during the week. On weekends he would fly up to teach his classes and be driven in a college car to our house in the orchard on Bennington's grounds for a late dinner. Our conversations were wide-ranging and full of stimulation and joy. It didn't take long for me to suggest that instead of having the college car pick him up, I could drive him to and from the airport myself; the trip took about an hour and would give us an extra two hours a week for our discussions. Also, as a younger colleague, I felt it was an honor as well as an obligation on my part to do what I could to facilitate things for him.

In addition to psychoanalysis and discussions of the Talmud (Fromm was a rabbi and a well-known Talmudic scholar), we had long conversations about the college and the goals of education. We also kept returning to one topic: *How to live right.*

I mused once, "Why don't we teach a course in the art of living?" Erich said, "The most important thing in life is living, and yet we pay attention to everything else and practically none to how to live." Continuing, he said, "We could even teach them how to be a son of bitch! That is, if that is what they wanted to be. But we would have to be sure to cover the price they would pay and the consequences of making that choice." Fromm was a philosopher. I was a pragmatist. The whole idea of actually teaching people "how to live" fascinated me and put into words a long-felt need not only to do something about my own life, but also to apply what I had learned in anthropology to the everyday life of the average individual.

Having spent my life trying to decipher the hidden rules for getting along with others, I had a personal as well as an academic stake in this fascinating project. Of course, there were some doubts, some wishful thinking, enthusiasm, and the powerful draw of a chance to make a contribution. As we discussed our plans, I saw that there was some haziness as to how we were really going to attack this gargantuan task, but I also had an implicit trust in Fromm and figured that this was a godsent opportunity to learn from the master.

It was a disappointment but hardly a surprise when the faculty turned down our idea for teaching a course called "The Art of Living." Some were outraged by our proposal but covered it with polite academic circumlocutions; others simply dug in their heels, and a few were openly hostile. What were we going to use for a textbook? It had never been done before! What department would it be listed under? The college was having enough difficulty trying to cope with a dilettante image. What would the parents say? Bennington was founded on the idea that it was a pioneering college that would explore new ideas and new approaches to education, but our idea was just too far out to be taken seriously.

Erich never lost track of the idea, nor did I. He later wrote a best seller, *The Art of Loving,* a subject he had been immersed in for years and which had brought him the friendship of people whom he greatly admired, such as Anthony Quinn. Fromm believed that most people were passive in regard to love and that they spent their time looking for someone to love them, which was not the way to go about it. He saw it as more important to know *how* to love: his approach was active rather than passive. The same principle can, of course, be applied to living; that is, it can be done actively or passively. Many people take a passive view toward their lives, accepting what life dishes out without really taking charge. But what do you take charge of? This may be the most crucial issue in the quest for living and was the very sort of thing I wanted to know more about.

Bennington was noted for its training in modern dance under the expert and dedicated tutorship of Martha Hill, a close associate of Martha Graham. Mostly because of students who came to me each week for counseling, it wasn't long before I found myself involved with the dance classes. The students' problems with dance (they were constantly having to create new dances) seemed to center on three problems, the most common of which was a tendency to indulge themselves in overly complex statements—a failure to simplify their dances. A girl would come into my office, collapse into a chair, sigh, and say, "I'm having trouble with my dance."

"What is your dance about?" I would ask.

"It's about Negro/white relations."

"Isn't that a bit complex for one dance? How about cutting it down to something more manageable, like, the relations between a black man and a white woman?" I would suggest.

This session would be followed by another, in which I would discover the second problem—that the young woman had failed to integrate what the dance meant to her personally. That is, she had not internalized the message she was trying to get across in her dance—she had not *made it her own* or worked out all the feeling tones and their shifts throughout the dance. The third problem had to do with technical matters of choreography, which turned out to be straightforward once the first two hurdles had been cleared.

Both the dancers and I saw the dance as a system of communication that was capable, in the hands of a trained and talented practitioner, of transmitting some rather complex ideas and situations to an audience. Without this experience with the dance students I am sure that later discoveries in the field of communication would have come to me much more slowly.

The most significant and completely unexpected consequence of the Bennington move was my association with the Transactional school of psychologists (Adelbert Ames, Hadley Cantril, Franklin Kilpatrick, and others). This came about because of our Fine Arts instructor, Alexander Dorner, author of a revolutionary book called *The Way Beyond 'Art.'* Dorner had been director of one of the avant-garde art museums in Germany which were closed during the Nazi period. He was an extraordinary man with a saber scar —a souvenir of his student days at Heidelberg—which he vehemently disowned, because it was symbolic of things he no longer stood for. Some of the less sensitive people, thinking they were doing the right thing, would say, "Oh, Dr. Dorner, I think your saber scar is so romantic." Dorner would turn on his heel and mutter, "Terrible. Terrible. I was a different person then. Not the same man at all. I hate what it represents." I used to lecture in his classes on how "seeing" (perception) was not automatic, but was instead a highly programmed process—a product of culture, the laws of which worked almost entirely outside of our awareness.

The transactionalists who visited us put me to shame, for they had an entire system evolved by Adelbert Ames (an optometrist, of all things) demonstrating that visual perception departed in many important respects from the models which we had acquired or been taught. Ames's experiments demonstrated that vision is far from passive, as is generally thought, but is instead quite arbitrary —like language—and is a dynamic, highly structured, selective process in which the entire visual system cooperates in creating from material passing before the eyes those images which the viewer will find most useful. At the same time, the system eliminates extraneous data by a process of "selective inattention." The system also showed that vision is not only arbitrary, but operates according to certain tacit rules of visual grammar. Just as changing the order of the words "man" and "dog" in the sentence "The dog bit the man" to "The man bit the dog" changes the meaning,

Ames demonstrated that altering certain key elements in the visual field can actually change what one sees! This system is too complex, too far from the stereotypes we have been brought up with, to be explained in a few sentences in this book, but the trapezoidal window and the distorted room are two demonstrations that are taught in most psychology courses today and can be seen in popular science museums such as Frank Oppenheimer's Exploratorium in San Francisco.

Most of us see *actively*, just as we talk actively. We project our own image onto the world and in many instances that image can be different from what other people are seeing. In the words of a friend and psychiatric colleague, Dr. David McKenzie Rioch, "What you see is what you intend to do about it!"

Vision is not only highly selective, it is a *transaction* between the viewer and the world—in effect, we humans put together our own perceptual worlds according to rules and principles which are quite arbitrary. Furthermore, perception is greatly modified not only by the psychological state of the individual but by culture as well. Even back in my days at the Aspen Ranch, I had noted that the cowboys and I would see things like bear and deer tracks and even the degree of exhaustion of a horse ridden past the ranch gate—things that others simply walked past without seeing at all.

The transactional approach did not jibe with the stimulus-response school of psychology, which is popular in our highly compartmentalized, one-cause-and-one-effect, don't-bother-me-with-the-details-just-give-me-the-bottom-line American culture.

Hadley Cantril (a leading light among the transactionalists) was one of the most delightful, intelligent, and nonthreatening human beings I have ever known. He taught at Princeton in the psychology department where he conducted an impressive assortment of experiments and demonstrations illustrating the basic principles of transactional psychology, such as the trapezoidal window and distorted room previously mentioned. When he died, the Princeton administrators could hardly wait to remove reminders of this heretical approach to perception.

. . . .

For the cultural anthropologist it is crucial to know that the likelihood of someone's literally *seeing* things differently from someone else is great. The demonstrated fact that everyday perception varies as a function of experience and psychological state represented a genuine breakthrough in my understanding of the human species.

Earlier I mentioned comprehensive thinking, a favorite phrase of Buckminster Fuller, whose daughter Allegra was my student at Bennington. When we first met, Bucky was not yet famous. I found him to be gregarious, loquacious, rotund, and energetic. He had been so nearsighted as a child that anything more than a few feet away was out of his range. A fire engine would go by on the street and his playmates would talk about it. Since Bucky didn't see the fire engine himself, but only heard it, he would make up the missing reality. He didn't know this was happening until someone found out he couldn't see and got him glasses. Until then they thought he was confabulating, which caused no end of trouble in his life. When he told me that story I couldn't help but think how much of life is that way; only a few of us know that we can't "see" and fill in the missing parts from our own experience and our own imagination.

Bucky lived in his head and had a strong drive to get all his thoughts out so that others could share the results of his thinking. He was not only fun to be with, he also stimulated students' minds. Over the years that we knew each other, I never tired of watching the way his mind worked. I was equally fascinated by the structures he could make by intersecting great circles, the structures that later were known as geodesic or Fuller domes. Intrigued by the way these structures distributed stress equally to all parts, I tried to build some of the more complex ones. Three and four great circles (a great circle is a line *around* a sphere at its maximum girth, such as the equator) was easy, but with each new circle everything changed. Seven or more great circles were not only complex, but quite beautiful. Bucky said I couldn't possibly build the more complex ones, since "you don't have the mathematics." Spending one summer between gardening and soldering domes out of copper wire in my basement, I ended up with fifteen great circles. The dimensions of each cord making up a strut in the structure had to be precisely worked out, otherwise the errors magnified and horrendous distortions were introduced. I never told him. What would have been the purpose? I accepted the challenge because I wanted to penetrate his thinking.

One of the advantages of a college like Bennington was that it was possible to integrate the material presented in one class with that of other classes, so the entire curriculum, instead of being fragmented, could be a more or less coherent whole. In fact the college had been founded on the idea that the curriculum should be comprehensive and in many ways it was. Some of the integration took place in the dorms as the girls interacted. The rest occurred whenever faculty would get together and cooperate in teaching classes or parts of classes. Then there were performances: dance, theater, music, poetry readings, and art exhibitions. Possibly as important as anything else were the hour-long weekly counseling sessions between faculty member and student.

None of this meant that Bennington didn't have problems. As with any other small group that has been together long enough to have developed a past, there were always conflicts, and we certainly had them among the faculty. Many of the people who were there at the time went on to become world figures, but this was no country club crowd. There was talent and there were raw edges. One could get badly skinned (literally), as Mildy and I discovered.

Shirley Jackson and her husband, Stanley Hyman, seemed to thrive on controversy. We had met them at a dinner party given by another faculty member and they later invited us to their house. Mildy—who is virtually blind in one eye and has only 20/200 vision in the other—stepped into a jagged hole in the floor just inside the front door. I barely managed to catch her before she sank up to her thigh in the hole. A torn stocking, abraded skin, and a distressed ego were the most obvious results. The fact that Jackson and Hyman thought this was all screamingly funny and merely stood there laughing while I struggled to pull my disheveled, startled wife out of the hole didn't help.

The faculty at Bennington during our years there included our friend Max Kampelman, who became the U.S. chief negotiator with the Soviets for years on end; Howard Nemerov, Stanley Kunitz, Kenneth Burke, Paul Feeley, Peter Drucker, Paul Boepple, Claude Frank, George Soule, and Martha Hill, all of whom became acknowledged masters in their fields. Fromm, of course, was already world famous.

All that talent in a tiny isolated community made Bennington a complex place to be. What was possibly most unsettling was its profligate treatment of talent. Every semester, it seemed, someone had to be sacrificed, either a faculty member or a student. None of us figured out how this informal system worked, though Shirley Jackson obviously had it in mind when she wrote "The Lottery," the most controversial story ever to appear between the covers of the *New Yorker*. In it, the people of a New England town draw lots each year to see who is to be stoned to death. At Bennington, as regular as clockwork, at least once a year a crisis would develop and the entire community would become involved. Someone would have stepped over one of the various ill-defined lines governing the social organization of our small community and the next thing you knew there would be community meetings in the barn. In the end someone would be forced to leave. It just seemed to be part of the Bennington ethos.

The Bennington years brought other than academic experiences. Ellen, our first child, was born on June 21, 1949, an event that changed our lives. Our friend Ashley Montagu said, "Now you have joined the human race." Driving home from the hospital with tiny Ellen in the back seat in a basket wrapped in baby blankets, I was overwhelmed by the apparent fragility of this infant being and the fact that Mildy and I were responsible for nurturing and protecting this still ethereal life that had just joined us on this planet. At first I was afraid that any bump in the road might disturb her, so I drove with an exaggerated care that undoubtedly made me a traffic hazard. For that entire summer our lives revolved around that beautiful, new, and very feminine baby. Now I really did have responsibilities. A new life was in our hands and we wanted to do everything possible to give that life the opportunity to develop as it should. Naturally, as almost any parent knows, in spite of all the books we had read, experts we had listened to, and all the mental preparation, we discovered that we knew absolutely nothing about parenting. The baby would burp. What did that mean? Mildy, dredging up a memory from her past, would pick Ellen up, put a soft blanket on her shoulder, rest Ellen there, and gently pat her back. Up would come a little milk and everything would be okay until the next new behavior would surface. I began to see the inescapable advantage of the extended family where there are kinfolk around who know all these things.

We loved Bennington, our stimulating friends, the students, the clean country air and our life in that beautiful little house in the orchard, and we probably would never have left if circumstances hadn't forced us to. As a couple, living as economically as possible, we barely made it on the $4,500 I was paid per year. Now that there were three of us, costs exceeded income. I realized that in making up the difference between my earnings and the cost of living, I was subsidizing the education of the daughters of the extremely wealthy. Even so, it was painful leaving.

The economic realities drove me into the arms of the State Department. State's recently formed Foreign Service Institute was looking for an anthropologist to design and run an orientation program for specialists who would be working in third world countries under President Truman's Point IV program. My earlier work with the Indians made me acutely aware of the need to shift the usual emphasis of technical assistance from the traditional fields of economics, politics, and history, so that intercultural relations was recognized as important in the conduct of such programs.

For one semester in the fall of 1950, teaching on weekends, I commuted between Washington and Bennington. I realized that a large bureaucracy would be different from the academic world but I had no notion of how critical the next few years would be, nor how deeply they would affect the rest of my life. Change is never easy and it is frequently painful. This one was both. But like the army and the years with the Hopi and the Navajo, it made its mark on my life. Fortunately throughout the entire process I had the active support and cooperation of Mildy. In fact, being a city girl, she took to Washington like a duck to water. One of her friends found us a nice house where the rent was affordable, on 34th Street in Georgetown. It was a good place to be.

Part IV

Washington, D.C. 1950–1963

FIFTEEN

The Diplomats at State

THIS CHAPTER covers a period in my life of creativity, excitement, frustrations, and lessons learned—a worm's-eye view of the middle levels of a large and powerful bureaucracy, the United States Department of State. I can't say I was prepared for what I had gotten myself into by accepting a job at the Foreign Service Institute. Given what I learned, I wouldn't have missed it for the world. It also brought me experiences with the people I was training and several years on the therapist's couch, which saved my life. The story is complex and separating out the various threads is not easy. In a sense it is a story of opposing forces, both outside and inside myself.

Since the time I first discovered anthropology, everything I have done has added to my appreciation of our remarkable species. The biological, the psychological, the perceptual, and the spiritual aspects of the human situation have all enriched my stay on this earth. Luckily, my learning has always been of a whole; knowledge gleaned in one area has reinforced and added to my understanding in all other areas.

The past is always with me, subtly stamping its indelible seal on everything I do and particularly so when I am least aware of it.

Understanding that past has been helpful to me in interpreting everyday life. The gradual and imperceptible shift from apes that had neither tools nor language to humans who produced the world as we see it today is a rich but still largely untapped lode, yet to be mined for what we can learn about ourselves. Like some other anthropologists I am convinced that we humans have literally created ourselves. But which part is a natural development? How to distinguish between the real and the illusory? Other, more specific questions came out of my past, such as: Why was it so difficult for the Indian Service employees to see that the Navajo and Hopi were not underdeveloped whites but simply different from us as well as from each other? Why were we driven to transform the Indians into ill-formed clones of ourselves and in the process drive them into alcoholism? What was it that made MacArthur's paratroopers react so violently to the presence of black American troops in the Philippines? What really lay behind the behavior of Denver's cops in the 1940s, their urge to beat up and sometimes kill Hispanics and blacks picked up on the streets of Denver? How could an organism that can be so loving and so altruistic and so creative also be so stubborn and just plain obtuse at times? I was bewildered that our leaders could even contemplate going to war all over again in Korea and later Vietnam. Was culture programming us all in insane ways, causing each group to act as though it was put on earth in order to wipe out all the others? Why did the representatives of each culture act as though its primary purpose in life was to dominate everyone else? And what was culture anyway?

The real answers to my questions are still not clear. They will be found, however, in a better understanding of the dialectic between human beings as products of biological evolution on the one hand and of cultural evolution on the other. More is known of the former than the latter.

Our first ancestors were food gatherers and, later, hunters. Humans evolved as members of very small groups—a dozen or so individuals making up a tiny primordial band. It is not clear to me whether the human species is designed to live in mass societies or even whether we can ultimately stand the stress from being crowded as we are in today's cities. But I am getting ahead of the story. No one really knows why or even how, but around 100,000 years ago early humans developed a tremendous brain and concurrently the ability to talk. Today the talking part seems to be overused and the brain part underused, even though we delude ourselves that the opposite is the case.

Freud opened an entirely new set of doors to reality and in the process demonstrated that in all of us there exists, sealed away from consciousness, another world which makes itself known through dreams, myths, and slips of the tongue and pen (Freudian errors). Is there a connection between this hidden psychological self and its cultural counterpart, to which so many of us are also blind? For example, I knew that I would sometimes do things which seemed natural enough to me yet would make others quite angry. Was this psychological or cultural or both? I sometimes felt as though I was living in one world and everyone else seemed to be living in another. What were the building blocks of these two worlds and, as an extension, by what rules could they be fitted together so as to make coherent statements?

It was questions such as these that kept popping into my head when I was making the transition from academic Bennington to bureaucratic Washington. I had been chosen to head up a new program at the State Department's training branch, the Foreign Service Institute (FSI). In 1949 Harry Truman had given an inspiring speech calling for the United States to aid third world countries. Congress enacted Truman's program into law in 1950. The program, in the words of its director, Dr. Henry Bennett, was essentially a "grubstake" to the countries of the third world—technical assistance to "underdeveloped" countries. Technical personnel of every conceivable type were to be sent to countries where needed as technicians assigned to programs including all aspects of such areas as public health, education, agriculture, marketing, forestry, aviation, roads, fisheries, diet—in fact, the technical specialties on which our complex civilization is based.

Dr. Bennett, a heavyset man in his late fifties, was one of the many remarkable men I have been privileged to know. He was an educator, a leader of the self-effacing type, a man of wisdom with deep insight and experience in what was needed to work with the third world. He flew his own airplane and wore high-button shoes and knew from the top of his head to the soles of those shoes that while American specialists were the best you could get, there were a few things they did *not* know. Only a few could be expected to have had experience working at the cultural interface between American-European cultures and the exotic cultures of the Southern and Eastern worlds. All these questions were of the type that Dr. Bennett was mulling over while setting up his agency. He needed someone with my background and my approach to technical assistance to supply the missing ingredients.

I was hired by FSI to design as well as to conduct the very program Dr. Bennett was looking for to orient his Point IV technicians, a program which, while it could draw on FSI's specialists in history, economics, geography, political science, linguistics, and area studies, would nevertheless be self-contained.

Then located in an old apartment building on C Street, FSI was the training branch of the U.S. State Department. It was an example of those propitious accidents which happen every so often in large institutions when they become truly creative. This miracle occurred because, during the war, the Modern Language Association had successfully implemented a program for teaching foreign languages—Japanese, Russian, Polish, Serbo-Croatian, French, German, Chinese (several dialects), Thai, Burmese, Hindustani, and several of the languages such as Hindi spoken in India—to the American armed forces using new methods developed by descriptive linguists. The government used properly trained linguists on a massive scale with little interference and in a way in which they could be most effective. (One wonders why we always seem to wait until we are at war before we begin to do the right thing.) During wartime, the center of power is in the military establishment, but with cessation of hostilities it shifts back to the State Department. It was logical that linguists running the army programs would be recruited by State to carry on. FSI's language and culture programs were the result.

What was fortunate about FSI in the fifties was the choice of Henry Lee Smith, a respected scholar and linguistic scientist with a feeling for public relations and management skills, and with the courage to innovate, to act as dean of the School of Language Studies. Haxie Smith gathered around him an unusually creative and innovative group of young linguistic scientists. They included men and women of the caliber of George L. Trager (one of Edward Sapir's most gifted students), Charles Ferguson, Eleanor Jorden, and John Stockman. Any university would have considered itself blessed to be able to assemble such an array of talent. They were a group I would soon learn to like and respect as colleagues.

I knew that if the program I was putting together for Dr. Bennett's technicians was to succeed, not only must there be a significant amount of material on the type of culture—the tacit variety—that later filled my books,[1] but it was essential that the linguists and I be able to work together. This was particularly important because I had to ask the School of Language Studies to do things they did not like to do. There wasn't time even to teach the technicians enough of the language to get around effectively, but just enough time to get my people started, to give them confidence in a method for learning from native speakers and a feeling for what it was like to learn by doing. For Haxie's school this meant recruiting additional native tutors and rearranging class schedules that did not mesh with the others. It meant freeing the time of individuals such as Carleton Hodge and Charles Ferguson, who were fully engaged in developing a writing system and an analysis of colloquial Arabic.

The training orientation model I had in mind was innovative in two ways: it was intercultural not intracultural, and the concentration was on what people took for granted and did not verbalize (whereas most cultural research was devoted to material that could be explicitly stated in words). Ruth Benedict's Columbia University–based ground-breaking program Research in Contemporary Cultures—initiated during World War II—was the exception and would have produced the type of material I envisaged had it been oriented toward third world countries. Nevertheless, Benedict's program helped. It was the only large-scale effort of its kind conducted by anthropologists which had as its goal the understanding of the mentality of complex cultures. I spent hours on end exchanging notes with members of Benedict's staff, such as Rhoda Metraux, who had a feeling for patterns. There were rare individuals here and there, such as the sociologist John Useem, whose 1946 article "Americans as Governors of Natives in the Pacific" demonstrated that there are two or more sides to every intercultural equation, not just the government's top-down administrative justification for its programs.

The point I wanted to make at FSI was that enforced programs based on European philosophies, degree of economic development, and good intentions, while balm to American souls, were highly unreliable, frequently irrelevant, and almost certain to be misunderstood by the people we were dealing with at the cultural interface. My message was frequently misunderstood and actively resisted by most of the administrators as well as by members of the Foreign Service (who had chosen instead to use a "*Realpolitik*—twist their arm, gun to the head" approach to Latin America and anywhere else where they could get away with it). Nevertheless, even though the State Department remained blind to these new dimensions of foreign affairs and the need for cultural know-how at the grass roots, such skills still constituted a mandatory tool in the kit of the foreign aid technician and were therefore necessary ingredients in the training for Point IV.

Because the dust had not had time to settle after the war and new policies were not yet set in concrete, I intuited a "window of opportunity" which might be open long enough to make a little progress on defining the basics of cultural understanding at FSI. I couldn't have been more right concerning the limited amount of time available.

As with orientation materials for blacks in the army, there were no materials on acquired culture, or what would later be known as the *tacit* dimension of culture. All that was available was the usual economic, political, and historical texts based on European intellectual needs. There was nothing to tell technicians how to deal with the kinds of cultural patterns I had observed with the Trukese, the Hopi, and the Navajo.

I knew that, given State's bureaucracy, it would have been so easy to have produced a training format that looked good, would have satisfied the local experts, would not have aroused anxiety, and would have left people just as uninformed as they were before they took the course. Since I knew what my audience would be getting into overseas, it simply would not have been honest not to do my best to prepare them.

I saw that there were several things I must take into account: First, it was important to make the culture concept as real as possible. Second, the anxiety aroused by leaving home and going out into a new and strange world must be recognized and dealt with. Third, there must be an opportunity to work with the language of the country of assignment. Fourth, the technicians needed basic and simple formulas for staying healthy in the tropics as part of the background information on the country. Fifth, they needed experience with someone (a living, breathing model) from the country to which they were assigned. In building my program I tried to view the world as seen through the eyes of the technician and then reinforce and strengthen what I already knew about work with other cultures.

Fortunately I was able to convince the linguists to put their shoulders to the wheels. Because the linguists and I conceptualized the orientation process similarly, their lectures, demonstrations, and exercises meshed perfectly—one reinforcing the other. I saw language as an expression of culture; they saw language as reflecting culture. These points of view were not uniformly accepted by either set of colleagues, a situation which was due in part to the fact that there was no unified theory of culture. I could see that my greatest need was for a conceptual model of how the complex constituent parts of language and culture were structured and how they fit together. Some of the answers to these important questions were locked up in the heads of the linguistic scientists. Others would have to be developed on the spot.

Fortunately at that time, this sort of creative work was possible at FSI. Our organization was small and it was new, so there hadn't been enough time for—what my friend Ashley Montagu used to call—psychosclerosis (hardening of the mental processes) to set in. No one looked over our shoulders, or asked us to punch a time clock, or chained us to a single desk. We were free to improvise and test our results. I was also lucky that great progress had been made in descriptive linguistics since my days in graduate school.

Linguistics at Columbia in the thirties and early forties was not the integrated subject that it was later to become. There was no coherent generally accepted theory of language as system, only theories and descriptions of individual languages and language families such as Indo-European. However, at the same time I was studying at Columbia, Edward Sapir, Leonard Bloomfield, and Benjamin Lee Whorf at Yale were pumping new life and new insights into linguistics. I was working with their students.

It was heartening as well as electrifying to see firsthand the new course linguistics had set for itself. The new insights generated at Yale were reinforced as a consequence of having to design an entirely new approach to language learning for the army and navy training programs. There is something about being able to apply your science and seeing the results that can have an extraordinarily beneficial effect on a field. Also, going through the refining process and having to explain what you are doing and why you are doing it to people who could not care less gets rid of a lot of excess intellectual baggage.

I had been using Haxie Smith to lecture on the practical side of linguistics to the Point IV technicians. They were being given a specially designed six-week short course in the language they needed most so that they could continue learning after arrival at their post. Haxie provided lucid lectures on language as language, but since it was essential for the cultural material we were teaching to mesh with and be reinforced by the theory and practice of the linguistic side, I was brought into direct contact with George Trager, FSI's director of linguistic research. Trager had worked out a way of approaching the descriptive linguistics of the times so that what had been quite abstract was transformed into a wonderfully precise set of procedures along lines closely parallel to my own work.[2]

What I found most exciting was how the way linguists managed to handle the difference between acquired language (the part that is not taught in schools because it is acquired earlier as a natural process of maturation) and what is taught in schools that is built on the "acquired" foundation. Though the schoolteachers didn't know it, not having taken courses in linguistics, what they were putting out as dogma about language was loaded with myth and misinformation, such as that the spoken language is an imperfect and pale reflection of the written language.

An unforeseen spinoff of the active participation of the linguists in my program was that I began to see insights impinging on the interpersonal process that could also be useful to my friends in the psychiatric community. I wondered if I could find some way of exposing them to what the linguists were up to. There were things the psychiatrists should know about nonverbal communication and about how the communications system on which humans depend most (language) is organized and works in terms translatable to psychiatry.

As a consequence I began mobilizing my friends and colleagues among the psychiatrists in Washington: Frieda Fromm-Reichmann; David Rioch, chief of psychiatric research at Walter Reed Hospital; Dexter Bullard's staff at Chestnut Lodge; Otto Will; and Harold Searles, a friend and an incredibly sensitive and accurate observer. These were just a few of the people I dragged down to FSI whenever the linguists were lecturing.

Also lurking around the fringes of my consciousness was an ill-defined, embryonic notion that by joining forces with the linguists our efforts might lead to some new ways of looking at both language and culture, as well as culture as a coherent system.

None of the issues above were as clear in my mind in the 1950s while teaching at FSI as they are now, as I am writing this. Then, I knew only that here was a new and vital approach to the whole process of human communication and that I must do something about it; I must take an active part in spreading the word.

THE EXCITEMENT of working with talented, innovative people was the positive side of FSI, and very positive it was, but working in the bowels of a big bureaucracy like State was often frustrating. Fortunately, Dr. Bennett and I saw eye to eye on the basic issues, but unfortunately, the State Department was not ready for anthropology. After talking with two of our more urbane, sophisticated former ambassadors, I discovered that the State Department had yet to transcend its outdated deficit model of human relations. Most of the bureaucrats who controlled our fate at FSI hadn't the remotest notion of what culture, as anthropologists refer to it, was really all about. These functionaries thought of culture as something one doffs and dons like a suit of clothes, not as a process that was intimately intertwined with the self. I was reluctantly compelled to face the fact that anthropologists, instead of being viewed as an asset, were actually an embarrassment to administrative types, who asked themselves such questions as "How do I explain the presence of anthropologists who study old bones and South Sea islanders to Senator Joseph McCarthy's House Un-American Activities Committee?" Fortunately, my program had been funded with twenty-one positions, two-thirds of which were skimmed off the Office of Personnel, which meant that if Personnel didn't like my program and its anthropologists, it would cost them fourteen positions. Also Dr. Bennett knew that what I was doing was what he had originally asked for and that it worked and was essential to the success of his program.

Most people I know, given a job to do, will bridle under obstructionism from above. I was no exception, but I wasn't alone either because the entire staff of FSI had problems getting through to Personnel. FSI's standing in the State Department was so lacking in power as to be laughable. Power and the symbols of power are the currency of our land and, lacking power, it was essential that we learn a new language—bureaucratese—and the appropriate behavior that went with it. The money was there, the positions were there, the paperwork stating what was to be done was complete, yet, like my camps on the Hopi reservation, things did not always go as they should. Old hands like Haxie Smith and Howard Sollenberger (a China hand familiar with Chinese bureaucracies) were smart enough and experienced enough to see that we had to find ways to get that massive machine above us to respond, and that it would be necessary for us to learn how to communicate with them; if we didn't learn the language of bureaucracy, it would be impossible to obtain the basic essentials for our work. In the process of learning, a clearer picture of the inner workings of government began to emerge.

In terms of a model I worked out years later, the Office of Personnel was low context; that is, it was essential to tell them precisely and in an unambiguous way what action was to be taken in such a way that the message could not be misinterpreted. The linguists and anthropologists at FSI were used to operating at a much higher point on the context scale which required leeway, imagination, and the ability to use one's head. Since in the culture of everyday life it is considered a put-down to tell people in specific terms how they should solve an administrative problem, we were (until we learned better) out of step with large sections of the Department.

The following example, of a memo from FSI to Personnel illustrates my point:

> Since we have received no notification concerning the assignment of an FSO [Foreign Service Officer] for training in Thai, we feel we should call your attention to the fact that the language officer now assigned to Bangkok is approaching the end of his second tour of duty. If training of his replacement does not begin immediately, there will be no qualified language officer in Thai to replace the present incumbent when he is rotated.

We were aghast to learn that when this memo from FSI reached the appropriate desk in Personnel, it was read with head-shaking followed by a sigh and "What do they want us to do?" We had presumed that the administrators in Personnel would *know* what they were supposed to do after we had described the situation to them, but we had neglected to tell them *what action to take*. That is, we should have ended the memo with the words "Action to be taken . . . and assign an FSO with the specified qualifications to FSI by *x* date."

I agree with Stephen Jay Gould that, without attention to what is frequently viewed as trivial, the field of science does not advance. It was communicative minutiae like this memo that determined whether we got what was needed to do our job, as well as how we were regarded by other arms of the Department, particularly the high-status political arms. What I could see of the bureaucratic processes at work was similar in many respects to what I had observed in the Indian Service and with Freddy in the army: there were two or more entirely different means of communication employed by two different groups. To get along, one had to be able to speak the language of both groups. I had been taught that I only had to learn how to use the proper channels, but there was an added dimension, the framing of the message itself—the situational dialect, if you will—that identified me as a member of the team who knew the signals. The framing of the message constituted a metacommunication that told everyone which group I belonged to.

What struck me was that the staff of FSI at that time was highly educated, with specialized interests in communication on a number of different levels, yet it took us almost as much time to learn the situational dialects of the State Department bureaucracy as it would have taken us to learn to function in another culture. The difference was, however, that when working with another culture we *knew* that we didn't know, whereas at home, on our own turf, we blamed the other party, rationalizing our lack of success as a function of bureaucratic recalcitrance. This being the case, what must it be like for foreigners and minorities, and what was it like for Dr. Bennett's technicians trying to deal with foreign bureaucracies in third world countries, many of them convinced that *they* had all the answers? FSI demonstrated how important it is to know more about culture than what is taught in our schools.

What had begun as a relatively straightforward orientation job in a small and quite wonderful institution had at times elements of a full-blown nightmare. Some things I seemed to learn only the hard way. My head was progressing; however, my psyche seemed to be standing still.

SIXTEEN

Definitions of Culture

ONE DAY upon my return from a trip through Latin America and the Middle East, I found George Trager, FSI's director of linguistic research, in the process of dismantling the language portion of my training program. I had underestimated the level of his interest in what I was trying to do, as a consequence I failed to involve him in the planning of my program (which was clearly a mistake). Yet when I visited him in his office directly above my own, not only was there no rancor or defensiveness in his demeanor, but he was as amiable as could be. Having established the fact that I really was sincerely interested in and valued deeply what he and the other descriptive linguists were doing we had no trouble communicating and he was as cooperative as anyone would wish. I had been told to expect him to be recalcitrant and confrontational and was pleasantly surprised by his cordial reception. Not only did we not fight over the program but, before either of us had realized it, we were immersed in the whole question of the nature of culture and the relationship of language to culture.[1] By mutual agreement we decided to set up a schedule of regular afternoon meetings to be devoted to an analysis of what our field was really all about.

Trager was a short, rotund man, bespectacled, almost bald, with a high-pitched raspy voice. There was an abrupt, cantankerous, professorial air about him. When he felt threatened, for whatever reason, he could be bullheaded and intractable. His earlier professional collaborations, while productive, had all ended on the trash heap; in one way or another, he had destroyed those relationships by his need for total independence and his hair-trigger temper. Even his closest friends would tell you that he was his own worst enemy. Nevertheless, he had a mind that was both quick and incisive, and he was considered one of the leading theoretical linguists in the country.

The time and the situation were both conducive to and appropriate for our collaboration. I entered on this collaboration with the expectation that at any moment Trager would revert to his traditional way of relating to collaborators. I knew Trager would eventually go his own way and might even disown our relationship later. My hope was that before that occurred we would have progressed far enough so that our joint efforts to produce a synthesis of the interrelation of language and culture might have taken on a life of its own. On the plus side was the knowledge that Trager usually finished tasks he had started with others.

Later, after we had begun working together, I developed a tremendous respect and even a real affection (tempered by exasperation) for him. One asset in our relationship was my own need to avoid confrontations, to steer away from conflict in the direction of harmony. There were times when Trager was as much as anyone could wish for by way of a collaborator; there were others when I could have strangled him quite cheerfully. As things turned out, this relationship, as with my earlier ones with Lorenzo Hubbell and Erich Fromm, had both pivotal and creative impacts on my thinking.

By the time I reached FSI I had come to the conclusion that the analysis of culture could be likened to the task of identifying mushrooms, using several different texts as references. Because of the nature of the mushrooms, no two experts describe them in precisely the same way, which creates a problem for the rest of us when we are trying to decide whether the specimen in our hands is edible. I hoped that in the analysis of culture we might be able to do better than that. While I didn't know where Trager and I were headed on this particular journey, I knew we had both spent years thinking about the task we were about to tackle and had ranked it at the top of our list of priorities.

Meeting every afternoon in Trager's Washington office one floor above mine, the two of us began to block out areas of agreement. Our first task was to define what we meant by the term "culture." Like the nineteenth-century concept of ether (the medium through which electromagnetic radiation traveled and which filled space), "culture" had too many meanings and was too nebulous to be useful. Why was this definition important? Culture is the medium evolved by humans to survive. *Nothing* in our lives is free from cultural influences. It is the keystone in human civilization's arch and is the medium through which all of life's events must flow. We are culture! In our quest to define the nature of culture we would also be shedding light on who and what we are.

Sitting there at the conference table next to the blackboard, we started by questioning the implicit aspects of our own belief system. We asked ourselves, "Instead of a system made of a *single* category of basic particles or elements, could it be that culture is instead a complex, or composite, of linked and associated but still quite different events?" If so, this might explain the many highly divergent theories of culture; each investigator was looking at different cultural systems or at different parts of the same system. We decided to investigate what would happen if, instead of looking at culture as a single entity, we turned our attention to a search for clearly defined, distinct fields which, if clustered together, might account for what anthropologists had been studying under the label of culture.

We started a review of social science as seen through these new eyes. In spite of its strongly academic slant, our work was a far cry from the ivory-towered, theoretical, philosophical approach of academia. Both of us knew that unless we could speak to our own constituencies in less abstract terms than had been used in the past, we might as well not be talking at all. Also, my people at FSI were technically trained specialists and needed something they could sink their teeth into, not somebody else's abstractions.

Trager and I agreed that language and culture were part and parcel of the same process, yet paradoxically, under certain restricted conditions, like the photon in physics, each could be analyzed as separate and distinct from the other; that is, language and culture reflect each other but are also discrete.[2] This suggested that there might be other, as yet unidentified, cultural systems comparable to language embedded in culture, and that instead of a single system made up of like particles, it would be more appropriate if we were to think of culture as a *set* of systems and deal with each system on its own terms. This was a momentous decision on our part and one with promising potential.

As a way of overcoming some of the compartmentalizing characteristics of our own culture, Trager and I found it was important to stress that language not only is a vehicle for messages, but has embedded in its structure and use all of the other cultural systems. That is, language distinguishes between the sexes, has tenses (time), spatial references, and differences in tone of voice for distance and rank, respect, and terms of endearment. All of these are built into the structure of the language so that meaning does not always have to be conveyed specifically and technically.

At this point my feelings were a combination of excitement, optimism, and relief. I was hoping we could actually introduce some order into a field that had been far from orderly. I did not believe we could define the discipline in the same way as the "hard" sciences, because each science must develop its own procedures, methodologies, and theories. But by breaking the job down into its component parts, the field could assume manageable proportions.

THE *information* HUMAN BEINGS ARE REQUIRED to process, because they have evolved themselves, their cultures, their theories, their technologies, and their languages, is of a different sort of complexity than physical phenomena. Our work was centered in and around information: how it was processed, reproduced, transmitted, organized, and broken down into its essential components. We believed that *culture* is *communication and no communication by humans can be divorced from culture.* This was a radical departure from the view of culture as a system of beliefs or of values, mores, customs, and the like.

All of it seems so simple in retrospect but at the time it was a little bit like navigating in a dense fog with only the swells of the sea to guide us. Certainly one of the most powerful influences on our work was that we had each other to talk to and had a goal on which we both agreed. Also we seemed to complement each other in our thinking and the way in which we attacked problems.

Having agreed that culture is a complex of related systems, our next problem was to select out the other basic core cultural systems. We also had to decide on the criteria to use in testing the validity of our choices. Trager and I concluded that the criteria that had proved so reliable for language as a componential unit of culture would be a good place to begin.[3]

In descriptive linguistics, some things were axiomatic. George's work in phonetics demonstrated that any valid phonetic system must be rooted in the biology and physiology of the speech apparatus. We also knew that language, one way or another, eventually gets into every nook and cranny of all culture, and that in spite of being reflected in all of culture, language, as a system, could be analyzed and taught independently of the rest of culture. Eventually we agreed that in order to qualify as a core system the following criteria would apply:

1. There should be no break in the evolutionary chain connecting humans with their mammalian ancestors. For example, all animals, including amoebas, organize space in such a way as to prevent overcrowding.
2. The system should be reflected in *all* other cultural systems. All languages, even though they may not have a word for time, have some built-in ways of dealing with time, for example, while all cultural events occur in space as well as time.
3. And, paradoxically, just as another language can be both learned and studied independently of other cultural systems, all such core systems should also be independent.[4]

Every afternoon I would leave my office, climb the back stairs, turn to the right at the top, and make a left turn into Trager's office, where I would find him waiting. We spent most of our efforts looking for reasons why core systems such as "territoriality" were valid and looking for other systems that might work.[5] We also kept searching the literature, our experience, and language itself for clues as to what some of the other systems might be.

In the end the answers to our search came not from any specific research, they sprang full-blown from my subconscious, which had been hard at work for months, even while I was sleeping.

It happened one afternoon as I made my usual trek to George's office. He was out, so I went over to the blackboard and wrote down ten words:

INTERACTION	and	MATERIALS
ASSOCIATION	and	DEFENSE
SUBSISTENCE	and	PLAY
SEXUAL DIMORPHISM	and	LEARNING
TERRITORIALITY	and	TEMPORALITY

These words made up five pairs of terms: language and technology, social organization and all defensive activities, work and play, two sexes and what they learn, and time and space.

I had seen the entire structure as a unified whole. When George returned, I said simply, "George, there it is. I can't find any more. And while I can't tell you why right now, the order is important. If we set these up as the two coordinates of a grid so that each basic system is reflected in all the others, we could then see what we would get." The two of us discussed each category I had written on the board, and all satisfied our criteria for core systems. We then set about creating a matrix on the blackboard, with all ten systems running both across the top (horizontal) axis and down the vertical axis. These ten-by-ten core systems were the basis of a one-hundred-compartment matrix with time and space in the middle. It was clear even from the beginning that each of those hundred slots in the matrix would designate an important area of human activity. The temporal aspects of recreation (play) are the times when the individual plays. The spatial aspects of play are the places where the individual plays. Substitute learning for play and one gets the times and the places where learning occurs. The institutional aspect is schools (in our culture) and so forth.

It was at this point that Haxie Smith and Ed Kennard joined in. Their interest and enthusiasm did not lag during the year the four of us worked together (with the help and cooperation of a dozen or so colleagues in and outside the Washington area). Others also became interested in what we were doing and involved themselves in our "game," by participating in the creation of a conceptual model of the systems of culture. Once the rules were learned they could play and, in the process, contribute to the testing of our matrix.

The creation of the matrix led to another task: to identify what fit into those slots from the interaction of the different systems of culture with each other. For example, it is difficult to consider time without space, one without the other. We knew our model was an outrageous simplification of reality and a far, far cry from the culture we were all living on a daily basis, but we had to start somewhere. Our first task was to see if our "machine," crude as it was, would fly. What would it tell us about relationships which might have been intuited but had never really been spelled out before? A year's additional work left us with the realization that we had created a primitive system of relationships—a modest beginning of a mathematics of culture.

From the viewpoint of practicality and the real world, we also now had a core system into which all of the specialties of the people we were training could be fitted. The agriculturalist occupied different slots in the matrix than did the educator, the public health doctor, or the agronomist. We began thinking of each discipline in its *archetypal* relationships. Healers are healers the world over, just as teachers are teachers wherever you find them. They practice their skills differently only because all are working in their own cultural matrix, which determines much of what they do. That is, the agriculturalist is in the center of those activities having to do with earning a living, health is associated with protective activities, and clearly education has to do with learning.

Our matrix didn't tell us what we would find, only where to look and what some of the adjacent and tangential influences might be. It also laid a foundation for fields like kinesics, proxemics, and chronemics, which were developed later and demonstrated why social organization was so important. What we had was a *map* of culture.[6]

Our hope was that our colleagues would recognize the importance of our work. In this we were to be disappointed—my own contributions, which had formed the corpus of the ten-by-ten matrix of basic cultural systems, had their roots in as many fields. Remember that American culture is not an integrating one but a compartmentalizing one. All of this worked against us. It was difficult for the average social scientists to make the leap to a comprehensive approach from their own highly specific research, in which every step along the way is carefully specified and every move accounted for and measured. If one followed what we had done, step by step, there was nothing complicated about it—it was just that people simply were not used to thinking in comprehensive terms. We were living in a fragmented world in the grip of a trend which was unfortunately growing, not diminishing.

One aspect of Trager's and my work that took at least thirty years to become recognized was that culture viewed as a multilevel system of communication (an extension of the genetic code) represented a new way of looking at things, a concept that people could work with and that provided avenues to awareness at the cultural interface which other definitions had not provided.[7]

SEVENTEEN

The Devil's Name Was Time

LITTLE SUNDAY, a Navajo, was a modest gentle little man who worked as a hand on one of my construction crews. The Navajos only laughed when I asked how he got that name, so I asked Fletcher Corrigan, a cousin of the Wetherills from Kayenta. An old-timer, Fletch would know. Fletch was Lorenzo's bookkeeper and ran the store when Lorenzo was away. Catching him at a moment when I saw he needed a break, I asked, "Fletch, how did Little Sunday get his name? What does it mean, anyway?"

Fletch smiled and told me the following story: "A few years ago, when there were only a few white men on the reservation, the traders used to close their trading posts on Sunday. The Indians didn't like that. They would come a long way in and their heads were full of the desire to trade. They anticipated coming into the store for many days and then finally they would hitch up their horses and make the long trip in from the other side of the Dinnebito wash or some other place way out in the country. And when they arrived at the store they were *ready!* But on Sunday, the store would be closed. They would bang on the door and shout, 'We know you are in there. Come open the door so we can trade.' Finally the trader's wife would tell him she couldn't stand all that pounding and shouting, so he would go open the door. You see, the trouble was that the Indians didn't have any days of the week. They didn't know one day from the other. So how could they tell what day it was, way out in the country where all the days were the same and one day just followed the other? Well, there was one Navajo, it seemed like he couldn't come on any day but Sunday and we started calling him Big Sunday, because he was a big man. The other one who was the runner-up in the contest to see how many times he could arrive at the store on Sunday was Little Sunday, because he was number two and because he was little."

Little Sunday never did learn to distinguish Sunday from the other days of the week. He lived by the month and the season. The days of the week were a strange and arbitrary abstraction existing only in the mind of the white man, not in reality. He had neither a calendar nor a watch and wouldn't have known what to do with them if he had had them. The moon told him the passage of the months but not the days of the week. So when he arrived at the trading store on a Sunday (having ridden four hours on horseback to get there) and found the store closed, he would naturally beat on the door until somebody came and let him in.

During my five-year stay on the reservations, I found that, in general, the Indians believed that whites were crazy, although they didn't tell us that. We were always hurrying to get someplace when that place would still be there whenever we arrived. Whites had a kind of devil inside who seemed to drive them unmercifully. The devil's name was Time.

For me there was nothing new or strange about the Indian approach to time. In Santa Fe when I was a child we would go visit our Indian friends at Tesuque Pueblo or at Santa Clara, and we always seemed to arrive when the men were at work in the fields or some other inconvenient time; when they came to visit us they would arrive early in the morning before we had gotten up and fixed breakfast. The scheduling of the Pueblo dances seemed to be regulated not by clocks but by something else, which made them unpredictable to us white folks. Even with my Hispanic neighbors in Santa Fe there had always been a different way of handling time than the one we Anglos used. By the time I was five years old I had already been immersed in three different time systems. In Mexico these differences were acknowledged in the language because everyone knew there were two kinds of time. When making appointments, we would ask, "*¿Hora mexicana o hora americana?*"

These differences in time fused at first into an undifferentiated gestalt in my mind. The dry sun-baked country, the adobe houses, the leisurely pace of the burros loaded with wood gave an organic quality to life that one can get only by living in a world without clocks. Riding on horseback in the mountains, as I did for several years, also had a way of disconnecting me from the clock and attaching me to the rhythm of the horse. These early experiences made it easier for me to get into sync with my Navajo and Hopi friends so that I didn't jar their rhythm the way most white people did. Rhythms made up part of the glue that held each group to its own. The reservation whites stuck together most of the week, spending as little time as possible outside their own group, while almost all my time was spent with the Indians. I remember one of our number, a man by the name of Hicks, who had been a carpenter and was later elevated to supervisor, which brought him into contact with all of us, and with the Indians. The Navajo rhythm was sort of free and easy, more like the way mountain lions or large African cats walk when they are not after prey but are simply walking from the sun to the shade. Hicks's movements were as jerky as if he were a marionette on strings; there was little coordination between his limbs and his body. Of course he simply could have been uncomfortable in his unaccustomed supervisory role. (But I had noticed that when he was sawing a board or doing carpentry of any type, the jerky quality was less pronounced.) Regardless of cause, there was no way to fit Hicks's rhythm into that of the Navajo.

As my reservation experiences demonstrated, there is a difference between natural time and imposed time driven by schedules. I couldn't see that we whites were any more organized than the Indians, and there were occasions when our white schedules worked at cross purposes with the more natural rhythms of the country, inducing a kind of culturally imposed schizophrenia.

I also experienced discontinuities in time during the births of my two children, Ellen and Eric. Ellen, our first child, was born in Bennington in 1949. The doctor didn't really care about either his patients or about the proper practice of medicine. The birth was lengthy, traumatic, and painful. Everything was out of sync, including the doctor, who, after Mildy had endured hours of labor, arrived at the same time as the baby. Eric was born in Washington, D.C., and, thanks to my colleague Ashley Montagu, who had extensive medical connections, we ended up in the capable sympathetic hands of Drs. Parks and Barter, who believed with us that babies did best if they were in the room with the mother and not in a nursery behind glass. The comparison with the first birth was unbelievable. This time I was with Mildy until she was taken to the delivery room. I held her hand as she lay on the gurney relaxed and at ease as the contractions, rhythmic and visible, were allowed to be a natural process proceeding at its own pace, neither advanced nor retarded to convenience the doctor. The choreography of the two births symbolized how natural things can be and how that nature can be distorted.

I don't know when I first became aware that I was deeply interested in time as behavior, not "what is time?" in the philosophical sense. Mine has been more of a phenomenological approach—that is, I have been most interested in how time is used and structured by different people in different situations and in the effects of these differences. For example, white Americans, particularly when living in Mediterranean countries and in Latin America, treat time as an unconscious language, the rules of which are binding. Arriving for an appointment five minutes late *means* something different from arriving twenty or thirty or forty-five minutes late. The time language is taken more seriously than words. I have watched and listened in foreign settings as my fellow Americans sat around drinking and socializing with each other in their fancy houses. In spite of the luxury and the status there were things that bothered them deeply about the way they were being treated in their home away from home, as though life were one ambiguity after another. They had status, special passports, and meetings with officials of cabinet rank, but they could never feel secure in that status because they were sometimes kept waiting forty-five minutes or an hour, as though they were nobodies. Almost without exception these were hard-working, sincere, well-motivated human beings who were easy to get along with, people who had left their homes, many for ideological reasons, and who were doing their utmost to be effective in their work. Their problems were problems of the cultural interface. Like that old children's game of Rock, Paper, Scissors,[1] it was though they were "rocks" living in a permanently "paper" world where paper won because it wraps the rock. Nothing in those foreign lands worked as it should, because they didn't know how to translate from one language of behavior and time to an entirely different language of behavior and time.

It wasn't hard for me to see that the Americans were taking time as a constant in social relationships and believed that it was something that could be relied on to give a truer reading of the nature of a relationship and how the other person felt than what was said in words for the sake of politeness and convention. They had internalized one time system and made it their own, integrating it into their personality, and the people of the country of assignment had done the same thing with an entirely different time system, and there was no one to translate for them.

The hidden side of culture was pushing people around, making them react harshly to behaviors that were merely different. The question in my mind was how to make such deeply personal aspects of the self real enough so that people could stop blaming the foreign environment. I had to learn how to say to Americans, "Look, it's not your fault that you feel this way. But it's not their fault either. At home you had to be on time because everything there was organized around a linear time base. Here this is not the case; time is only secondary and everything is organized around networks of people and their relationships with each other. They would not survive if they were to adopt your system just as you would not survive if you were to carry their system back to Washington."

I have found that it was impossible to change people by telling them to change. But people can learn for themselves if they are given the proper examples, which is what occurred in my classes for the Point IV technicians, where we discussed time as a system of organization and of communication. In my classes, I could even tell which part of the country people were from by the way they used time. There were differences not only in when people arrived but how they felt about it. Once everyone was seated I would get the ball rolling by asking the students to tell us about time in Utah, the home of many Mormons. We had noted that all the Mormons would be seated in the classroom, notebooks open, sitting erect and attentive in a small group a few minutes before the appointed hour. The Southerners, on the other hand, were seldom on time, and they observed about Northerners, "Why all the rush—what difference does it make if you are a few minutes late?" The Midwesterners mirrored the eastern seaboard pattern except that their rhythms were slower. Students from the Northwest Coast demonstrated that the eastern patterns were in effect with the exception that these students didn't *feel* as strongly about deviations and were much more relaxed about time in general.

These regional differences did seem to help get my point across. Things were no longer abstract, but were demonstrated in the conference room before my students' very eyes. None of what they learned changed the Mormons, the Southerners, or anyone else, but it did open a door to a new vista on their lives.

One thing my class taught me was that the grammar of the United States time system was, for the most part, almost completely out of awareness. How time was structured was an unexplored but vital avenue to understanding the profound and subtler aspects of out-of-awareness culture.

During the Point IV program I was simply gathering data in any way possible but with emphasis on *natural communications in natural settings* as people lived and experienced them without intervention on my part. In linguistics and in all my work during the previous years with other cultures, I had learned that regardless of what I thought or felt or was inclined to do, it was imperative that I not intervene in other people's behavior. To let life's stream flow freely before my eyes was the only way to avoid contaminating my data.

George Trager and I thought it might be possible to use time as a new kind of mirror for the purpose of examining the tacit qualities, as well as the manifest characteristics, of culture as a way of shedding new light on other cultural systems.

We decided to make and record some naturalistic observations. The two of us began to collect raw data. We took care not to ask questions about time or even to appear to be interested in time. We simply recorded what people said and did in the course of their everyday lives that had anything to do with time. For instance, a colleague poked his head around our door and said, "I'll be gone for a while." We would record "a while" and question "How long is a while?" Noting when he returned, we saw that "a while" meant more than the quarter or half an hour that was usual to be away from one's desk. We would sit around our conference table discussing one of the language training programs and one of our members would say, "The most efficient use of time when learning a language is one hour a day every day of the week." We would record the context and "one hour a day." Another member, discussing the Hopi Indians, would say, "The Hopi concept of time is different from ours. It's an entirely different system. Of course they have religious calendars but the meaning of time is different. They can't understand how whites can let this artificial thing inside us push us around the way it does. They don't get technical about time the way we do." We wrote "technical time and Hopi time."

Later, with notepads full, the two of us sat down at the table in his office. We started reading down the lists, looking for categories or slots general enough to hold the wide variety of phrases and statements we had recorded. From the beginning of our analysis it was clear that some of the problems people were having with each other could be traced to the use of an inappropriate *type* of time. We could see that such statements as "a while" and "later" were in one category. There was another category we take for granted which required no explanation because "everyone" was familiar with its definition: a year, a month, a day, hours, minutes, seconds.

Then, looking up, Trager suddenly barked out, "There are three kinds of time: formal, informal, and technical!" I knew immediately that he was right and told him so, then asked, "But does this formal, informal, and technical distinction apply to anything else, any other part of culture?" It didn't take long to see that this pattern overlay other cultural systems. There were formal, informal, and technical ways of doing *everything*. After reflection and review, we could see that this pattern was one important source of intracultural stress.

A good case for the formal, informal, and technical distinction could be made for virtually every aspect of a culture:

The *formal* deals with *givens*, or systems that are treated that way—things that people take for granted such as the seven-day week in the Western world.

The *technical*, such as law, philosophy, mathematics, and physics, makes statements as precisely as possible.

The *informal* bridges the gap between the formal and the technical and has a wonderful integrated (and integrating) quality to it.

Good jazz is informal; church music is, as a rule, formal; symphonies are technical. Each is taught and learned in its own way. Formal learning shouts to the treetops that what is being learned is serious business. Technical learning is precise and linear. Informal learning is nonlinear, cooperative, and not controlled by anyone except the group; it is an organic, inside-out process.

I couldn't help but be excited by our discovery and by finding that our basic interpretation of culture worked so well. I knew that by applying a test of which system is being used in a particular situation in a foreign culture, I could help others function effectively in those cultures too.

George Trager and I had provided the world with some new ways of talking about time. Even though Einstein had done the same thing for physics, the public still viewed time as an absolute measure, which resulted in misreading the intentions of others who viewed time differently. Our work demonstrated that *time could no longer be viewed as an absolute.*

Our few weeks of research on how time was actually used on the eastern seaboard had proved to be unusually productive. In fact it opened up unanticipated ways of viewing *and* categorizing behavior and provided me with a flexible, powerful system for the analysis of culture (and personality, incidentally).

All this was satisfying and, professionally, I had made great strides. However, the great gap between the world of words and ideas and dialectics and the real world of events was proving to be increasingly stressful and I knew that the time was approaching when I was going to have to do something about it. It was not surprising when it turned out that some of my stress was the result of having to spend my working hours in highly structured temporal situations. The bureaucrats never seemed to feel comfortable unless everyone was seated at her or his desk. This need to control was not restricted to Washington but could be observed in the field, where there was every reason for many people to be away from their desks out among the people, making friends, networking and learning the culture so they could be more effective. I was beginning to see that, insofar as controls were concerned, they could be applied from the outside *or* the inside but not from both (which is why Latino administrators, in order to counter the free-flowing character of Latino society, institute systems of tight control). The North American preoccupation with control is of a different nature, however. Employers have to assure themselves of their employees' loyalty—that they are "team players." I have never been a team player, because my loyalty is not to institutions but to science—to discovering what is really going on underneath the surface of daily life.

In other words, there was a monumental conflict between myself and my culture, much of it buried and ill-defined. The problem was that the sharper the image of how cultural systems worked, the greater the strain between myself and the bureaucratic context in which I found myself embroiled. Now that I was beginning to be able to read the language of time, I could see what the bureaucracy was really doing to me. The message of State's time-clock mentality (which was consistent with the rest of the culture) was that anyone who had to account for his or her time and who had to stay glued to a desk was not only unimportant but had no control over the work. I was being told, "You are a subordinate and *we* will tell you how best to use your time. We know better than you do." How could they possibly tell me what was important and what not, and how to set my priorities? After all, I was a professional and operating according to academic standards.

Although I did my best to keep from openly acknowledging it, I have seldom felt more alienated or more discouraged than during the FSI years. All I ever really wanted to do was to be able to continue to decode this mysterious and wonderful language we humans had evolved, which I had identified as "culture." Somehow, in spite of the bureaucratic squeeze and the suffocating atmosphere, with luck there was a short period when we were allowed to do our job, albeit without support from above, but also without too much interference either. These little windows of creative opportunity don't come very often. I was lucky to be there when one of them did.

EIGHTEEN

The Psychiatrists

OUR WASHINGTON FRIENDS were drawn primarily from three groups: psychoanalysts, the media, and government, plus a smattering of academicians, lawyers, writers, artists, and intellectuals, but the psychoanalysts were the pivot around which our social life turned. They included the Chestnut Lodge crowd, a budding National Institute of Mental Health group, neo-Freudians pulled together by Harry Stack Sullivan at the Washington School of Psychiatry, and a number who were in private practice.[1] There was a high degree of overlap between Sullivan's school and Chestnut Lodge as well as an alliance with the William Alanson White Institute in New York City. The psychiatrists were an active, alive group, the members of which were reaching out in all directions for anything that would add to the effectiveness of treatment and the understanding of the psychotherapeutic process. The fact that Sullivan the psychiatrist and Sapir the linguist bridged the gap between the two disciplines set the stage for much of the imaginative pioneering work that was done in the late 1940s and the 1950s.

My wife was then chief administrative officer for the Washington School of Psychiatry and I was on the school's faculty and a member of its Council of Fellows, so we were actively involved in the inside circles of this group, which included Frieda Fromm-Reichmann (Erich's ex-wife), David and Margaret Rioch, Bob and Mabel Cohen, Dexter and Anne Bullard, Winifred Whitman, Otto Will, Jim Barber, and others. David and Margaret Rioch were special friends. She was unusually attractive, articulate, intelligent, and serious about everything. Margaret and Mildred did much of the formal entertaining in our circle of friends. We were joined from time to time by attorneys Abe Fortas, one day to be named a Supreme Court justice by Lyndon Johnson, and his wife Carol Agger. Short, slight of build, and intense, Abe was actively involved in the Washington School of Psychiatry and had done much to help us. He was one of the most scintillating, brilliant individuals I have ever known. In addition he had a great sense of humor and, while self-assured, was unpretentious. He was a champion of the positive role of psychiatry in those dark, witch-hunting days when to see a psychiatrist was thought subversive. Deeply concerned with the philosophical and social implications and consequences of the law, he delved into such esoteric realms as the *power* of words as tools which could be used for either good or evil. Abe's wife, Carol, wouldn't marry him until he hired a housekeeper so she could concentrate on what she did best. She was quick, sharp, with a subtle sense of humor, excelling in everything she did, including ballet, figure skating, skiing, and ballroom dancing. One hell of a good lawyer, she was once a great help to me and to my mother and stepfather.

Energized by the new discoveries in descriptive linguistics at FSI, as well as by the progress Trager and I had made in defining culture, I would invite selected members of the psychoanalytic group to attend orientation sessions where we explained the basics of our approach to the analysis of language and behavior. I knew that the models and the procedures being developed had therapeutic applications. While I thought that the psychiatrists could benefit from some nonjudgmental ways of treating cultural differences, it was our refinements in the observation and recording of behavior that were applicable to a more systematic approach to psychiatry. In fact, the whole notion of nonverbal communication which we had jointly developed at FSI should have been fraught with meaning for the psychiatric world.[2] The notion was new, however, and few analysts were used to thinking in communications terms, particularly at the nonverbal level. This was in spite of the fact that Freud taught that slips were as communicative as behavior itself. It was as though they had built a wall blocking their own thought process from moving one iota beyond their own dogma. It was the virtually complete overlap between the concept of the unconscious and my notion of out-of-awareness level of culture seen as a system of communication that I was trying to get across to them. Here was a ready-made device that did not have the twists and turns and uncertainties of the unconscious but which could be observed and recorded.

The power of the psychiatrists' models holds them tightly to their own way of seeing things. Like a black hole from which light cannot escape, the psychiatrists see everything through eyes altered by their training and their association with each other. For many of them there didn't seem to be any room left for other explanations or ways of analyzing behavior. A patient who was habitually late was often treated as a case of "resistance," whereas I was trying to tell them that if the patient was a Latino, cultural considerations should be taken into account. In addition to the wide range of nonverbal behavior in middle-class American culture which was almost totally out of awareness and deeply personal to boot, my goal was to introduce them to some of what the linguists and I were discovering about the everyday differences in culturally patterned behavior such as the handling of time, distancing, and the variations in the structuring of relationships. I wanted to give them some new tools which might help them read their patients' behavior with greater assurance and accuracy.

A few were interested in an academic way in what we were doing but failed to see that it had anything to do with psychiatry. I was counting on their being able to use their heads and synthesize the two systems of thought. But in order to reach them, I would have had to outline everything that Freud and Sullivan had said on the subject and then outline in a similar way the details of our own work.[3] Also, I had yet to realize that just because *I* could see something didn't mean everyone else could. David Rioch and Abe Fortas were two of the exceptions.

What I was doing was not a one-way street. For, as I soon learned, my psychiatric colleagues had much to offer me as well. They brought me, from time to time, little offerings which by themselves would have been worthless, but which, seen in the context of my own work, were invaluable.

David Rioch was chief of psychiatric research at the army's General Walter Reed Hospital. His position involved him in all sorts of interesting and important issues that others had neither the time, talent, nor inclination to deal with. He brought a refreshingly original approach to traditional subjects such as troop morale, battle fatigue, and the relative performance of military units under differing conditions. His approach was so unusual and made so much sense that I wondered how he had survived in the army environment. Our interests were parallel in many ways. Information flow was one of these ways. Unlike most people, David avoided the Aristotelian trap of reasoning from self-evident principles, and went instead directly to the field to see what was happening on the spot.

During the Korean War, one of the more creative generals wanted to know what made some infantry companies perform better than others. David discovered that the company with the best morale and the highest performance was the one with the freest flow of information at all levels of command. The sergeants felt free to discuss anything with Captain Beatty (not his real name), the commanding officer of the company. They even felt free to make suggestions for organizational changes. Once, on the eve of combat, Captain Beatty was approached by his NCOs. With some foot shuffling, indicating that what they had to say was really important, one of them blurted out, "Captain, we talked things over and while you and we have gotten along just fine, now that we are going into combat there are men in the company who would do a better job of leading us in battle than we can. We think you should take our stripes and give them to those other guys." The switch was made. The company performed with distinction and received a battle commendation. After the battle, as soon as they were setting up camp in their new area behind the lines, the combat NCOs arrived in force at the captain's tent, saying, "Captain, you might as well take our stripes back now while we are still friends, because we are going to fuck up anyway." The stripes reverted to the original NCOs.

Rioch's story confirmed something I already knew but which is seldom acknowledged by institutions. Unlike many countries and cultures, where leadership is based on class (and other criteria) and is functional in all situations, leadership in the United States happens to be *situational.* Leadership does not carry over from situation A to B. The army had, to my knowledge, not really taken advantage of this feature of American culture, and this failure cost us dearly when our troops were taken prisoner by the Chinese during the Korean War. Because the Chinese were unfamiliar with our informal situational leaders and tried to impose leaders on the prisoners, new leaders could not evolve in the new situation and there was a leadership vacuum. Without leaders, both behavior and morale among the prisoners sank to the lowest level possible. Needless lives were lost as a result.

One time David had come down to FSI to see me and was directed to Trager's office where we were working on the "culture map." We had filled all the one hundred slots in our matrix on the blackboard. The way it was organized, all the slots had to balance and agree as functions moved in rings out from the center where there was a four-slot grid with space and time in two separate cells, and time considered as space and space considered as time in the other two. David watched while we talked and struggled, and then I heard him say in his deep authoritative voice, "What you fellows are doing is playing!"

Playing! How could such serious scholarly work be playing? But of course he was right. Play originated in Cenozoic times with the emergence of mammals and playing has always been the way mammals first learn and then polish the necessary skills for survival. The creeping, crawling and pouncing of young felines is play when they are kittens and is deadly serious once they are adults. Play is a way of testing various techniques and perfecting strategies before it is necessary to use them. To explore the possibilities and potential of any new system it is important to play with it. Play and creativity are closely linked.

The depth, relevance, and sheer audacity of David's thinking never ceased to amaze me. Opening a meeting of psychoanalysts, he put things in perspective and introduced an element of real life by announcing, "If people had friends, you fellows would soon be out of business."

Once while we were lunching at Walter Reed, the subject of aging came up. David said, "Aging is nothing more nor less than the condition of your circulatory system!" Though I had said nothing to him about it, my interest in the subject centered on the fact that office life tied to a desk was not healthy for me and I felt like I was beginning to get old. Fifty was staring me in the face. David must have sensed this because his comment on aging gave me the answer I had been looking for. All I needed to do was to start running (a good fifteen years before it became a craze), and I could feel the difference almost immediately. Another point which everyone reaches—some sooner than others—is that life does not go on forever. You cross a divide and see laid out before you the few years remaining in which to accomplish whatever it is you are going to do. On a trip to New Mexico with my son and daughter, I had taken them up to Aspen Basin outside of Santa Fe. I learned for the first time that just because a mountain was there didn't mean you could climb it. To my horror and chagrin I discovered I didn't have the stamina to climb even a hundred or so feet at that elevation. Standing there in that beautiful mountain basin with alpine flowers in the meadow encircled by dark green fir trees, I looked wistfully up at Lake Peak, which seemed almost close enough to touch in that crystal clear air. At an elevation of 12,400 feet, Lake Peak had never been much more than an hour's walk from Aspen Basin and I had no idea how many times I had made the climb when I was young. Standing there looking at that mountain just asking me to climb it again and look out from the top of the world once more, I realized that I might very well never see the top of that mountain again, that I might not ever again experience the exhilarating experience of scanning 45,000 square miles of the West from the tops of New Mexico's highest peaks.

I had grown up in those mountains and felt at home in them. They had given me health, happiness, and a strong body. In later years Stanley Noyes, a poet and western writer who was my walking companion, and I would think nothing of walking twenty-five miles with three thousand feet of climbing as a warm-up early in the season for what would later be a forty-miler. I had never been much on exercise just to exercise. This was because in the West my life had always given me what I needed: carrying water, chopping wood, cleaning the ditch, repairing the corral, riding my horses, walking, and doing all the things that were part of western life.

The thought was intolerable. I didn't know whether it was possible to get myself in good enough shape to climb the mountains again, but I set about doing something about it. A combination of bicycle riding and running five to six days a week for about an hour was all I needed. On the next visit I made it to the top of Lake Peak, and the world was once more mine to behold.

Later on I came to the conclusion that David Rioch was right, and that chronological age has never been a satisfactory criterion for anything: life insurance, driver's licenses, retirement. The condition of the body is a more reliable index of potential performance, physical and mental, than is chronological age. Yet our institutions and our culture continue to assess the ability to perform solely on the basis of chronology. David's formula was so simple and elegant, and could be the basis for ending useless discrimination against the old who are young in body and spirit.

Another time David and I were discussing perception and how it changes under differing conditions and is particularly molded by culture. My remarks were a review of the perceptual landscape and the many different views held on the subject. This time David's condensed wisdom emerged as "What you see is what you intend to do about it!" His statement was so elegant, so direct, and so tightly packed, it almost took my breath away.

My wife administered the research projects sponsored by the Washington School. David used to drive her crazy because he insisted that the school could only charge a maximum of 5 percent overhead on research. The normal overhead in those days was 25 to 45 percent. Today it can be up to 60 percent or higher. There was no way in which any institution could work on 5 percent, but David wouldn't budge. The school never really covered expenses, so people like David would then pitch in to make up the difference.

He used to speak from time to time about Colonel Glass, a friend and subordinate whom he admired. David was not temperamentally suited to coping with the bureaucratic folderol generated by a massive organization like the army. Colonel Glass not only made things work for him but took great care to look at the system from the inside and the bottom up, as it was experienced by the average GI. One tour de force of the team of Rioch and Glass was their recognition that soldiers would do anything to hide battle fatigue from their officers. They didn't want to let their buddies down and they knew that if they were pulled out of the line and sent for treatment at a hospital far behind the lines, the next step was what was called a "repledepo" (replacement depot) where troops were pooled, classified, and reassigned to outfits who needed them. Once in a repledepo, a man didn't stand a chance of getting back to his own outfit. When told of the situation, David said, "That's very simple. Why don't we move our clinics up behind the front lines? That way we can treat the men right there and, because they will still be under the control of the field commanders and not Com-Z [the non-combat area behind the front lines which was under a separate command], we can send them right back to their own outfits. There is no reason for them to be reassigned. It's bad for everyone."

After Mildy and I moved away, we made certain to visit Washington often so we could see Margaret and David. The last time we were there, David had retired, and the two of them were to join us for dinner after drinks at their place in Bethesda. David had a cold and wasn't feeling too well but we managed to tease him out of his room to join the party. We all had the most incredible time together. David told more of his stories about people he had known in the most unexpected places, all of whom had solved some human problem by observing the patterns of the group with which they were working. Each story was a little gem, illustrating how problems should be solved. As we left, David was looking so happy and energized that I said, "David, you really must write this stuff down, otherwise it's going to disappear from this earth." The next morning Margaret left a message on our answering machine that David had died that night in his sleep.

I really loved that man. Although sometimes difficult to deal with, he was an impressive human being; he had presence and brains and the welfare of the human race at heart. He was not as well recognized as he might have been, simply because the world was not ready for those who can see and who don't need to be told what is there.

ROLLO MAY, even though he was not living in Washington at the time, was a favored associate of many of our friends and colleagues. He would appear at parties and was chosen to give several of the Washington School's public lectures.

He was a quiet, self-effacing man who wore dark conservative suits and horn-rimmed glasses. I never really got to know him but was always impressed by his work. A gifted therapist and philosopher, he wrote *The Meaning of Anxiety*, a carefully crafted study of the cultural and behavioral building blocks that combine to create that hidden, pernicious, and ineffable state called anxiety. The book has always been underrated and has never received the recognition it deserves. Its message is that humans receive information from all channels but as a rule only attend to one or two. But, whether they attend or not, all the messages by hook or by crook still get through. If the messages contradict each other, the damage to a human being can be catastrophic. We go through these agonies because few people have learned to be honest with others, to say nothing of themselves. What is seldom recognized is that the "truth" can almost never be found in words, and certainly *not only in words* if words are stripped of the supporting or contexting channels which give them meaning.

May's research as described in *The Meaning of Anxiety* carried a subtle but significant message to those of us reared on the works of Ibsen, Tennessee Williams, and Henry Miller, all of whom spoke to the various dimensions, phases, modes, and permutations of hypocrisy—those cultures which live by the lie. In the category of culturally accepted lies, among the most used and most abused is the expression of maternal love among the middle and the upper classes. I am referring to those occasions when the mother unconsciously resents the child or does not allow leeway for situational mood shifts, yet continues to display signs of affection. There is ambiguity in the communication, which Gregory Bateson termed "the double bind." It was the mechanisms which reveal that words are carrying one message and nonverbal cues another that I was doing my best to communicate to the psychiatrists. May's work revealed the results—the anxious personality—but not the mechanisms that make for ambiguity in communication. It was up to those of us dealing with nonverbal messages to untangle that particular snarl in the complex and rich tapestry we call the mind.

Frieda Fromm-Reichmann was without a doubt one of the most gifted therapists in Washington and was the linchpin around which much in our circle revolved, but, like all therapists, she was not right for everyone. She had a weakness for brains and she let David Rioch engage her with his mind when what David needed was to be more at ease with himself. Because his mind overshadowed equally impressive traits, the other parts of his personality did not get the attention they deserved. Psychoanalysis is a tricky business at best, but I suspect that Frieda could have done more work on David's other less developed talents, such as a deep capacity to see through the cultural fluff that most of us surround ourselves with, to reveal the talent underneath and the capacity for loving which he so carefully hid. Nevertheless, their relationship must have been a strong one because hints of it show up in her book.[4]

Frieda was one of the most persuasive and gentle (yet iron-willed) individuals I knew. She loved ideas, yet she had the capacity to empathize with seriously disturbed patients and to establish contact with them regardless of how distorted their communications were. Nonverbal communication was an idea she could identify with and she appreciated the depth of its usefulness to psychiatry. She found it worthwhile to attend the FSI lectures that I put on for the analysts' benefit. She was also a good friend because of our close relationship to Erich and our mutual interest in the improvement of the human situation. The heart of her therapeutic program at Chestnut Lodge was the light she shed on the relationship between productivity and health. Her experience with seriously regressed patients convinced her that the suppression, repression, or diversion of the creative stream of people's lives could have devastating consequences, leading to depression and, in some cases, even to psychosis. For example, we once lived next to a family with a lot of children. All of them were bright, healthy youngsters, all except one. Albert was a genius. It was a delight to watch his young mind work. He was so bright it was almost painful. The tragedy was that Albert's teachers were not bright and were made anxious by his unbridled intelligence. There was nothing they could teach Albert because he was way ahead of them, so they made him dumb so they could teach him. Unfortunately, because he was a fast learner and knew that what the teachers really wanted was a dummkopf, he became a dummkopf and ended up in a special-ed class for students with learning disabilities!

Otto Will, a psychoanalyst, used to visit our home, bringing toy cars and special effects for my son Eric's Lionel train which I had set up in the basement. Since Otto and I were both from the West (he from Colorado), we carried with us a longing for those open spaces. I found a way to reproduce the effect of the great plains with the whistle of the model Santa Fe Super Chief's diesel locomotive as it pulled a chain of cars around a loop, through tunnels and grade crossings. The "Vfwoo, vfwooo, Vfwoo vfwoo vfwooo" of that whistle as the train approached a grade crossing conjured up visions of lonely dark nights and a distant train as it worked its way from across the prairie between La Junta and Trinidad on the way to Raton, Lamy, Albuquerque, Gallup, Winslow, and Flagstaff. Each engineer had his own characteristic way of blowing his train's whistle. Which engineer I was imprinted with I do not know, but he is there deep inside and I would bring him out and let him toot for Otto. The two of us stood there with my son as we were transfixed and temporarily transported back to a time and place that no longer was.

Like me, Otto valued the outdoors in the same way that we valued vitamins. We could do without them for a while but not forever. He told me once, "You know, Ned [he would drawl the Ned], I think about the West and all those open spaces and even if

I am not there, the fact that they are there and available for me to visit when I need them puts my mind at rest. If for some reason I were to learn that something had happened to them, that they were taken away and that I could no longer visit them, my anxiety level would increase intolerably."

Otto was exceptionally tall and had a permanent stoop left over from his war duty as a surgeon on a four-stacker destroyer where he had to duck every few feet while walking along passageways and through the steel doors of that ancient tub. Somewhat resembling Boris Karloff, he had a dramatic manner that made him even more impressive. Otto had a strong attraction to anthropology and we used to exchange notes. One evening he arrived, settled his long frame on the couch in our living room, and then told me this story:

For some time he had been treating an unusually attractive, vivacious female. Things were going along quite well when without notice or any warning movements, she picked up an ash stand with a bulbous bottom and took a swing at Otto's skull. If he hadn't been a former boxer with lightning reflexes, he could not have survived. Sobered by his close call with death, Otto knew it was essential that he devise an "early warning system," for the next time he might not be so lucky. Since there had been no visible outward signs foreshadowing the attack, he took a chance that his body might pick up clues that his conscious mind and perceptual systems missed. With this in mind, whenever he was with this particular patient he started keeping one finger on his pulse. Sure enough, there would be times when his pulse would begin to race, signaling an imminent attack and giving Otto time to defend himself. The fact that signals were being exchanged between these two people without either one's being aware of what was being communicated and how it was being read and received was an affirmation of some of my own work in nonverbal communication.

Otto had long been preoccupied with envy, seeing it as a particularly corrosive dynamic. He wanted to know more so he finally decided to put together a study group devoted to the subject. Its members were Herb Staverin, Bob Kvarnes, and the two of us. We met every other week at the house of one of the group. As a non-psychoanalyst I considered it a great privilege to be included as an equal in such a group. Not only did I enjoy our discussions, but I picked up a good deal concerning the culture of thought among psychoanalysts; it was almost like learning a new language. The group itself, the way it behaved and the way my friends were behaving in it, had a detached theoretical quality that I had not experienced with my anthropological colleagues or even with Erich Fromm—a kind of fear of coming out and saying something definitive. They would bring their insights and observations to the group in a tentative way. Every so often I would feel that we had reached a point where it looked as though we could summarize what amounted to a consensus. At this point I would sit and state in writing what we all obviously had agreed on so that the statement could be amended to make it more precise. Instead of taking issue with my analysis, correcting it, making suggested changes, or even agreeing, I was greeted instead with an extraordinary response. It wasn't that what I said was rejected; it was that, by stating our position and marking progress, I had made everyone quite anxious. It wasn't until years later that I recognized a similar pattern as a consequence of the process of self-discovery: namely, a resistance to closure. The group never did reach a point where it was possible to publish even a preliminary statement on the subject of envy. However, the subject is one that has intrigued me throughout my life. Envy is an archetype and seems to be present even in the mammals I have had around me. It is especially strong among the Hispanics and appeared in the Japanese folk tales my mother read to me as a child.

Ironically, our group dissolved when one of the members bought a big fancy house in an elite neighborhood and aroused so much envy among the others that we couldn't carry on. Envy was no longer an abstraction but had reared its ugly head right there in our midst. Envy proves to be just one of those things which the human race must overcome on its long, long road to ultimate fulfillment.

Because of my preoccupation with proxemics as well as with psychiatry as a sort of laboratory, I kept a continuous log of clinical data reported to me by my psychiatric colleagues. These colleagues were widespread and included people such as Humphry Osmond, director of a large mental health establishment in Saskatchewan; Paul Sivadon, a Belgian who headed up the mental health treatment centers for the French schoolteachers' union; and Harold Searles, a therapist at Chestnut Lodge. Hidden in all the data they brought me were hints as to the nature of some types of mental illness, indicating that much that we labeled as mental illness could also be described as abnormalities and aberrations in the perceptual and communicative systems; that is, serious distortions in the *processing of information.* Searles's work was particularly relevant.

It was known that paranoid schizophrenics were not only particularly sensitive to intrusions into the personal space bubble, but that the bubble was significantly larger than for nonschizophrenics. It was also known that many French and American schizophrenics suffered from an expansion of the body boundary. When one of Searles's patients said, "Doctor, you don't know what it's like looking at the world through square eyes," or another one said, "Doctor, it is very uncomfortable when I am here, having you inside my head all the time," these statements, out of context, sounded crazy. They were not crazy at all once it was known that the perceptual boundaries of the schizophrenics' bodies had expanded to a point far in excess of the physical boundaries. Both patients were speaking both the truth and sense. The perceived body field of the first filled the room. If the windows had been round he would have sounded less crazy, but like most windows they were square. The second apparently did not quite fill the room but the distortion was large enough to include the doctor.

In another series of observations, both nurses and staff physicians revealed that patients occupying rooms on a corridor facing and perpendicular to the nurses' station were able to remain reasonably stable in their condition but would deteriorate if moved around the corner, outside the "field" of the nurses' station. This suggested that the patients quite logically experienced a loss of mass and feared they would float off in space if removed from the "gravitational field" of the nurses' station. I said as much to Searles at a time when, as luck would have it, he had just finished seeing a patient who had brought him a drawing of a female figure looking like a blimp. She explained that she had drawn lead shoes on the figure to keep it from flying off into space. Her purpose in making the drawing was to try to explain to her doctor what it was like to be in her condition. The entire syndrome suggested an additional dimension to what had been considered simply a psychiatric problem.

My office was in the same building as the Washington School of Psychiatry, so I knew everyone in the building. It was an ideal situation for reviewing how psychiatrists used space in the course of therapy. One, a rather distant young man, had a large office and would put his patients as far away from himself as he could, up to eighteen feet away. Another, a Greek, picked the smallest office in the building (there were closets that were larger), which meant that he was literally on top of his patients, well within their "personal" bubbles and verging on intimate distance. When I asked how the patients responded to the close quarters, he told me that he liked the intimacy of that small office but that there were patients who had problems and left. One of his female patients had a shoji screen made for the window because the brick wall of the building next door was so solid and immediate as to be actually intrusive. Another therapist had his chair placed right up against the head of the couch. His explanation was, "It's so I can whap 'em. Freud whapped 'em when they weren't producing."

One of the doctors was especially good with dependent patients. He would keep a hand or a foot in the patient's personal bubble and would know that the patient's dependency on him was beginning to weaken when his hand or foot would automatically withdraw from the bubble.

Another colleague, Warren Brody, made more direct use of my work than the others. He first approached me because he was treating a couple, neither of whom appeared to be particularly neurotic, yet who were having a lot of trouble. When he gave them a copy of my book *The Silent Language* to read, the source of their troubles became patently clear. She was a New Englander. He was from southern Italy. She didn't like to be touched. He couldn't live without touching. When they understood what had been going on they began (with Brody's help) to compare notes. Her family ate at a dining room table. His family preferred the breakfast nook in the kitchen and were only really at ease when all were squeezed in so that their fannies were touching. There was a real catharsis as they explored the different facets of the proxemic patterns in which each had been raised.

Brody was fascinated with the senses, as I was. At one time we conducted an extensive series of seminars with some talented blind men. The men were chosen because they could "travel"—that is, they could move about in public with nothing but a cane. I used to watch one of our blind trios crossing Massachusetts Avenue at Columbus Circle in Washington. What a feat! This group could go just about anywhere. To travel they depended almost entirely on their ears but were also tuned in to such spatial clues as the heat radiated from walls, which they used as locator signals: warm, cold, cold, cold, warm, blank (no wall), warm, cold—this was the pattern of one of their routes just before they reached Connecticut Avenue. To my surprise, our research showed that the blind feel more claustrophobic in a windowless room than sighted people do. Because the windows are more transparent to the sound of street noises, the blind can not only keep track of what is happening outside but can get a better feeling of the shape of the room inside. Indoors they can identify each individual in the room by the characteristic noises of breathing, something I didn't know before because the sound of breathing in "normal" people is masked out by the auditory part of the brain and classified as not significant. It's the same process familiar to anyone who has made tape recordings of conversations and discovered all sorts of background noises which they were not aware of at the time of the recording.

Not only could our group travel around Washington, but they also liked to hunt! They could identify the game, locate it in space with sufficient accuracy to kill it, and track it if the first shot was not fatal. Many sighted hunters simply shoot at anything that moves or whenever they hear something moving in the bushes. The first year I was teaching in Denver, more than thirty hunters were killed during hunting season. If the sighted hunters had been as sensorially sophisticated as our blind group, all those men would have been alive at the end of the hunting season.

. . . .

THERE WAS NOT EVEN THE SHADOW of a doubt in my mind of the intimate relationship between microcultural studies and what the psychiatrists were doing. I was therefore deeply indebted to my friends and colleagues in psychiatry because of what I learned from them about the deeply personal aspects of the human transactions. As this is being written almost forty years later, the fields of anthropology and psychology are still separate. If there is a link, however, it is where the two fields intersect in the dynamics of everyday life.

NINETEEN

Broken Idols

To grasp the truth you must first break your idols.
—B. J. O. Nordfeldt

B. J. O. NORDFELDT was an old Santa Fe friend and an expressionist painter of no small stature who had been deeply influenced by Cézanne. While I was in graduate school, "Nordy" divorced his wife, left Santa Fe, and moved to Lambertville, New Jersey, across the Delaware River from New Hope, Pennsylvania. With my five years in the army plus three in the academic world, it had been at least eight years since I had seen my friend, so since we were now both on the East Coast I made it a point to look him up. I had always admired his work, but there were personal things about him that I also liked such as his quick subtle wit, his sense of humor, his courage, and the fact that we had known each other for a long time in different contexts and were of compatible temperaments. There weren't many people like Nordy in my world. A short gnomelike man, he had an expressive face and twinkling eyes. Far from flashy and unlike many other artists I had known, Nordy was neither narcissistic and introverted nor competitive and extroverted. He just went about his work in a quiet, unassuming way.

Nordy had a kind of independence of spirit that didn't bow down to adversity. He never compromised his work. I knew about commissions Nordy had turned down because he didn't like the cut of a potential client's jib. He terminated one commission when the patron was presumptuous enough to criticize his work before it was finished.

He was one of several men who became models for me of what a man should be. It was his quiet, unassuming manner, the way he did things, and his basic attitude toward life that impressed me most.

Once while we were still at Bennington, Mildy and I were visiting New York and saw a notice of a Nordfeldt show at the Passedoit Gallery on Fifty-seventh Street. Seeing the show was almost like seeing my friend. We were particularly taken with and bought a powerful oil painting he had done in Taos, New Mexico. Though we have owned that painting for over forty years, I never pass it without my spirits lifting.

When Mildy and I would visit Nordy at his Lambertville house and studio, we would first be ushered into the kitchen to sit and chat over coffee. Later, we would be taken to the studio.

On my first visit to his new home in the East I was struck by a dramatic change in his paintings. Massive, strong seascapes in an entirely new palette and style greeted us. "Gosh, Nordy, you really are off on a new tack this time!" I said. "Well, Ned, there comes a time in every man's life when he must break his idols."

Not until I had done a good deal more living did I realize that Nordy's remark was not restricted to painters and their styles nor to those obvious models one follows as a child, but could be applied to all of life. The idols symbolized fields or activities and beliefs. Maturation could be viewed as a process of eliminating outmoded models.

Long association with artists—particularly my mother (who was a reputable painter in her own right), Heinz, who was first-rate, and E.Boyd—had imprinted me with a certain mind-set. I knew I could never be an artist, but once I found the courage to buy that first Nordfeldt painting, Mildy and I began to build what grew to be a modest but good collection of contemporary art and photography. This was a decisive risk on our part, because we really didn't have the money to pay for it. Collecting also provided an outlet for Mildy's unusual gift for spotting talent.

Our collection has threatened to fill every available foot of space in our house. If Mildy or I saw a particularly appealing artistic statement, if it was priced even near our range, we had to have it. Neither of us could imagine what it would be like to live without our friends there to greet us each day. Most people think you must have money to buy art and that art is luxury, which it most certainly is not. We didn't have money, because professors don't make that much. For us art was on a par with such necessities as food, shelter, and education.

The artists in my past had, without my knowing it, programmed me so that I could never be content with clichés, particularly if I had anything to do with creating them. This marked me as a nonconformist. Yet in the Department of State, I was working for the government, the kingdom of the cliché and the buzzword. No breaking of idols was tolerated there!

When George Trager and I started to work together and as our thinking took on tangible form, it began to look as though we might have discovered something worthy of recognition. Yet instead of making a name for ourselves, the opposite happened. Our obvious departure from the older ambiguous or narrow concepts of culture was met with deafening silence, in spite of the fact that by all conventional academic standards our statement warranted recognition. To the group at FSI our work was seen as a big step forward. To hard scientists in the Washington community it was taken as a definite advance, the first theory in anthropology where there was an attempt to be systematic on an extensive scale. However, in a conceptual no-man's-land of our own making, it soon became apparent that we were drawing fire from not just one, but two directions: from our own bureaucracy and, where it was most painful, from our colleagues. In the larger sea of anthropology our innovative comprehensive approach, including little-explored aspects of culture such as the unconscious/tacit side, as well as culture as *communication*, attracted little attention.

Now I can see that there were several reasons for the neglect and even the rejection of our work, all stemming from the very processes we had been studying. The reception (or lack of it) was in fact a classic example of the processes we described. Since about

450 B.C., the time of Socrates and Plato, Western culture has been obsessed with a restricted view of what constitutes science: measurement as a way of ascertaining the degree to which things are or are not similar to each other, with causation and explanations—*why* does something happen? These were not our obsessions. Trager and I simply wanted to know, in a more specific way, what it was that we were studying and, further, how people learned and integrated this massive system which had come into being as an extension and partial substitution for the genetic code. Culture is a system involving a lot of information processing and takes the place of instincts, which makes humans infinitely more adaptable than they otherwise would be. Trager and I wanted to know how to systematically divide up the field yet still be consistent. Both of us had assumed that if we played by the academic rules we had been taught, people would as a matter of course recognize our contribution. What we failed to take into account was both American culture and the informal infrastructure of our very own field. We were learning the hard way how the culture of academic anthropology really worked, as distinct from what people said about how it worked.

If either of us had been one of the "popes of the field" (to use the expression of that wonderful man Albert Szent-Gyorgyi[1])—men and women such as Alfred Kroeber, Robert Redfield, Clyde Kluckhohn, or Ruth Benedict—the response to our work might have been different. But we weren't. We hadn't earned our spurs as big shots. In the United States, one must be a big shot before most people think it is safe to listen. My error was in not realizing soon enough that my work was like that of the anonymous people who first saw that language, like everything else in the universe, was systematic and then began the arduous task of reducing language to writing. These people changed the world. They introduced a new level of reality so that people didn't have to learn something new from scratch but could read what others had done and build on the solid foundation of an acquired skill. And that was what I really wanted to do—to build onto what was already there so that people could make it their own. My observations and insights into the human dimensions of territoriality and temporality seemed to be this kind of work. Space and time are used as a kind of language; people knew that when they were kept waiting it communicated something, but they didn't have a way of pinning down what others were saying when their spatial or temporal mores were violated. No one had figured it out and explained it before. The fact that neither of these cultural systems was universal (as had been supposed) but were tied to a particular culture was a genuine breakthrough which helped to remove some of the distortions inherent in all cross-cultural interactions.

Essentially I had managed to do five quite different, but related things:

1. Dip down into the cultural unconscious, the part that I was later to define as being identified with the self, and raise that unconscious part to awareness so that its role in both behavior and communication could be examined and appraised.
2. Reveal that shibboleths[2] distinguishing one ethnic group from another were not restricted to words but to the rest of culture and particularly to out-of-awareness culture.
3. Demonstrate that there is more to culture than words. In fact, it seems that eighty to ninety percent of communication might eventually be situated in this nonverbal unconscious realm of culture.
4. Link culture to its ecological roots in ten different dimensions, including space (territoriality) and time (temporality).
5. And connect culture—via this highly personalized realm—to psychiatry and from there to personality.

I believe that to grasp the full significance of my work and the general framework which Trager and I developed, one should possess a bit of what Buckminster Fuller called "comprehensive thinking." Unfortunately, most people who have been indoctrinated by our schools have comprehensive thinking pretty much knocked out of them, to be replaced by highly *compartmentalized* thinking. (It gets worse in graduate school.) Yet what the world needs today is many more comprehensive thinkers. Otherwise, how does the human race link its fate with that of its environment?

My frustration with the reception given my work seemed intolerable. No matter where I looked, there seemed to be no way to dethrone the idol of compartmentalization and to link people to themselves again. It was frustrating beyond belief. I had worked for years on the whole problem of bridging cultures, I was actually able to do something specific for the Point IV program technicians, and yet I was still unable to convince more than a tiny cadre of colleagues that my work was worthwhile.

Clearly I had to know more about how to make a bridge into the culture of the bureaucracy, or the formal culture, as well as the process of defining culture. And I would have to know more about myself as well, both from the psychological and the cultural viewpoint. In the meantime I had to earn a living and be careful whose toes I stepped on. But there were also events over which I had no control. By spurning the intellectual continuity of the field and not consulting the popes, Trager and I had desecrated the revered idols of our colleagues.

When you embark on change, you must be prepared for the consequences. Our colleagues were living in a *word* world and we had said, "Words are not enough. There is much more to this picture than you imagine." We had taken some of the mystery out of anthropology and made it simple (or, if not simple, at least direct). I knew that many Americans made the mistake of believing that anything simple could not be profound. But I simply could not bring myself to complicate something I had worked so hard to make accessible to the average layperson.

Out of all this came a penetrating insight: it is much more difficult to apply what you know to your own culture than to a foreign one. Why? Because people have too much at stake! Look at what happened to Galileo! Because there is always a status quo and because you know too much. Either through experience or intuition, you are aware of where the power lies and it is hard to keep your scientific statements from being transmuted from nonjudgmental objective science into politics. You are confronting the underground power structure—the one obsessed with the notion that everyone should prove loyalty to the team by conforming, and the one which requires that you recant and say that what you have said isn't really true. In the old days heresies were put down by the Church. By the 1950s, while we had effectively lost the Church, we had gained a more obdurate guardian of the gates of knowledge. Instead of recanting, people conformed.

Nowhere was the rush to conform demonstrated more clearly than in the period of notorious self-serving witch-hunting at the head of which was the late Senator Joseph McCarthy. The State Department—lacking a constituency like the other departments—was selected by McCarthy for "special treatment." He knew we were defenseless and couldn't strike back, so he went all out. His speeches resounded with cries and accusations that our agency was a "hotbed of subversion" and "riddled with Communists." What was extraordinary and frightening was the way State's personnel folded with a cowardly "I'll do anything you want, as long as I don't get fired" response. Too many Americans had really lost their courage and let themselves be kicked around by such an obvious fraud and bully as McCarthy, a man who did more to subvert our institutions and to destroy morale than anyone in recent history. The travesty of it all was that he was manipulating the culture in a particularly insidious and malevolent way.

The 1950s were not a good time in my life. Our phones were tapped and I was working for a frightened bureaucracy. Finally, one of our linguists who was teaching Spanish to the President's brother got the President to remove the phone taps, but this did not stop the eavesdropping by administrators within our own organization. Our entire program was under attack from two directions at once: McCarthy on the outside and our own bureaucracy on the inside. Pretending that everything was okay while striving to decipher the administrative code, I felt a bit like the Indians on the reservation trying to find out what the white man was going to do next. It came as no surprise when I learned that the last two directors assigned to us by the Office of Personnel (senior members of the Foreign Service) had been given strict orders to "clean out the anthropologists."

The truly creative side of the Foreign Service Institute, the academic part, had never been firmly rooted in bureaucratic soil. But it was a strategic shift in the departmental policy that proved to be the straw that broke the camel's back. There had been a move on for some time to staff the State Department predominantly with

Foreign Service officers. To do this meant absorbing large numbers of departmental personnel into the Foreign Service. With one stroke of the pen we were finished as an academic institution. Instead of using professional economists, geographers, anthropologists, and area experts to train our diplomats, Foreign Service officers were assigned to do training. Everything changed overnight. Our little period of productivity, the bright spot in a pedantic effort, became a thing of the past.

Clearly there was nothing subversive about our little corner of academia unless it was subversive to be innovative, but we were treated that way. I kept asking myself, What is behind this? Why the pressure to get rid of the academicians? Some of the problem centered on the fact that, being in the forefront of change, we were reporting back to the Department some evidence that the world was changing, that new policies were in order, and new forms of information must be gathered from the field. We were raising the question of whether those in charge shouldn't be taking a fresh look at things, as well as what skills and perspectives were needed.

One day as I returned from lunch, I came into my office to find an inquisitor sitting in the chair behind my desk going through my desk drawers. Remaining in my chair, he told me to sit down and proceeded to grill me. He was a fat man with a round pale face, trifocal glasses, and the expression of a professional informer. While I had had little experience with his type, it was clear that he was the hound and I was the hare. All the while, sitting there rooting around in my drawers, reading pieces of paper, looking under everything including the desk blotter, questions like rifle shots came out: "Are you loyal to the United States?" Instead of asking what gave him the idea that I wasn't, or reminding him that I had taken an oath to that effect when I went to work for the State Department, I said yes and that I had served five years in the army in World War II, five campaigns in Europe, and so on. "Do you know any Communists?" "Are you a Communist?" "Are any members of your family Communists?" He asked for the usual background data: date and place of birth, foreign travel, my job description, questions about my family, was I related to any foreigners, and so on. It felt like Nazi Germany.

This interview shook me up, highlighting one thing very clearly: something was radically wrong in my life. I had been breaking my idols left and right, and from the wreckage emerged a fact I had been avoiding: I needed to go into therapy.

Under normal circumstances I could have just gone to see one of my psychiatrist friends. But now I was in the State Department and in the 1940s and 1950s to be unable to solve one's problems oneself and to see a psychiatrist was viewed as prima facie evidence of unreliability akin to subversion and brought the possibility of being fired as a "security risk." Nevertheless, I had to risk it. Phoning my friend David Rioch, I asked him to lunch. In Washington, an invitation to lunch signals that you have something serious on your mind.

TWENTY

The Underlying Truth

DAVID RIOCH was not just a colleague, he was an admired and valued friend. So I turned to him as the individual whose judgment I trusted most, to advise me in selecting an analyst. Good psychoanalysts were hard to find then. The ones who had time for a new patient were even more rare. If anyone could help it would be David.

I wasted no time coming to the point. I told him I needed help, that things were getting out of hand and that I was acutely uncomfortable. His eyebrows twitched a bit as he thought. He did not act surprised, only supportive, and said, "It must be pretty tough. I have been in a bind like that. While most therapists leave a good deal to be desired, there is one who has had some success. I think I can arrange something for you with her. You're in luck because she is just finishing up with a patient."

A handsome woman trained at Johns Hopkins Medical School, Winifred Whitman had fine gray hair that had once been brown, regular features, and an unusually smooth skin with a classical bone structure. She was solidly built, walked with a cane, and exuded an air of professional competence. In the course of our initial interview, she identified the core of my problem and she left me feeling confident that she could help me.

I was amazed at how hard it was to describe my problem to Dr. Whitman. I simply didn't know what was wrong. All I knew was that it was as though I had been living in a fragmented world lacking logic, justice, and coherence, a world over which I had little control. There I was, sitting in a chair facing Dr. Whitman, with the world inside me coming apart, and all I could offer her were generalities: an outline of my history, my parents' divorce and my mother's leaving, where I had lived, my education, my marriage to Mildy, my two children, Ellen and Eric, my previous marriage to E.Boyd, and a thumbnail sketch of my job situation. Winifred sat there taking it all in, listening quietly. Just as the hour was about to end, she said, "I can't tell for sure, because you haven't given me much to go on, but beneath all that I have heard there is an undercurrent that tells me you are *depressed.*" She told me that her diagnosis was based more on intuition, a nonverbal hunch, than on anything concrete.

Depressed! How did she know? I didn't even know myself. But when she said it, I knew she was right. Suddenly I was facing something about myself that I had been avoiding most of my life. Along with that reality came the first hint of a sense of relief that I had known in years. At least it would no longer be necessary to fight against some ill-defined malady of the soul. For the first time I had an inkling that the real problems were inside me and not outside, and that if I could square them away, I could do anything. I knew that a few rare people grew up without internal conflicts, but I was not one of them and whatever I got I would have to work for. Then I heard Winifred saying, "We should see each other on Mondays and Wednesdays. I don't know how long it will take, but it may take a long time. My fee will be fifteen dollars an hour." Shaken, but with the sense that I was doing the right thing and that I was in competent hands, I left.

We spent a lot of time, Winifred and I, over the next few years reviewing my life history and pursuing the will-o'-the-wisp that lay behind my depression. She thought it was my parents' divorce, an idea with which I did not agree for reasons I was unsure of. I kept asking myself, "How could something they had done so long ago have such a deep effect on me?" I was trying to reassure myself that I was free of my parents.

I had started the analysis sitting in a chair opposite Winifred. But at a certain point she suggested I should try the couch. Lying there, looking down past my feet, I could see out the window but I couldn't see her behind me. It was impossible to monitor her reactions; I had no tangible way to keep track of her emotions, and there were no cues as to what she was feeling or thinking. But there was one time when I did know. I had been reviewing the events following my parents' divorce and leading up to my life on the Hopi reservation when Lorenzo Hubbell had taken me under his wing. She interrupted to ask, "How long had it been since you had seen your mother?" There was a pause while I mentally reviewed the years from 1927 when she left to 1931 when I joined her and Heinz in Paris. I finally answered, "Four years" and then added, "Between 1927 and 1935, I saw her three times." Usually the only sounds in the room were those made by my voice. But this time there was an audible gasp from Winifred. That gasp was reality talking; like a speeding bullet it hit me where I least expected, punching a hole in my hidden defenses. But it was almost a year later that, one day on the couch, my defenses crumbled and something triggered a repressed memory. I saw myself at eleven years of age, riding in the car beside Mother down the road toward the golf club as she told me she was leaving.

The thirty-one-year-old lump in my chest grew and grew until there was no holding it back. The dam broke with a torrent of emotion. This time there was no mother there to be made anxious at the slightest sign of distress. Released from the fortress so carefully built to contain my feelings, I could no longer control my emotions and my body took over. The wrenching sobs of pain released by that memory of loss gushed forth in a torrent of grief. As I lay there gasping, my chest heaving, I realized how I had been hurt and deceived by Mother. I was face to face with a part of myself that I had kept hidden from prying eyes—even my own—for many years. Along with relief came a flash of recognition of what a heavy price I had paid for what I had done—or rather failed to do: let my mother know how I felt as she destroyed my world. Removing the wall I had built around that memory freed up tremendous energy as well as grief that had been repressed.

What was extraordinary was that, in spite of the abandonment by both my parents and the clear signs that neither of them could handle the responsibility of being parents, I had bought into their own myth. I had told myself that they were normal, fine, upright people who did their best under difficult circumstances. I had no idea how odd they were when judged by conventional standards, which both my parents (particularly Mother) had labeled as "bourgeois." Their attitude had immeasurably complicated relations with others—even estranging me from my own culture. However, that remoteness enabled me to see things I might not have otherwise seen. And having been distanced I was not so easily taken in by the ubiquitous verbal and visual tricks of hucksters, politicians, and merchants of power.

Analysis continued like punctuation marks in the sentences and paragraphs of my life for seven years. When I began to dress differently,—a sign I had noted in friends in analysis—I knew I was getting better. Such changes had reflected improvements in my friends' self-image and in their relations with others. Now I could feel these changes taking place in myself. To give a minor example, at that time men wore two kinds of ties—regular four-in-hands and bow ties. I had never worn bow ties. Men who wore them seemed kind of cocky and self-assured (like McGeorge Bundy). Yet all of a sudden I realized I wanted to wear a bow tie. The trouble was that they were harder to tie. I was damned if I was going to wear a clip-on; I figured if you were going to wear a bow tie you should be able to tie it for yourself. So I simply took the trouble to master the skills necessary to tie a bow tie, which, strangely enough, gave me a much needed dram of confidence. I started writing *my first real book, The Silent Language*, one hour a day between five and six in the morning when no one could bother me.

My analysis proceeded. I knew there was no nirvana, but I was happier and not as withdrawn as before, and even though there were times when things were difficult, my relations with others were, on the whole, less strained. A clearer picture of how the significant events in my past had molded the present was beginning to form in my mind, as well as a knowledge that there was no law on the books saying you should remain overwhelmed and crippled by the past.

Still, the therapeutic process continued to baffle me. My interest wasn't just a matter of personal curiosity; it was related to everything I was doing and writing about in my professional life. In addition to the more obvious connections between mental health and culture, there must be another relationship, that of the nonverbal, between tacit culture and psychiatry. But nothing of what I had read connected culture with psychoanalysis. As my therapy unfolded, I could see part of what was happening inside *me*, but I had difficulty pinning down what was happening between me and Winifred. I had no trouble separating the therapeutic from my day-to-day encounters. However, with Winifred, not only was the process different (even when she appeared to be doing and saying nothing) but there was something happening I had not experienced before—a silent, intangible, nonjudgmental intervention—that was actively helping me to sort things out even when nothing seemed to be going on.

I had been brought up to believe that some things, quite arbitrarily, were things I should do, and they kept other people comfortable. Other things would get you into trouble. These other things were supposed to be "bad" and were to be avoided. But some of the things that kept others comfortable, such as kowtowing obsequiously, I could not bring myself to do, regardless of cost. The result was that I never really learned how to use the culture as a way either of getting along with others, or of persuading others to do things for me.

Something that is seldom recognized is that culture can be a deadly tool in the hands of those who see their fellow human beings only as objects to be exploited. While culture accomplishes multiple tasks, when used as an instrument for gain or destruction it plays no favorites and can be lethal in the hands of the unscrupulous. Just look at Hitler and what he did with his knowledge of the culture and psychology of the German people.

As my psyche slowly rearranged itself, I finally gave up trying to sort out the dynamics of therapy. It could just as well have been shamanism for all the immediate sense it made. I say this only as a statement of my own wonder and awe. During my therapy I simply had to accept, to take on faith, that whatever was happening was happening. I not only had no control over it, but, if I had, that control would have defeated the entire process. My psyche was leading the way and I was following.

It finally dawned on me that I had been looking for explanations in the wrong way and possibly for the wrong reasons. I knew that the psyche is infinitely complex, but I was being too linear. I had thought that if I could rationalize the therapeutic process, it would speed things up (which was the voice of my culture speaking). But I had to reconcile myself to the fact that progress was far from linear and that I could not impose my thinking mind on the rest of my psyche. In the army, I had to learn to do things the army way. I now had to learn how to do things *my* way, but according to a part of my self that had been repressed by my parents and my culture.

The striking thing about the analytic process was that it was so unpredictable. I would be lying on that couch working my way through an incredible maze of annoyances, some trivial and some not so trivial, when out of the blue I would be face to face with some new facet of myself, a whole new frame of reference. A door would open and with it a world of insights. One dream I had was particularly germane. In the dream three men were fighting each other with chairs and knives, dancing around with the chairs held like lion tamers in a cage. Those that didn't have a knife had a chair, so that while no one was getting hurt, no one was happy either. The dream was puzzling, yet I knew that behind that symbolism there was a message. When I told Winifred the dream, she explained that these three men stood for three parts of myself which were in conflict. The metaphor I came up with, since it was difficult at first to think of parts of myself actually fighting with each other, was that each part could be likened to a governmental agency competing with other agencies for funds and power; each being more concerned with standing the others off than with the welfare of the nation. It was my true self that created that dream, a metaphor for inner conflict, a message from my unconscious to my conscious self telling me what I was doing to myself and to get my act together. What an extraordinary process!

Each little step forward in the psychoanalytic process meant giving up an old internal defense and, because it left me feeling defenseless, demanded courage. I was to discover that insights are easy to come by, but they can be deceptive. We tend to think we have done something when we have had an insight. But insights not acted on are a bit of a fraud. My three men were just the beginning. They would have to be identified. I would have to know who they represented and what they stood for, and, much more to the point, how they should be handled, all of which could take years.

But what was even more formidable when it came to changing was garnering the raw courage to confront my entrenched habits of dealing with relationships: how to stand up to people whose only claim to authority over me was power (physical, political or cultural); how to handle mother figures who expected me to hide any feelings about the way they were behaving and how they were treating me; how to accept my presence here on earth as a natural and intended event; how to convince myself that I was here for a purpose, that I had a right to be here and that it was bad for me when I bought other people's ideas as to who I should be; how to stop treating everything as a matter of life and death. I began to see that for me, life, instead of being a natural process in which there were successes and failures, fun, pleasure, gentleness, and even love, had for a long time been merely a struggle for survival. I had to develop new ways to relax and to let some situations unfold, particularly when I was not personally involved in the outcome.

Living in Washington with so many friends in the psychoanalytic world, I nevertheless persisted in wanting to know more about how therapy worked, why some therapists and some patients never connected, why other therapists were so successful with one kind of patient but not with others. In the simplest terms, analysis seemed to go better when the therapist identified with the patient and was more concerned with the patient's welfare than with whether the psychoanalytic dogma or mores of the culture were being breached. What wasn't good was when the therapist was exploiting the patient in some way, was overly preoccupied with following accepted procedures, hadn't worked out in her or his own psyche something the patient was having trouble with, or simply lacked the important component of courage.

Each therapist I knew was different from the others: Frieda, with her iron will and soft penetrating wisdom; David, with his no-nonsense subtle mind, always looking for the real-life patterns that underlay verbose explanations; Otto, with his theatrical, humorous, insightful approach; Bob, with his difficulties in closure; Cecil and his distancing; Dinos the Greek, who had to be physically close; Jimmy, who was so good with dependent patients; Leon, who lectured them on "the good life"; perceptive Searles, whose insights into the psychotics' distorted perceptual view of their relation to the world enriched my own insights into the dynamics of the perception of space; insightful, sensitive Herb, who treated his patients sitting at drugstore counters and in his automobile; Warren, who used the insights of *The Silent Language* when treating cross-cultural marriages; and Mark, who whapped 'em because Ernest Jones said Freud whapped 'em.

What I really saw were friends who had been doing something long enough so that they had mastered what amounted to a craft, a craft which in many ways was not all that different from other crafts, except that it took longer to learn, more commitment to master, and required certain personality traits such as the ability to identify with other human beings in the true sense of the word while not being made anxious by the patient's pathology. Naturally there were those who were more skilled at their craft than others. Winifred was one of them. There were those who were born healers, just as there are born musicians, and there were those who would never develop a high level of skill. Part of the craft involved knowing what you could and could not do and where your strengths and weaknesses lay. Everyone seemed to know who was good with dependent patients and who was not, who knew how to treat alcoholics (difficult to treat), who could handle hostility, who had a high tolerance for anxiety, or who was good at dreams and myths.

But there was structure to therapy, despite the diversity of methods. There was still a gap between theory and practice, between the world as it is and how it is perceived. Yet somehow these people had mastered that structure even though they had not completely defined it, nor were they fully aware of it. This process could be compared to learning French not in the traditional classroom, but from hearing it spoken and using it in France without having to go through the laborious process of analyzing the language in terms of its classroom vocabulary and rules of grammar.

During the entire seven years of my analysis with Winifred, a hidden part of myself, the unconscious, was gradually coming through. Though it would be years before a comfortable relationship with my unconscious (or my primeval self) was established, and even though I didn't know its nature, at least I knew it was there, waiting to be brought out and put to work. Far beneath my surface emotions, attitudes, thoughts, and ways of reacting was this other part of me—a hidden self wherein was to be found the valid principles against which all my acts could be evaluated. It was in this part of the self that I should look for the truth. And if I could learn to listen, it would not let me down.

In the perspective of my more than seventy years I can see that, as self-sufficient and independent as I was, there were still times when I needed healing help from others. This help came in many forms and guises, mostly while I was merely engaged in the process of living, and frequently it came from unexpected sources which I did not recognize as a corrective in the pattern of my life until much later (the relationship between myself and Mildy, my wife and partner, was such a corrective). My "therapists" were mostly not professionals. Many weren't even what I would call harmonious, sympathetic individuals. At times their medicine was cruel and bitter. Yet almost inevitably, when viewed in retrospect, these individuals appearing throughout the fabric of my life taught me things about myself which I could not have learned in any other way and which set me back on course again. What I have finally come to appreciate is that, when all is said and done, *my entire life has been therapeutic, even my parents' divorce.* It just took work and living and the sense that it was important to live right and not to blame others, to learn that lesson.

NOTES

CHAPTER ONE

1. My father's branch of the family spelled the name "Twichell," a variant of the original family name, "Twitchell." I chose to use the original spelling for my own name, Edward Twitchell Hall.

2. A source of resentment on my mother's part against my father was that he had all of us christened with names from his family and of his choice. Edward Twichell Hall, Delight Dawson Hall, Richard Walkley Hall, and Priscilla Alden Hall. Poor D! It took years for Mother to find things she liked and admired and felt comfortable with in my sister, but it did finally happen.

CHAPTER THREE

1. "Open range" was an expression used prior to World War II for unfenced land between towns where anyone who chose to do so was free to graze cattle.

2. A snubbing post is a large post six or more inches in diameter placed in the center of a corral. Its purpose is to assist the cowhand after he has roped an animal. Two or three loops are thrown around the post to take the strain off the cowhand by transferring the pull of a bucking animal from the cowhand to the post, so the critter can't drag him around the corral.

Tapaderos are leather shields mounted around the fore end of wooden western stirrups. Their function is to protect the rider's feet in tough country through thorny bushes or cactus. Tapaderos traditionally were functional and unadorned, but when used for show could also be very fancy. Appleton's were the fanciest.

3. This entire area, once so pristine, is now the site of a bustling ski resort served by a paved highway.

CHAPTER FOUR

1. Starting at the top of the Camino and working back toward town there were: Fremont Ellis, Will Shuster, William P. Henderson, Josef Bakos, Willard Nash, Frank Applegate, Andrew Dasburg, and Datus Meyers, who were immediate neighbors. Others were B. J. O. Nordfeldt, Gerald Cassidy, John Sloan, Albert Schmidt, Sheldon Parsons, Martha Field, Olive Rush, Lynn Riggs, Randall Davey, Raymond Johnson, Carlos Vierra, E.Boyd, Cady Wells, Witter Bynner, Ansel Adams, John Marin, and Mabel Dodge Luhan.

2. At the time, while it was not forbidden to speak Spanish in our school, Spanish was a "foreign" language, the use of which was to be discouraged.

CHAPTER FIVE

1. Elizabeth Boyd White Andrews Van Cleve—E.Boyd, pronounced as one word. She was one of the pioneer scholars of Spanish colonial art in New Mexico.

CHAPTER SIX

1. Anasazi is the technical name for the prehistoric ancestral group of the Pueblo Indians.

2. Actually it was one of John Collier's sons who recommended me for a position in the lower ranks of the "new" Indian Service. I had known his sons (John, Jr., Charles, and Donald) in the late 1920s and early 1930s because of our mutual interest in the Pueblo people of New Mexico.

CHAPTER SEVEN

1. IECW (Indian Emergency Conservation Work) was the Indian equivalent of the Civilian Conservation Corps run by the army for civilians as a substitute for relief during the Depression.

2. Polychronic (a term I coined years later) refers to doing many things at once. Polychronic cultures are also characterized as facilitating the flow of information (there are no compartments to slow it down). See my book *Beyond Culture*, 1976.

CHAPTER EIGHT

1. The price of certain items fluctuated, because their value was tied to off-the-reservation markets, such as the price paid for lambs, wool, and blankets.

2. It is in the nature of intercultural relations that uncertainty as to what one is really communicating is about the only thing that one can be certain of. Here were all these white males, out on the reservation, observing the accepted patterns of their own culture and leaving the Navajos with the uncomfortable feeling that their mere presence was unpleasant. One Navajo said to another: "Ever notice how most of those *Bilekana* [white] men look angry all the time?"

3. The split between the "friendlies" and "hostiles" came about with the appearance of the Catholic fathers shortly after Coronado's conquest of the Southwest in the 1540s. The "friendlies" were in favor of accepting the presence of the whites as in the order of things and learning to live with this new force in their lives. The "hostiles" took the opposite view.

CHAPTER NINE

1. The contemporary reader should keep in mind that in the fifty-six years between these events and the writing about them, times have changed. Shine's explanation was part of an act—his way of facilitating his being allowed to pitch in and help out. Also he happened to be right when he said there was no way they could have made it up that twenty-five-mile hill through the sand dunes without help. To negotiate that hill it was necessary to let most of the air out of the rear tires to provide traction in the soft sand. When the top of the hill was reached the tires had to be pumped up again. Shine could handle both. Besides, his added weight in the back seat was an asset in traversing those desert sand dunes.

CHAPTER ELEVEN

1. The army recognized—in fact, stipulated—that there would be two armies: the United States Army for the regulars and "the Army of the United States" for conscripts.

2. He was not Hispanic, and not wanting to use his real name, I had to call him something appropriate.

3. A lieutenant colonel from Mississippi who had been relieved of the command of a battalion was assigned to us. He was no Colonel Henry. The less said the better.

CHAPTER FOURTEEN

1. Harry Stack Sullivan was one of the truly innovative psychiatrists in the United States. In many ways his thinking paralleled my own concerning the interpersonal as well as the cultural aspects of psychiatry.

CHAPTER FIFTEEN

1. The terms "tacit culture," "acquired culture," and "out-of-awareness culture" have all been used to refer to those levels of culture which have yet to be reduced to writing or otherwise technically described.

2. For more about language as a system of culture, see my book *The Silent Language* (1959).

CHAPTER SIXTEEN

1. A satisfactory bedrock definition of culture, like the elixir of life in days gone by, had continued to elude even the greatest anthropologists.

2. The parallel between Planck's discoveries in physics and ours concerning the nature of cultural data was not recognized until recently, when I was working with physicists. The interpretation is somewhat complex and beyond the scope of this book. It hinges however on the fact that the effect of Heisenberg's indeterminacy principle is even more profound in my work than it appears to be in physics—that is, the role of the observer cannot be separated from the events observed.

3. Our task was eased because I had already identified and worked with two nonlanguage, biologically based cultural systems (time and space) that were not only communicative and distinct from each other, but satisfied the criteria we were in the process of establishing for identifying all basic cultural systems. Social organization and learning were also solid candidates—learning because culture is

above everything else learned, while social organization is characteristic of most, if not all, species ancestral to our own.

4. The basic cultural systems can be and frequently are analyzed in their own terms as *closed systems* without reference to other systems. Language is an example. That is, most language teaching is done without reference to the cultural matrix in which the language is set. It is this compartmentalization of culture which leads to incredible difficulties in translating from cultures like the Japanese that do not compartmentalize.

5. I later named the field of *proxemics* as the study of space as the human aspect of territorial studies in animals.

6. For a description of our map of culture, see my book *The Silent Language.*

7. All of culture is an extension of what were once hard-wired physiological functions. That is, even though the idea is not much more than forty years old, all behavior in the animal kingdom *evolved* and, like physiology, is rooted in the genetic template. For more on this see *The Silent Language.*

CHAPTER SEVENTEEN

1. In this game rocks break scissors, scissors cut paper, and paper wraps rocks. At a signal, two children playing the game, would make a fist, double their forearms towards the shoulder, lower their arms in synchrony with each other three times. On the last "throw" each player trying to guess what their opponent was going to do had to choose whether to display two separated fingers (scissors) and open palm (paper) or a fist (rocks). The winner got to slap the loser on the wrist.

CHAPTER EIGHTEEN

1. Chestnut Lodge, in Rockville, Maryland, was a prestigious, family-owned private mental hospital run by Dexter Bullard, who was famous for pioneering the use of dynamic psychotherapy in the treatment of psychotics. Many of our psychiatric friends either worked there or had been on Bullard's staff at one time or another.

2. Frieda Fromm-Reichmann wrote about the importance of paying attention to the nonverbal part of the therapeutic process, possibly because of her association with Harry Stack Sullivan and David Rioch, or possibly because of her own strong intuition. Her interest in this subject was one of the many bonds I had with this gracious, talented woman.

3. As time progressed, particularly after I had written *The Silent Language*, there was some progress. Psychiatrists like Warren Brody actually began to make use of the cultural side of psychiatry in the treatment of patients.

4. *Principles of Intensive Psychotherapy*, 1950.

CHAPTER NINETEEN

1. "Dionysians and Apollonians," *Science*, vol. 176, June 2, 1972, p. 966.

2. This term is used in its original meaning—a word used by the Gileadites to identify the fleeing Ephraimites, because they could not pronounce the sound *sh* (Judges 12:4–6).

BIBLIOGRAPHY

BARNETT, LINCOLN. *The Universe and Dr. Einstein.* New York: Time Incorporated, 1948.

BOYD, E. *Popular Arts of Spanish New Mexico.* Santa Fe: Museum of New Mexico Press, 1974.

CARSON, RACHEL. *Silent Spring.* Boston: Houghton Mifflin, 1962.

CATHER, WILLA. *Death Comes for the Archbishop.* New York: Alfred A. Knopf, 1927.

COWAN, JACK D., and DAVID H. SHARP. "Neural Nets and Artificial Intelligence." *Daedalus*, vol. 117, Winter 1988, p. 85.

DOI, TAKEO. *The Anatomy of Dependence.* Tokyo: Kodansha International, 1973.

———*The Anatomy of Self.* Tokyo: Kodansha International, 1986.

DORNER, ALEXANDER. *The Way Beyond 'Art.'* New York: New York University Press, 1958.

DYK, WALTER, and RUTH DYK. *Left Handed: A Navajo Autobiography.* New York: Columbia University Press, 1980.

EINSTEIN, ALBERT. *The Meaning of Relativity.* Princeton: Princeton University Press, 1946.

FEYNMAN, RICHARD. *Surely You Must Be Joking, Mr. Feynman.* New York: W. W. Norton, 1988.

FROMM, ERICH. *The Art of Loving.* New York: Harper, 1956.

———. *Escape From Freedom.* New York: Farrar & Rinehart, 1941.

FROMM-REICHMANN, FRIEDA. *Principles of Intensive Psychotherapy.* Chicago: University of Chicago Press, 1950.

GALEANO, EDUARDO. *Memory of Fire: Faces and Masks.* New York: Pantheon, 1987. (Excerpted in *Harper's* magazine, February 1987.)

HALL, EDWARD T., *The Dance of Life*. Garden City, N.Y.: Anchor Press/Doubleday, 1983.

———. *Beyond Culture*. Garden City, N.Y.: Anchor Press/Doubleday, 1976.

———. *The Hidden Dimension*. Garden City, N.Y.: Anchor Press/Doubleday, 1966.

———. *The Silent Language*. Garden City, N.Y.: Anchor Press/Doubleday, 1959.

———. "The Freudian Error as an Aid in Determining Attitudes." *International Journal of Opinion and Attitude Research*, Spring 1949.

———. "Race Prejudice and Negro-White Relations in the Army." *American Journal of Sociology*, March 1947.

———and GEORGE L. TRAGER. *The Analysis of Culture*. Washington, D.C.: American Council of Learned Societies, 1953.

HARDIN, GARRETT. *Exploring New Ethics for Survival: The Voyage of the Space Ship "Beagle."* New York: Viking Press, 1972.

———. "The Tragedy of the Commons." *Science*, vol. 162, December 31, 1968.

HERRIGEL, EUGENE. *Zen in the Art of Archery*. Translated by A. F. C. Hull. New York: Vintage, 1971.

HOFFMAN, PAUL. "The Man Who Loves Numbers (Paul Erdos)." The *Atlantic*, November 1987.

JUNG, CARL G. *Memories, Dreams, and Reflections*. New York: Pantheon, 1963.

KELLER, EVELYN FOX. *A Feeling for the Organism: The Life and Work of Barbara McClintock*. W. H. Freeman, 1983.

KROEBER, A. L., and CLYDE KLUCKHOHN. *Culture: A Critical Review of Concepts and Definitions*. Cambridge, Mass.: Papers of the Peabody Museum, vol. 47, no. 1, 1952.

KUNG TSU. *The Great Learning*. (Ta Hsio) reference in Thomas Merton, *Mystics and Zen Masters*. New York: Farrar, Straus and Giroux, 1976.

LETVIN, J. Y., H. R. MATURANA, W. S. MCCULLOCH, and W. H. PITTS. "What the Frog's Eye Tells the Frog's Brain." *Proceedings of the Institute of Radio Engineers*, vol. 47, 1959.

LORENZ, KONRAD. *Man Meets Dog*. Boston: Houghton Mifflin, 1955.

MACLEAN, P. D. "On the evolution of three mentalities." In *Man-Environment Systems*, vol. 5, 1975.

———, J. J. ROTH, and E. C. ROTH. "The Ecology and Biology of Mammal-like Reptiles." In *The Ecology and Biology of Mammal-like Reptiles*. Washington, D.C.: Smithsonian Institution Press, 1986.

MARRIOTT, ALICE. *The Ten Grandmothers*. Norman: University of Oklahoma Press, 1945.

MERTON, THOMAS. *Mystics and Zen Masters*. New York: Farrar, Straus and Giroux, 1967.

PADDEN, CAROL, and TOM HUMPHRIES. *Deaf in America: Voices from a Culture*. Cambridge: Harvard University Press, 1988.

PAVLOV, I. P. *Conditioned Reflexes: An Investigation of the Physiological Activity of the Cerebral Cortex*. London: Oxford University Press, 1927.

SAPIR, EDWARD. *Selected Writings of Edward Sapir*. In *Language, Culture and Personality*. Berkeley: University of California Press, 1949.

SHEEHAN, NEIL. *A Bright Shining Lie: John Paul Vann and America in Vietnam.* New York: Random House, 1988.

SIMMONS, LEO W., ed. *Sun Chief: The Autobiography of a Hopi Indian.* New Haven: Yale University Press, 1942.

SKINNER, B. F. *Science and Human Behavior.* New York: MacMillan, 1953.

STONE, I. F. *The Trial of Socrates.* Boston: Little Brown, 1988.

SULLIVAN, HARRY STACK. *Conceptions of Modern Psychiatry.* New York: William Alanson White Psychiatric Foundation, 1947.

SWENZEL, RINA, and TITO NARANJO. "Nurturing: the Gia at Santa Clara Pueblos." *El Palacio*, Summer-Fall, 1986.

SZENT-GYORGYI, ALBERT. "Dionysians and Apollonians." *Science*, vol. 176, June 2, 1972.

TINBERGEN, NIKO. "The Curious Behavior of the Stickleback." *Scientific American*, vol. 187, no. 6, December 1952.

TOLSTOY, LEO. *War and Peace.* Abridged Edition, translated by Louise and Aylmer Maude. New York: Washington Square Press, 1963.

USEEM, JOHN. "Americans as Governors of Natives in the Pacific." *Journal of Social Issues*, August 1946.

VON UEXKULL, JACOB. *Streifzuge durch die Umwelten von Tieren und Menschen.* Berlin: J. Springer, 1934. In English: "A Stroll Through the Worlds of Animals and Men." In C. Schiller, ed., *Instinctive Behavior.* New York: International Universities Press, 1964.

WHORF, BENJAMIN LEE. *Language, Thought and Reality.* New York: Technology Press and John Wiley, 1956.

INDEX

About the Author

Edward T. Hall is also the author of *The Hidden Dimension*, *The Dance of Life*, *Hidden Differences* (with Mildred Reed Hall), and *Beyond Culture*. He is a fellow of the American Anthropological Association and of the Society for Applied Anthropology, as well as president of the Anthropological Film Research Institute and a founding director of the National Building Museum. He received the first Edward J. Lehman Award from the American Anthropological Association for demonstrating anthropology's relevance to government, business, and industry. He lives in Santa Fe, New Mexico, with his wife, coauthor, and partner, Mildred Reed Hall.